적중 100

영어 기출 문제집

중2

동아 | 이병민

Best Collection

구성과 특징

교과서의 주요 학습 내용을 중심으로 학습 영역별 특성에 맞춰 단계별로 다양한 학습 기회를 제공하여 단원별 학습능력 평가는 물론 중간 및 기말고사 시험 등에 완벽하게 대비할 수 있도록 내용을 구성

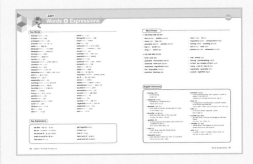

Words & Expressions

Step1	Key Words 단원별 핵심 단어 설명 및 풀이
	Key Expression 단원별 핵심 숙어 및 관용어 설명
	Word Power 반대 또는 비슷한 뜻 단어 배우기
	English Dictionary 영어로 배우는 영어 단어
Step2	실력평가 단원별 수시평가 대비 주관식, 객관식 문제풀이
Step3	서술형 대비 학업성취도 및 수행능력평가 대비 서술형 문제풀이

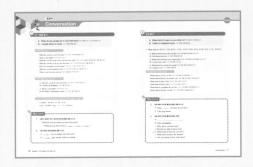

Conversation

Step1	핵심 의사소통 의사소통에 필요한 주요 표현 방법 요약
	핵심 Check 기본적인 표현 방법 및 활용능력 확인
Step2	대화문 익히기 상황에 따른 대화문 활용 및 연습
Step3	기본평가 시험대비 기초 학습 능력 평가
Step4	실력평가 단원별 수시평가 대비 주관식, 객관식 문제풀이
Step5	서술형 대비 학업성취도 및 수행능력평가 대비 서술형 문제풀이

Grammar

Step1	주요 문법 단원별 주요 문법 사항과 예문을 알기 쉽게 설명
	핵심 Check 기본 문법사항에 대한 이해 여부 확인
Step2	기본평가 시험대비 기초 학습 능력 평가
Step3	실력평가 단원별 수시평가 대비 주관식, 객관식 문제풀이
Step4	서술형 대비 학업성취도 및 수행능력평가 대비 서술형 문제풀이

Reading

Step1	구문 분석 단원별로 제시된 문장에 대한 구문별 분석과 내용 설명
	확인문제 문장에 대한 기본적인 이해와 인지능력 확인
Step2	확인학습A 빈칸 채우기를 통한 문장 완성 능력 확인
Step3	확인학습B 제시된 우리말을 영어로 완성하여 작문 능력 키우기
Step4	실력평가 단원별 수시평가 대비 주관식, 객관식 문제풀이
Step5	서술형 대비 학업성취도 및 수행능력평가 대비 서술형 문제풀이
	교과서 구석구석 교과서에 나오는 기타 문장까지 완벽 학습

Composition

|영역별 핵심문제|
단어 및 어휘, 대화문, 문법, 독해 등 각 영역별 기출문제의 출제 유형을 분석하여 실전에 대비하고 연습할
수 있도록 문제를 배열

|서술형 실전 및 창의사고력 문제|
학교 시험에서 점차 늘어나는 서술형 시험에 집중 대비하고 고득점을 취득하는데 만전을 기하기 위한
학습 코너

|단원별 예상문제|
기출문제를 분석한 후 새로운 시험 출제 경향을 더하여 새롭게 출제될 수 있는 문제를 포함하여 시험에 완벽
하게 대비할 수 있도록 준비

|단원별 모의고사|
영역별, 단계별 학습을 모두 마친 후 실전 연습을 위한 모의고사

on the textbook
교과서 파헤치기

- **단어Test1~2** 영어 단어 우리말 쓰기와 우리말을 영어 단어로 쓰기
- **대화문Test1~2** 대화문 빈칸 완성 및 전체 대화문 쓰기
- **본문Test1~5** 빈칸 완성, 우리말 쓰기, 문장 배열연습, 영어 작문하기 복습 등 단계별 반복 학습을
  통해 교과서 지문에 대한 완벽한 습득
- **구석구석지문Test1~2** 지문 빈칸 완성 및 전문 영어로 쓰기

이책의 차례 Contents

Lesson **7** **Can I Trust It?** 05~56

Lesson **8** **Be like Sherlock!** 57~108

Special Lesson **Frindle** 109~124

〈**Insight on the textbook**〉 교과서 파헤치기 01~52

〈책 속의 책〉 정답 및 해설 01~34

Lesson 7

Can I Trust It?

 의사소통 기능

- 추천 요청하기

  A: Can you recommend a musical for me?

  B: How about *The Lion King*?

- 만족 여부 묻고 답하기

  A: How do you like your bicycle?

  B: I'm really happy with it.

 언어 형식

- so ~ that

  The movie is **so** boring **that** I want to cry.

- 목적격 관계대명사

  In the ad, "Best Picture" is the award **which** the movie won.

Words & Expressions

Key Words

- **adventure** [ədvéntʃər] 명 모험
- **advertisement** [ədvərtáizmənt] 명 광고
- **author** [ɔ́ːθər] 명 작가
- **award** [əwɔ́ːrd] 명 상
- **backpack** [bǽkpæk] 명 배낭
- **belief** [bilíːf] 명 신념, 생각
- **boring** [bɔ́ːriŋ] 형 지루한
- **connection** [kənékʃən] 명 관련성, 연관성
- **desert** [dézərt] 명 사막
- **difference** [dífərəns] 명 차이점
- **else** [els] 부 또 다른
- **especially** [ispéʃəli] 부 특히
- **explain** [ikspléin] 동 설명하다
- **express** [iksprés] 동 나타내다, 표현하다
- **fantasy** [fǽntəsi] 명 공상
- **friendship** [fréndʃip] 명 우정
- **genre** [ʒáːnrə] 명 장르
- **lie** [lai] 동 거짓말하다
- **lift** [lift] 동 들어 올리다
- **meal** [miːl] 명 식사
- **mix** [miks] 동 섞다

- **navy** [néivi] 명 남색
- **novel** [návəl] 명 소설
- **opinion** [əpínjən] 명 의견
- **perfect** [pə́ːrfikt] 형 완벽한
- **pocket** [pákit] 명 주머니
- **prove** [pruːv] 동 증명하다
- **purple** [pə́ːrpl] 명 보라색, 자색
- **recommend** [rèkəménd] 동 추천하다
- **side** [said] 명 옆면, 측면
- **simple** [símpl] 형 간단한, 단순한
- **solve** [sɑlv] 동 해결하다, 풀다
- **strongly** [strɔ́ːŋli] 부 강력하게
- **touching** [tʌ́tʃiŋ] 형 감동적인
- **traditional** [trədíʃənl] 형 전통적인
- **trip** [trip] 명 여행
- **trust** [trʌst] 동 믿다, 신뢰하다
- **truth** [truːθ] 명 진실, 사실
- **unlike** [ənláik] 전 ~와 달리
- **wisely** [wáizli] 부 현명하게
- **worth** [wəːrθ] 형 가치가 있는
- **yet** [jet] 부 아직

Key Expressions

- **based on** ~을 바탕으로
- **check out** ~을 확인하다
- **for example** 예를 들면
- **from now on** 지금부터
- **full of** ~로 가득한
- **hold on** 기다려, 멈춰

- **look for** ~을 찾다
- **main character** 주인공
- **make a choice** 선택하다
- **number one** (인기 순위) 1위
- **right now** 지금
- **worth it** 그만한 가치가 있는

Word Power

※ 서로 반대되는 뜻을 가진 어휘

- **simple** 간단한, 단순한 ↔ **complex** 복잡한
- **true** 사실의, 진실의 ↔ **false** 거짓의
- **boring** 지루한 ↔ **exciting** 신나는
- **perfect** 완벽한 ↔ **imperfect** 불완전한
- **ancient** 고대의 ↔ **modern** 현대의

- **worth** 가치가 있는 ↔ **worthless** 가치가 없는
- **wise** 지혜로운 ↔ **foolish** 미련한, 어리석은
- **fact** 사실 ↔ **opinion** 의견
- **like** ~처럼, ~같이 ↔ **unlike** ~와 달리
- **similarity** 유사점 ↔ **difference** 차이점

※ 색을 나타내는 단어

- **navy** 남색
- **orange** 주황색
- **burgundy** 진홍색
- **purple** 보라색
- **ivory** 상아색
- **violet** 보라색
- **gray** 회색
- **silver** 은색
- **brown** 갈색
- **khaki** 카키색

English Dictionary

- **advertisement** 광고
  → a notice, picture or short film telling people about something
  사람들에게 무언가에 대해 이야기하는 게시, 그림 또는 짧은 영화

- **award** 상
  → a prize such as money, etc. for something that somebody has done
  누군가가 한 무언가에 대한 돈 등과 같은 상

- **connection** 관련성
  → the way in which two things are related to each other
  두 개가 서로 관련되어 있는 방식

- **explain** 설명하다
  → to tell somebody about something in a way that is easy to understand
  이해하기 쉬운 방식으로 무언가에 대해 누군가에게 이야기하다

- **express** 나타내다, 표현하다
  → to show what you think or feel
  당신이 생각하거나 느끼는 것을 보여주다

- **lie** 거짓말하다
  → to say or write something that is not true
  사실이 아닌 무언가를 말하거나 쓰다

- **lift** 들어 올리다
  → to move something to a higher position
  무언가를 더 높은 위치로 옮기다

- **meal** 식사
  → the foods eaten or prepared at one time
  한 번에 먹거나 준비되는 음식

- **mix** 섞다
  → to add something to something else
  무언가를 다른 무언가에 더하다

- **opinion** 의견
  → ideas or feelings about something
  무언가에 대한 생각 또는 느낌

- **pocket** 주머니
  → a small bag that is attached to something
  무언가에 붙어 있는 작은 자루

- **prove** 증명하다
  → to use facts, evidence, etc. to show that something is true
  무언가가 진실이라는 것을 보여 주기 위해 사실, 증거 등을 사용하다

- **trust** 신뢰하다, 믿다
  → to believe that something is true
  무언가가 사실이라고 믿다

- **truth** 진실, 사실
  → the real facts about something
  무언가에 대한 실제의 사실

01 다음 짝지어진 단어의 관계가 같도록 빈칸에 알맞은 말을 쓰시오.

> tall : short = _____ : complex

02 다음 영영풀이가 가리키는 것을 고르시오.

> a prize such as money, etc. for something that somebody has done

① penalty
② award
③ fare
④ fee
⑤ price

중요

03 다음 중 밑줄 친 부분의 뜻풀이가 바르지 <u>않은</u> 것은?

① I saw an <u>advertisement</u> for a ski camp in Toronto. 광고
② There is a <u>connection</u> between pollution and the death of plants. 관련성
③ The steak was <u>especially</u> good. 특히
④ Give me a chance. I'll <u>prove</u> it to you. 제공하다
⑤ My favorite color is <u>purple</u>. 보라색

서답형

04 다음 우리말에 맞게 빈칸에 알맞은 말을 써 넣으시오.

(1) 말로는 내 기분을 표현할 수 없다.
  ➡ Words cannot _____ my feelings.
(2) 같은 광고가 3개의 잡지에 등장했다.
  ➡ The same _____ appeared in three magazines.
(3) 그는 승리할 것이라는 자신의 능력에 강한 신념을 갖고 있다.
  ➡ He has a strong _____ in his ability to win.

중요

05 다음 주어진 문장의 밑줄 친 touching과 같은 의미로 쓰인 것은?

> The movie was so <u>touching</u> that I cried a lot.

① My daughter is <u>touching</u> a pet.
② Who is the boy <u>touching</u> an ant?
③ What a <u>touching</u> love story!
④ Avoid <u>touching</u> your eyes and nose with dirty hands.
⑤ <u>Touching</u> the keyboard, she told me about the plan.

06 다음 문장에 공통으로 들어갈 말을 고르시오.

> • My father served three years in the _____.
> • I dressed my son in the new _____ suit.
> • It's not bad, but I prefer the _____ skirt.

① navy
② pink
③ yellow
④ purple
⑤ brown

서답형

07 다음 문장의 빈칸에 들어갈 말을 〈보기〉에서 골라 쓰시오.

> ┤ 보기 ├
> beliefs, purple, genre, friendship

(1) Do you know the girl wearing the _____ jacket?
(2) You must respect other people's _____.
(3) Which _____ do you like most?
(4) A strong _____ grew between the two people.

01 다음 짝지어진 단어의 관계가 같도록 빈칸에 알맞은 말을 쓰시오.

> similar : different = similarity : _____

02 다음 우리말에 맞게 빈칸에 알맞은 말을 쓰시오.

(1) 나는 네게 거짓말하지 않았다. 모든 것은 진실이야.
➡ I didn't _____ to you. Everything is true.

(2) 주머니에 구멍이 났다.
➡ I have a hole in my _____.

(3) 그 만화 영화는 소설을 바탕으로 한다.
➡ The animation is _____ on a novel.

03 다음 문장의 빈칸에 들어갈 말을 〈보기〉에서 골라 쓰시오.

> ─ 보기 ─
> fantasy, traditional, connection, author, desert, award

(1) I'm interested in _____ Korean culture.

(2) The land of Australia is primarily _____.

(3) This novel was written by a famous _____.

(4) There is a _____ between health and eating habits.

(5) Emma was really happy when she won the _____.

(6) I like to read _____ novel.

04 다음 우리말을 주어진 단어를 이용하여 영작하시오.

(1) 지금부터 축구 경기를 시작하겠습니다. (from, start, let's, playing)
➡ _____

(2) 나가기 전에, 전등을 다시 확인해 주세요. (light, you, check)
➡ _____

(3) 누가 이 영화의 주인공입니까? (main, this)
➡ _____

05 다음 우리말과 일치하도록 주어진 어구를 모두 배열하여 영작하시오.

(1) 게임 규칙을 설명해 줄 수 있나요?
(explain / the game / can / of / the rules / you)
➡ _____

(2) 당신이 빨간색과 파란색을 섞으면 보라색을 얻을 수 있어요.
(purple / get / you / blue / red / with / mix / you / can / if)
➡ _____

(3) 그가 유리창을 깨지 않았다는 것을 증명할 수 있어요.
(that / I / the window / didn't / can / break / prove / he)
➡ _____

(4) 신문에 난 그 광고 봤니?
(you / see/ did / the advertisement / the newspaper / on)
➡ _____

Conversation

교과서

1 추천 요청하기 및 추천하기

> **A** Can you recommend a musical for me? 제게 뮤지컬을 추천해 줄 수 있나요?
> **B** How about *The Lion King*? *The Lion King*은 어때?

■ 'Can you recommend ~?'는 '~을 추천해 줄 수 있나요?'라는 뜻으로 상대방에게 무엇인가를 추천해 달라고 부탁하는 표현이다. 대답으로 "How about ~?", "Why don't you ~?", "I recommend ~", "Try ~", "I think ~." 등의 표현을 사용해 추천해 줄 수 있다.

추천 요청하기

- What would you recommend? 무엇을 추천하나요?
- What do you think would be the best? 무엇이 가장 좋다고 생각하나요?
- Can you suggest a good movie? 좋은 영화를 추천해 줄 수 있나요?

추천하기

- How about *Frozen*? The music is so beautiful. *Frozen*은 어때? 음악이 매우 아름다워.
- Why don't you read *Frindle*? The story is really touching.
  *Frindle*을 읽어 보는 게 어때? 이야기가 정말 감동적이야.
- I recommend *Beauty and the Beast*. 나는 미녀와 야수를 추천해요.
- Try Antonio's. It's a good restaurant. Antonio's에 가 봐. 좋은 식당이야.
- I think this backpack is much better than that one. 제 생각에 이 배낭이 저것보다 월씬 나을 거 같아요.

핵심 Check

1. 다음 주어진 우리말과 일치하도록 빈칸을 완성하시오.

(1) **A:** Can you _____ a movie for me? (영화를 추천해 줄 수 있나요?)

   B: _____ _____ *Spider Man*? It's interesting. (Spiderman 어때? 재밌어.)

(2) **A:** _____ _____ _____ a good novel for me? (제게 좋은 소설을 제안해 주시겠어요?)

   B: _____ don't you read *Harry Potter*? (Harry Potter를 읽어 보는 게 어때요?)

(3) **A:** _____ _____ _____ _____ _____ _____ the best musical?
   (최고의 뮤지컬이 무엇인 거 같아요?)

   B: I think *The Phantom of the Opera* is the best. (저는 오페라의 유령이 최고인 것 같아요.)

2 만족 여부 묻고 답하기

A How do you like your bicycle? 네 자전거는 마음에 드니?
B I'm really happy with it. 정말 마음에 들어.

■ 'How do you like ~?'는 '~이 마음에 드니?'라는 뜻으로 특정 물건이나 장소 등에 대해 만족하는지를 묻는 표현이다. 이에 대한 대답으로 만족을 표현할 때는 'I'm happy with ~.'로, 불만족을 표현할 때는 'I'm not happy with ~.'로, 표현할 수 있다.

만족 여부 묻기

- How do you like your new sneakers? 새 운동화가 마음에 드니?
- What do you like about the movie? 그 영화의 무엇이 마음에 드니?

만족 여부 답하기

- I'm satisfied with my job. 내 일에 만족해.
- I'm disappointed with the decision. 나는 그 결정에 실망했어.
- I'm pleased with the food. 음식이 마음에 들어.
- It's perfect. 완벽해.
- It's fantastic. 매우 좋아.

핵심 Check

2. 다음 주어진 우리말과 일치하도록 빈칸을 완성하시오.

(1) **A:** _____ _____ _____ _____ your new pants? (새 바지가 마음에 드니?)
   B: I'm really happy with them. (정말 마음에 들어.)

(2) **A:** How do you like your jacket? (재킷이 마음에 드니?)
   B: _____ _____ _____ _____ _____. (만족스럽지 않아.)

(3) **A:** _____ _____ _____ _____ about the bicycle?
   (그 자전거의 무엇이 마음에 드니?)
   B: It's light and fast. (가볍고 빨라요.)

Listen and Speak 1 - B

W: ❶May I help you?

B: Yes. I'm ❷looking for a ❸backpack. Can you recommend ❹one?

W: ❺How about this red one? Red is the most popular color ❻these days.

B: My old backpack was red, so I want a different color.

W: How about this navy one? It has side pockets.

B: Oh, that looks good. I'll take ❼it.

W: 도와드릴까요?
B: 네. 배낭을 찾고 있어요. 하나 추천해 주시겠어요?
W: 이 빨간 배낭은 어떤가요? 빨간색은 요즘 가장 인기 있는 색이에요.
B: 제 옛 배낭이 빨간색이어서 다른 색을 원해요.
W: 이 남색 배낭은 어떤가요? 양옆에 주머니가 있어요.
B: 오, 좋아 보여요. 그걸로 살게요.

❶ 'May I help you?'는 '도와드릴까요?'라고 도움을 제안하는 표현으로 'How can I help you?' 또는 'Do you need any help?' 등으로 바꾸어 표현할 수 있다.
❷ look for: ~을 찾다　　❸ backpack: 배낭　　❹ one = a backpack
❺ 'How about ~?'은 '~하는 게 어때?'라고 추천하는 표현으로 'What about ~?'으로 바꾸어 쓸 수 있다.
❻ these days: 요즘 cf. those days: 그 당시에
❼ it은 the navy backpack with side pockets를 가리킨다.

Check(√) True or False

(1) The boy already had a red backpack.　　　　　T ☐ F ☐

(2) The boy bought the backpack with side pockets.　　T ☐ F ☐

Listen and Speak 2 - B

Jack: Hi, Suji. ❶How did you like your trip to Gyeongju?

Suji: I was very happy with it.

Jack: Where did you visit?

Suji: I visited Cheomseongdae. It was great.

Jack: Where else did you go?

Suji: Bulguksa. It was a wonderful place.

Jack: Sounds like the perfect trip.

Suji: Yeah, but ❷walking up to Seokguram was difficult.

Jack: But I'm sure it was ❸worth it.

Jack: 안녕, 수지야. 경주 여행은 어땠니?
Suij: 매우 즐거웠어.
Jack: 어디를 방문했니?
Suij: 첨성대를 방문했어. 좋았어.
Jack: 또 어디를 방문했니?
Suij: 불국사. 멋진 곳이었어.
Jack: 완벽한 여행이었던 것 같네.
Suij: 응, 하지만 석굴암까지 걸어 올라가는 것은 힘들었어.
Jack: 하지만 그것이 그만한 가치가 있었을 것이라고 확신해.

❶ 경주 여행이 마음에 들었는지 묻는 표현이다.
❷ 동명사가 주어이므로 동사는 단수 형태로 쓰였다.
❸ worth it: 그만한 가치가 있는

Check(√) True or False

(3) Suji was happy with her trip to Gyeongju.　　　T ☐ F ☐

(4) It was not hard for Suji to walk up to Seokguram.　T ☐ F ☐

Listen and Speak 1-A

Brian: Can you ❶recommend a good movie?

Emily: Try *Star Wars*. I really liked ❷it.

Brian: Oh, I haven't seen ❷it yet.

Emily: ❷It's the ❸number one movie ❹right now.

❶ recommend: 추천하다
❷ it은 *Star Wars*를 가리킨다.
❸ number one: 1위의
❹ right now: 지금

Listen and Speak 1-C

A: Jiho, can you recommend a musical for me?

B: ❶How about *The Lion King*? The dancing is fantastic.

A: Okay. ❷Sounds good.

B: ❸I'm sure you'll like ❹it.

❶ How about ~?: ~는 어때?(=What about ~?)
❷ Sounds good.에는 앞 문장을 받는 주어 That이 생략되었다.
❸ I'm sure ~.: 나는 ~라고 확신해.
❹ it은 *The Lion King*을 가리킨다.

Listen and Speak 2-A

Sue: Tom, you got a new smartphone.

Tom: Yes, I did. I'm really happy with ❶it.

Sue: ❷What do you like most about ❶it?

Tom: I love the camera. It ❸takes great pictures.

❶ it은 a new smartphone을 가리킨다.
❷ 무엇이 마음에 드는지 묻는 표현이다.
❸ take a picture: 사진을 찍다

Real Life Talk – Step 1

Brian: Mina, can you recommend a good pizza restaurant?

Mina: ❶Why don't you try Antonio's? ❷It's my favorite.

Brian: What do you like about ❷it?

Mina: The food is delicious. I recommend the bulgogi pizza.

Brian: How are the prices?

Mina: I think the prices are good, too.

Brian: Sounds like a good restaurant. How do you like the service?

Mina: It's ❸a little slow on the weekends.

Brian: Okay. I'll ❹check it out. Thanks.

Mina: No problem. Enjoy your meal!

❶ How about trying Antonio's?로 바꾸어 쓸 수 있다.
❷ It은 Antonio's를 가리킨다.
❸ a little: 조금
❹ check out: ~을 확인하다

Real Life Talk – Step 2

Amy: Yujin, can you recommend a book for me?

Yujin: How about *The Little Prince*?

Amy: What do you like about ❶the book?

Yujin: I like the ❷main character. ❸He is very special.

Amy: Sounds good. I'll read it.

❶ the book은 *The Little Prince*를 가리킨다.
❷ main character: 주인공
❸ He = the main character

● 다음 우리말과 일치하도록 빈칸에 알맞은 말을 쓰시오.

Listen & Speak 1-A

Brian: Can you _____ a good movie?

Emily: Try *Star Wars*. I really liked it.

Brian: Oh, I haven't seen it _____.

Emily: It's the _____ _____ movie right now.

해석

Brian: 좋은 영화를 추천해 줄래?
Emily: 'Star Wars'를 봐. 정말 좋았어.
Brian: 오, 나는 아직 그 영화를 본 적이 없어.
Emily: 지금 1위 영화야.

Listen & Speak 1-B

W: May I _____ you?

B: Yes. I'm looking for a _____. Can you _____ _____?

W: _____ _____ this red one? Red is the most popular color _____ _____.

B: My old backpack was red, so I want a _____ color.

W: How about this _____ one? It has side _____.

B: Oh, that looks good. I'll _____ it.

W: 도와드릴까요?
B: 네. 배낭을 찾고 있어요. 하나 추천해 주시겠어요?
W: 이 빨간 배낭은 어떤가요? 빨간색은 요즘 가장 인기 있는 색이에요.
B: 제 옛 배낭이 빨간색이어서 다른 색을 원해요.
W: 이 남색 배낭은 어떤가요? 양옆에 주머니가 있어요.
B: 오, 좋아 보여요. 그걸로 살게요.

Listen & Speak 2-A

Sue: Tom, you _____ a new smartphone.

Tom: Yes, I did. I'm really happy with it.

Sue: What do you _____ _____ _____ _____?

Tom: I love the camera. It _____ great pictures.

Sue: Tom, 새 스마트폰을 샀구나.
Tom: 응, 그래. 나는 정말 만족스러워.
Sue: 무엇이 가장 마음에 드니?
Tom: 카메라가 정말 좋아. 멋진 사진을 찍어.

Listen & Talk 2-B

Jack: Hi, Suji. How did you _____ your _____ to Gyeongju?

Suji: I was very _____ with it.

Jack: Where did you visit?

Suji: I visited Cheomseongdae. It was great.

Jack: _____ _____ did you go?

Suji: Bulguksa. It was a _____ _____.

Jack: Sounds like the _____ _____.

Suji: Yeah, but _____ _____ to Seokguram was difficult.

Jack: But I'm sure it was _____ _____.

해석

Jack: 안녕, 수지야. 경주 여행은 어땠니?
Suij: 매우 즐거웠어.
Jack: 어디를 방문했니?
Suij: 첨성대를 방문했어. 좋았어.
Jack: 또 어디를 방문했니?
Suij: 불국사. 멋진 곳이었어.
Jack: 완벽한 여행이었던 것 같네.
Suij: 응, 하지만 석굴암까지 걸어 올라가는 것은 힘들었어.
Jack: 하지만 그것이 그만한 가치가 있었을 것이라고 확신해.

Real Life Talk – Step 1

Brian: Mina, _____ _____ _____ a good pizza restaurant?

Mina: _____ _____ you try Antonio's? It's my favorite.

Brian: What do you like _____ it?

Mina: The food is _____. I _____ the bulgogi pizza.

Brian: How are _____ _____?

Mina: I _____ the prices are good, _____.

Brian: _____ _____ a good restaurant. _____ do you like _____ _____?

Mina: It's a little _____ on the weekends.

Brian: Okay. I'll _____ _____ _____. Thanks.

Mina: No _____. _____ your meal!

Brian: 미나야, 괜찮은 피자 식당을 추천해 줄래?
Mina: Antonio's에 가 보는 게 어때? 내가 가장 좋아하는 곳이야.
Brian: 무엇이 좋은데?
Mina: 음식이 맛있어. 나는 불고기 피자를 추천해.
Brian: 가격은 어때?
Mina: 가격도 괜찮다고 생각해.
Brian: 괜찮은 식당 같네. 서비스는 어때?
Mina: 주말에는 좀 느려.
Brian: 알겠어. 내가 확인해 볼게. 고마워.
Mina: 천만에. 맛있게 먹어!

Real Life Talk – Step 2

Amy: Yujin, can you _____ _____ _____ _____ _____ _____?

Yujin: How _____ *The Little Prince*?

Amy: _____ do you _____ about the book?

Yujin: I like the _____ _____. He is very _____.

Amy: _____ good. I'll read it.

Amy: Yujin아, 내게 책을 추천해 줄래?
Yujin: '어린 왕자' 어때?
Amy: 책의 무엇이 마음에 드니?
Yujin: 나는 주인공이 마음에 들어. 그는 매우 특별해.
Amy: 좋은 책 같네. 내가 읽어 볼게.

[01~02] 다음 대화를 읽고 물음에 답하시오.

> Brian: _____?
> Emily: Try *Star Wars*. I really liked it.
> Brian: Oh, I haven't seen it yet.
> Emily: It's the number one movie right now.

01 위 대화의 빈칸에 들어갈 말을 〈보기〉에 주어진 단어를 모두 배열하여 영작하시오.

┌─ 보기 ─┐

you / recommend / a / movie / can / good

➡ _____

02 위 대화의 내용과 일치하지 <u>않는</u> 것은?

① Brian은 Emily에게 좋은 영화를 추천해 줄 것을 요청하였다.
② Emily는 *Star Wars*를 볼 것을 추천하였다.
③ Emily는 *Star Wars*가 정말 좋았다.
④ Brain은 아직 *Star Wars*를 보지 않았다.
⑤ Brian은 지금 1위 영화를 보았다.

[03~04] 다음 대화를 읽고 물음에 답하시오.

> Sue: Tom, you got a new smartphone.
> Tom: Yes, I did. I'm really happy with (B)it.
> Sue: (A)무엇이 가장 마음에 드니?
> Tom: I love the camera. (C)It takes great pictures.

03 위 대화의 밑줄 친 (A)의 우리말을 주어진 단어를 모두 배열하여 영작하시오.

┌─ 보기 ─┐

you / it / about / what / most / do / like

➡ _____

04 위 대화의 밑줄 친 (B)와 (C)의 it이 가리키는 것을 각각 찾아 쓰시오.

➡ (B) _____ (C) _____

[01~03] 다음 대화를 읽고 물음에 답하시오.

Jack: Hi, Suji. ①How did you like your trip to Gyeongju?

Suji: I was very happy ②with it.

Jack: Where did you visit?

Suji: I visited Cheomseongdae. It was great.

Jack: Where else did you go?

Suji: Bulguksa. It was a wonderful place.

Jack: ③Sounds like the perfect trip.

Suji: Yeah, ___(A)___ walking up to Seokguram ④were difficult.

Jack: ___(A)___ I'm sure it was ⑤worth it.

01 위 대화의 ①~⑤ 중 어법상 어색한 것을 찾아 바르게 고치시오.

➡ _____

02 위 대화의 빈칸 (A)에 들어갈 말로 적절한 것은?

① and / And   ② but / But
③ so / So   ④ for / For
⑤ because / Because

03 위 대화의 내용과 일치하지 않는 것은?

① Suji was satisfied with her trip to Gyeongju.
② Suji visited both Cheomseongdae and Bulguksa.
③ It was difficult for Suji to walk up to Seokguram.
④ Jack didn't think that it was worth while walking up to Cheomseongdae.
⑤ Suji thought that Bulguksa was a great place.

[04~05] 다음 대화를 읽고 물음에 답하시오.

Amy: Yujin, (A)내게 책을 추천해 줄래?(can)

Yujin: How about *The Little Prince*?

Amy: What do you like about the book?

Yujin: I like the main character. He is very special.

Amy: Sounds good. I'll read it.

04 위 대화의 밑줄 친 (A)의 우리말을 주어진 단어를 사용하여 영작하시오.

➡ _____

05 What does Yujin like about *The Little Prince*? Answer in English.

➡ _____

[06~08] 다음 대화를 읽고 물음에 답하시오.

Brian: Mina, can you recommend a good pizza restaurant?

Mina: (A) It's my favorite.

Brian: (B) What do you like about ⓐit?

Mina: (C) The food is delicious. I recommend the bulgogi pizza.

Brian: (D) How are the prices?

Mina: (E) I think the prices are good, too.

Brian: Sounds like a good restaurant. How do you like the service?

Mina: ⓑIt's a little slow on the weekends.

Brian: Okay. I'll check it out. Thanks.

Mina: No problem. Enjoy your meal!

06 위 대화의 (A)~(E) 중 주어진 문장이 들어가기에 적절한 곳은?

> Why don't you try Antonio's?

① (A) ② (B) ③ (C) ④ (D) ⑤ (E)

서답형

07 위 대화에서 밑줄 친 ⓐ와 ⓑ가 각각 가리키는 것을 찾아 쓰시오.

➡ ⓐ _____ ⓑ _____

08 위 대화의 내용과 일치하지 <u>않는</u> 것은?

① 미나는 괜찮은 피자 식당으로 Antonio's를 추천하였다.
② Antonio's는 미나가 가장 좋아하는 곳이다.
③ 미나는 Antonio's의 불고기 피자를 추천하였다.
④ 미나는 Antonio's의 가격이 괜찮다고 생각한다.
⑤ Antonio's의 서비스는 주중에는 좀 느리다.

[09~10] 다음 대화를 읽고 물음에 답하시오.

W: May I help you?
B: (A) Yes. I'm looking for a backpack. Can you recommend one?
W: (B) Red is the most popular color these days.
B: (C) My old backpack was red, so I want a different color.
W: (D) How about this navy one? It has side pockets.
B: (E) Oh, that looks good. I'll take it.

09 위 대화의 (A)~(E) 중 주어진 문장이 들어가기에 적절한 곳은?

> How about this red one?

① (A) ② (B) ③ (C) ④ (D) ⑤ (E)

10 위 대화를 읽고 대답할 수 <u>없는</u> 질문은?

① What was the boy looking for?
② What did the woman recommend at first?
③ Why didn't the boy want the red backpack?
④ What did the boy decide to buy?
⑤ How many pockets did the boy's old backpack have?

[11~12] 다음 대화를 읽고 물음에 답하시오.

Sue: Tom, you got a new smartphone.
Tom: Yes, I did. _____ (A) _____
Sue: What do you like most about it?
Tom: I love the camera. It takes great pictures.

11 위 대화의 빈칸 (A)에 들어갈 말로 <u>어색한</u> 것은?

① I'm really happy with it.
② I'm satisfied with it.
③ I'm disappointed with it.
④ I'm pleased with it.
⑤ It's fantastic.

12 위 대화를 읽고 대답할 수 <u>없는</u> 질문은?

① What did Tom get?
② Does Tom like his new smartphone?
③ What does Tom like most about his smartphone?
④ Why does Tom love the camera in his smartphone?
⑤ When did Tom take great pictures?

[01~03] 다음 대화를 읽고 물음에 답하시오.

Brian: Can you recommend a good movie?
Emily: Try *Star Wars*. I really liked it.
Brian: Oh, (A)나는 아직 그것을 본 적이 없어. (yet)
Emily: It's the number one movie right now.

01 위 대화의 밑줄 친 (A)의 우리말을 주어진 단어를 사용하여 영작하시오.

➡ _____

02 What movie did Emily recommend to Brian?

➡ _____

03 What is the number one movie now?

➡ _____

[04~06] 다음 대화를 읽고 물음에 답하시오.

W: May I help you?
B: Yes. I'm looking for a backpack. Can you recommend one?
W: How about this red one? Red is the most popular color these days.
B: My old backpack was red, so I want a different color.
W: How about this navy one? It has side pockets.
B: Oh, that looks good. I'll take it.

04 What is the most popular color nowadays?

➡ _____

05 What is the feature of the navy backpack?

➡ _____

06 Why didn't the boy want to take the red backpack?

➡ _____

[07~08] 다음 대화를 읽고 물음에 답하시오.

Jack: Hi, Suji. ___(A)___ did you like your trip to Gyeongju?
Suji: I was very happy with it.
Jack: ___(B)___ did you visit?
Suji: I visited Cheomseongdae. It was great.
Jack: ___(C)___ else did you go?
Suji: Bulguksa. It was a wonderful place.
Jack: Sounds like the perfect trip.
Suji: Yeah, but walking up to Seokguram was difficult.
Jack: But I'm sure it was worth it.

07 위 대화의 빈칸 (A), (B), (C)에 들어갈 알맞은 의문사를 쓰시오.

➡ (A) _____ (B) _____ (C) _____

08 위 대화의 내용과 일치하도록 Suji의 일기를 완성하시오.

Sun, Nov 3rd, 2019
I took a trip to ___(A)___ . It was a really nice and beautiful city. I visited ___(B)___ as well as Cheomseongdae. They are wonderful places. When I walked up to ___(C)___ , I was tired but it was worth while to do it. I was so happy with the perfect trip to Gyeongju.

➡ (A) _____ (B) _____ (C) _____

Grammar

1 so ~ that

> • The hot chocolate was **so** hot **that** Jeremy couldn't drink it.
> 그 핫 초콜릿은 너무 뜨거워서 Jeremy는 그것을 마실 수 없었다.
>
> • I am **so** hungry **that** I could eat a horse.
> 나는 배가 너무 고파서 말 한 마리를 다 먹을 수 있을 정도야.

■ 'so+형용사/부사+that ~'은 '너무 …해서 ~하다'는 의미로 원인과 결과를 나타낼 때 사용한다.

• This book is **so** interesting **that** I can't put it down. 이 책은 너무 재미있어서 내려놓을 수가 없어.

• The sun is **so** hot **that** I have to drink lots of water. 태양이 너무 뜨거워서 나는 많은 물을 마셔야만 한다.

• The fox was **so** playful **that** he wanted to make play with the crane.
그 여우는 장난기가 너무 많아서 학을 골탕 먹이고 싶었다.

■ 'so ~ that 주어 can't …'는 '너무 ~해서 …할 수 없다'는 의미로 'too ~ to V'로 표현할 수 있고, 'so ~ that 주어 can'은 '너무 ~해서 …할 수 있다'는 의미로 '~ enough to V'로 표현할 수 있다.

• I am **so** tired **that** I can't play with you.

= I am **too** tired **to** play with you. 나는 너무 피곤해서 너와 함께 놀 수 없어.

• Julia was **so** tall **that** she played basketball very well.

= Julia was tall **enough to** play basketball very well. Julia는 충분히 키가 커서 농구를 아주 잘했다.

핵심 Check

1. 다음 우리말과 같도록 빈칸에 알맞은 말을 쓰시오.

(1) 불빛이 너무 밝아서 나는 눈을 뜰 수 없어.

➡ The light is _____ _____ _____ I can't open my eyes.

(2) 그것은 너무 작아서 사람들은 그것을 보기 위해 현미경이 필요해요.

➡ It is _____ _____ _____ people need a microscope to see it.

(3) James는 너무 게을러서 모두가 그를 싫어한다.

➡ James is _____ _____ _____ everyone hates him.

② 목적격 관계대명사

> • Mr. Han **whom** everyone respects teaches English.
> 모두가 존경하는 한 선생님은 영어를 가르친다.
>
> • The jacket **which** Sam got from his mother looks fancy.
> Sam이 엄마에게서 받은 재킷은 멋져 보인다.

■ 관계대명사는 두 개의 문장을 하나로 이어주는 접속사 역할을 하면서 동시에 (대)명사 역할을 한다. 전치사의 목적어 혹은 동사의 목적어였던 (대)명사를 목적격 관계대명사로 만들어 문장을 하나로 이어준다.

  • There were many children at the zoo **which** Tom and Jane visited. 〈동사의 목적어〉
    Tom과 Jane이 방문했던 동물원에는 아이들이 많았다.

  • Those boys **who[whom]** the woman is looking after look very cute. 〈전치사의 목적어〉
    그 여자가 돌보고 있는 저 소년들은 매우 귀여워 보인다.

■ 목적격 관계대명사 who(m), which는 that으로 대체할 수 있으며, 생략 가능하다. 관계대명사가 전치사의 목적어로 사용된 경우 전치사는 동사 뒤에 그대로 두거나, 전치사를 관계대명사 앞으로 보낼 수 있다. 단, 관계대명사 that은 전치사의 목적어로 쓰일 수 없음에 유의하자.

  • The hotel (**which/that**) you stay in is famous for its breakfast.
    = The hotel **in which** you stay is famous for its breakfast.
    = The hotel in that you stay is famous for its breakfast. (×) 네가 머물고 있는 그 호텔은 아침식사로 유명하다.

  • The missing girl (**who(m)/that**) people were looking for was found at the train station.
    = The missing girl for **whom** people were looking was found at the train station.
    = The missing girl for that people were looking was found at the train station. (×)
    사람들이 찾던 그 실종 소녀가 기차역에서 발견되었다.

  • Tell me about the cats (**which/that**) you take care of on the streets.
    네가 길에서 돌보는 고양이들에 관해서 말해 줘.

핵심 Check

2. 다음 우리말과 같도록 빈칸에 알맞은 말을 쓰시오.
  (1) 나는 Elizabeth가 만든 드레스를 입고 싶다.
    ➡ I want to wear the dress _____ _____ _____.
  (2) Chris는 그가 어제 잃어버린 지갑을 찾고 있다.
    ➡ Chris is looking for the wallet _____ _____ _____ yesterday.
  (3) 나는 Molly가 정말 좋아했던 책을 가지고 있다.
    ➡ I have the book _____ _____ _____ _____.
  (4) 그녀는 꿈에서 본 남자를 찾고 있어.
    ➡ She is looking for a man _____ _____ _____ in her dream.

01 다음 문장에서 어법상 <u>어색한</u> 부분을 바르게 고쳐 쓰시오.

(1) The areas who you mentioned have some problems.

_____ ➡ _____

(2) Tell me about the patients which you cared for in the hospital.

_____ ➡ _____

(3) This necklace is very expensive that you will be shocked.

_____ ➡ _____

(4) Suji was so tired to do her homework.

_____ ➡ _____

02 다음 우리말과 같은 의미가 되도록 빈칸에 알맞은 말을 쓰시오.

(1) Tom이 많이 좋아하는 그 소녀는 내 친구이다.

= The girl _____ _____ _____ so much is my friend.

(2) 그 문제는 너무 쉬워서 모두가 그것을 풀 수 있다.

= The problem is _____ _____ _____ everyone can solve it.

(3) 그는 매우 부유해서 그가 원하는 어떤 것도 할 수 있다.

= He is _____ _____ _____ he can do anything _____ he wants.

(4) 내가 앉아 있는 이 의자는 편안하다.

= This chair _____ _____ _____ _____ is comfortable.

03 주어진 어구를 바르게 배열하여 다음 우리말을 영어로 쓰시오. 필요하다면 어형을 바꾸고 단어를 추가하시오.

(4) commute: 통근 (거리)

(1) 그녀는 좋아하지 않는 음식에 손도 대지 않았다. (she / she / didn't / didn't / like / touch / the food / that)

➡ _____

(2) 그 여자가 돌보고 있는 저 아기들은 매우 귀여워 보인다. (very cute / those babies / look after / look / whom / is / the woman)

➡ _____

(3) 구두가 너무 꼭 끼어서 내 발이 아파. (tight / hurt / the shoes / my feet / are / that)

➡ _____

(4) 그녀의 출퇴근 거리가 너무 멀어서 그녀는 차를 샀다. (a car / her commute / bought / so / she / far / was)

➡ _____

01 다음 우리말을 영어로 바르게 옮긴 것은?

> 그녀는 너무 피곤해서 일찍 잤어.

① She is very tired to go to bed early.
② She was too tired to go to bed early.
③ She was so tired that she couldn't go to sleep.
④ She was so tired that she went to bed early.
⑤ She went to bed so early that she was tired.

 02 다음 중 어법상 바르지 <u>않은</u> 것은?

> The woman ①whom I ②met yesterday ③was ④very friendly ⑤that I wanted to be friends with her.

①　　②　　③　　④　　⑤

03 다음 주어진 문장의 빈칸에 들어갈 말로 적절한 것을 <u>모두</u> <u>고르시오.</u>

> The sofa _____ they bought last week looks expensive.

① whose　　② which　　③ who
④ that　　⑤ what

서답형
04 목적격 관계대명사를 이용하여 다음 두 문장을 하나의 문장 <u>으로 쓰시오.</u>

> • The book was written by my mother.
> • You borrowed the book from the library.

➡ _____

_____

 05 주어진 문장과 같은 의미의 문장은?

> Tom was too scared to go out at night.

① Tom was scared enough to go out at night.
② Tom was very scared of going out at night.
③ Tom was so scared that he couldn't go out at night.
④ Tom was so scared that he could go out at night.
⑤ Tom was scared to go out at night.

06 다음 중 어법상 바르지 <u>않은</u> 것은?

① Minji is so smart that she can solve all the problems.
② The bike which Jason rides are fancy.
③ I know the house in which we used to live.
④ Some friends you invited are a little rude.
⑤ I was so upset that I didn't answer her phone.

 07 다음 빈칸에 들어갈 말이 바르게 짝지어진 것은?

> James kicked a ball so _____ that his foot hurt. The ball _____ James kicked was not found.

① hardly – whose　　② hardly – that
③ hard – who　　④ hard – whose
⑤ hard – that

서답형

08 주어진 단어를 활용하여 다음 우리말을 영어로 쓰시오.

> 그 컴퓨터는 너무 작아서 내가 가지고 다닐 수 있다. (so / carry around)

➡ _____

_____

09 다음 중 밑줄 친 부분을 생략할 수 <u>없는</u> 것은?

① The boy <u>whom</u> you ran across was one of my students.
② The banana <u>which</u> Jane ate was not hers.
③ Where are the coins <u>that</u> were under the sofa?
④ The car <u>that</u> Jimmy washed looked clean and shiny.
⑤ The children <u>whom</u> you play with are there.

10 다음 중 that의 쓰임이 나머지 넷과 <u>다른</u> 하나는?

① It is certain <u>that</u> Brady is alive.
② <u>That</u> he worried about you is true.
③ I lost the hat <u>that</u> you had bought me.
④ I told her <u>that</u> he was playing the piano.
⑤ Do you think <u>that</u> there will be lots of homework?

서답형

11 주어진 상황을 읽고 하나의 문장으로 표현하시오.

> There was an important examination. Julia studied hard to pass the exam. At last, she passed it.

➡ _____

_____

서답형

12 주어진 단어를 이용하여 알맞은 대답을 쓰시오.

> **A:** Why were you late?
> **B:** (that / traffic / heavy / here / be / on time)

➡ _____

_____

13 다음 빈칸에 공통으로 들어갈 말로 가장 적절한 것은?

> • The movie was so boring _____ most people fell asleep.
> • The plants _____ you cared for look very similar.

① who   ② which   ③ that
④ what   ⑤ whose

14 다음 중 서로 의미가 같지 <u>않은</u> 것은?

① Amelia was too talkative to listen to others.
= Amelia was so talkative that she couldn't listen to others.
② I lent you some money. What will you do with it?
= What will you do with the money that I lent you?
③ The boys are too noisy to be in the library.
= The boys are so noisy that they can't be in the library.
④ Jacky wrote a popular song. People loved the song.
= Jacky wrote a popular song which people loved.
⑤ Where is the dog? It follows you all the time.
= Where is the dog you follow all the time?

15 같은 의미가 되도록 빈칸에 알맞은 말을 쓰시오.

> • The concert made me excited.
> • We watched the concert last week.
> = The concert ＿＿＿＿＿＿ made me excited.

➡ ＿＿＿＿＿＿＿＿＿＿＿＿＿＿＿

16 다음 빈칸에 들어갈 말로 가장 적절한 것은?

> • My teeth were so painful that I went to the dentist.
> = I went to the dentist ＿＿＿＿ my teeth were so painful.

① although ② because
③ when ④ as soon as
⑤ unless

17 다음 우리말을 영어로 바르게 옮긴 것은?

> 그 노래가 나를 너무 슬프게 해서 나는 라디오를 껐다.

① The song was sad that I turned off the radio.
② The song made me so sad that I turned off the radio.
③ The song was too sad to turn off the radio.
④ I was so sad that I turned off the radio.
⑤ The song made me sadly so that I turned off the radio.

서답형

18 같은 의미의 문장이 되도록 빈칸에 알맞은 말을 쓰시오.

> • The song was beautiful.
> • They sang the song together.
> = The song ＿＿＿＿＿＿＿＿ .

➡ ＿＿＿＿＿＿＿＿＿＿＿＿＿

19 주어진 문장과 같은 의미의 문장은?

> I was so busy that I couldn't have lunch.

① I was busy although I couldn't have lunch.
② I was busy enough to have lunch.
③ I was busy because I couldn't have lunch.
④ I was busy having lunch.
⑤ I was too busy to have lunch.

20 다음 중 어법상 옳은 문장은?

① The necklace you wear look beautiful.
② The dress was so beautiful that I can't take my eyes off it.
③ The students whose you teach are noisy.
④ The apple you brought is tasty.
⑤ The man was so diligently that everyone liked him.

서답형

21 괄호 안의 말을 써서 주어진 문장과 같은 의미의 문장을 쓰시오.

> I can't talk in front of many people because I am too shy. (so ~ that)

➡ ＿＿＿＿＿＿＿＿＿＿＿＿＿

서답형

22 다음 우리말을 영어로 쓸 때 빈칸에 알맞은 말을 쓰시오.

> 내가 흥미 있는 과목은 영어입니다.
> (subject / interested)

(1) The subject ＿＿＿ ＿＿＿ ＿＿＿ ＿＿＿ in is English.
(2) The subject in ＿＿＿ ＿＿＿ ＿＿＿ ＿＿＿ is English.

Grammar **25**

01 주어진 단어를 바르게 배열하여 다음 우리말을 영어로 쓰시오.

네가 나에게 소개해 준 그 소녀는 매우 인기 있어.
(very / is / me / popular / the girl / introduced / you / to / whom)

➡ _____

02 다음 대화를 읽고 빈칸에 알맞은 말을 쓰시오.

A: Why didn't Sandra carry the box?
B: It was too heavy.

➡ The box _____

_____ .

03 다음 두 문장을 하나의 문장으로 쓸 때 빈칸에 알맞은 말을 쓰시오.

Ross wrote a poem. The poem was so amazing that I was moved to tears.

➡ The poem _____

_____ .

04 다음 빈칸에 알맞은 말을 쓰시오.

(1) The cats _____ you take care of look happy.
(2) The guests _____ are in the hall want something cold to drink.
(3) Some people _____ we can see over there are interested in our artworks.

05 주어진 문장과 같은 의미의 문장을 지시에 맞게 쓰시오. 주어 Penny로 문장을 시작할 것.

Penny was too sick to eat anything.

(1) because를 써서

➡ _____

(2) so ~ that을 써서

➡ _____

06 자연스러운 문장이 되도록 두 문장을 연결하시오.

• The car is not his.
• Kevin picked some roses.
• I know the person.

• Catherine planted roses.
• You took a trip with him.
• Tom is driving a car.

(1) The car _____ .
(2) Kevin _____ .
(3) I _____ .

07 다음 대화를 읽고 빈칸에 알맞은 말을 쓰시오.

A: Do you need to buy a coat, Avian?
B: I don't need to buy another coat because I already have a coat which is really warm.

➡ Avian's coat is _____

_____ .

08 〈보기〉와 같이 두 문장을 하나의 문장으로 쓰시오.

> ┌─ 보기 ─
>
> I was very grateful to her. I made a pie for her.
> → I was so grateful to her that I made a pie for her.

(1) Sally speaks English very well. You would think it is her native language.

➡ _____

(2) The music was very loud. You could hear it from miles away.

➡ _____

(3) Gabriel is very beautiful. Any man would love to be with her.

➡ _____

09 원인과 결과를 나타내는 구문을 이용하여 다음 문장과 같은 의미의 문장을 쓰시오.

> The soup burned my tongue because it was too hot.

➡ _____

10 주어진 단어를 활용하여 다음 우리말을 영어로 쓰시오.

> Jody는 Ms. Galler가 찾고 있는 학생이다.
> (look for)

➡ _____

11 다음 우리말을 영어로 쓰시오.

(1) 네가 어제 본 소년은 나의 남동생이야.

➡ _____

(2) 그녀가 입고 있는 드레스는 유명한 사람에 의해 디자인된 거야.

➡ _____

12 주어진 단어를 바르게 배열하여 다음 우리말을 영어로 쓰시오.

> 내가 가장 자주 전화하는 사람들은 나의 엄마와 내 여동생들이다.
> (my sisters / I / my mother / are / and / often / call / the people / most / whom)

➡ _____

13 다음 대화를 읽고 빈칸에 알맞은 말을 쓰시오.

> A: Lisa must be really happy.
> B: Why do you say so, Jason?
> A: I can see her dancing in the room.

➡ According to Jason, Lisa is _____ she is dancing in the room.

14 주어진 문장을 'so'를 이용하여 하나의 문장으로 표현하시오.

> The party was very enjoyable. Therefore, no one wanted to leave.

➡ _____

15 주어진 단어를 활용하여 다음 우리말을 영어로 쓰시오.

> 그녀는 너무 일찍 일어나서 피곤했어요.
> (so / early)

➡ _____

Making Good Choices

Emma: What are you doing, Kyle?

Kyle: Oh, Emma. I'm watching <u>the movie, *Y-Men 7*</u> <u>on</u> my computer.
the movie = *Y-Men 7* 동격   ～로(수단)

Emma: How is it?

Kyle: Don't ask. <u>It's so boring that I want to cry.</u>
원인과 결과(너무 ～해서 …하다)

Emma: I'm sorry <u>to hear</u> that.
감정의 원인

Kyle: I'm so mad. The movie advertisement said it was "The Most Exciting Movie <u>of</u> the Year."
of+명사(비교의 범위를 나타냄)

Emma: Well, you can't believe everything <u>that</u> you read.
목적격 관계대명사

Kyle: They lied on the advertisement. I'm going to ask for my money back.

Emma: Hold on, Kyle! They didn't <u>really</u> lie <u>because</u> they used <u>opinions, not facts.</u>
(부정문에서) 꼭, 사실   이유를 나타내는 접속사
A. not B: B가 아니라 A

Kyle: Huh? <u>I'm not following you.</u>
I can't understand you. = I don't get it.

Emma: Opinions express people's feelings <u>like</u>, "The desert is beautiful." You can't say <u>that</u> it's true or not. But, facts <u>can be proven</u>. For example, "The Atacama Desert is in Chile," is a fact. You can check <u>that</u> on the map.
전치사(～와 같은)
say의 목적어를 이끄는 명사절 접속사
조동사가 있는 수동태
= The Atacama Desert is in Chile.

Kyle: Okay…. But what's the connection with movies?

boring 지루한
advertisement 광고
believe 믿다
lie 거짓말하다
ask for A back A를 돌려달라고 청하다
opinion 의견
express 나타내다, 표현하다
for example 예를 들어
check ～을 확인하다
connection 관련성

📎 확인문제

- 다음 문장이 본문의 내용과 일치하면 T, 일치하지 <u>않으면</u> F를 쓰시오.

1   Kyle feels like crying because of the movie. ☐

2   Emma tells Kyle to believe what he reads. ☐

3   It is hard to say that they told a lie on the advertisement. ☐

Emma: Let me explain. What's your favorite movie?
let+목적어+동사원형: 목적어가 ~하게 하다

Kyle: It's *Forrest Gump*.

Emma: Okay. Let's look for its advertisement. What does it say?
it = Forrest Gump   = its advertisement

Kyle: It says, "Winner of 6 Academy Awards including Best Picture."
~라고 되어[쓰여] 있다   수상작   전치사(~을 포함하여)

Emma: See? It uses facts unlike the *Y-Men 7* advertisement. Do you
전치사(~와는 달리)

see the difference?
알다, 이해하다

Kyle: Not exactly. The *Y-Men 7* ad says "Most Exciting Movie" and the
정확히는 아니다

Forrest Gump ad says "Best Picture." Aren't they both opinions?
= 'Most Exciting Movie' and 'Best Picture'

Emma: That's a great question, Kyle. When people use words like
전치사(~와 같은)

"best" or "most," they are usually expressing opinions. But in the

Forrest Gump ad, "Best Picture" is the award which the movie
목적격 관계대명사(선행사: award)

won. We can check that on the Internet. That's a fact.
"Best Picture" is the award which the movie won

Kyle: Aha! From now on I'm only going to trust ads with facts.
지금부터   ~을 가진, ~이 있는

Emma: It's not that simple. Most ads mix facts with opinions. So you
지시부사(그렇게, 그 정도로)

have to make a smart choice based on both of them.
facts and opinions

Kyle: Got it! Emma, do you want to watch the rest of *Y-Men 7* with me?
알았어!

Emma: Thanks, but no thanks. Enjoy the rest of the movie!
상대방이 권해 줘서 고맙지만 거절하고 싶을 때 쓸 수 있는 표현

explain 설명하다

favorite 가장 좋아하는

difference 차이

both 둘 다

trust 믿다

simple 간단한

mix A with B A와 B를 섞다

make a choice 선택하다

based on ~을 바탕으로

rest 나머지

📎 **확인문제**

● 다음 문장이 본문의 내용과 일치하면 T, 일치하지 않으면 F를 쓰시오.

1 Emma's favorite movie is *Forrest Gump*. ☐

2 *Forrest Gump* won seven Academy Awards. ☐

3 People use words like 'best' or 'most' when telling opinions. ☐

4 Kyle wants Emma to watch the movie with him. ☐

● 우리말을 참고하여 빈칸에 알맞은 말을 쓰시오.

1 Emma: What _____ you _____, Kyle?

2 Kyle: Oh, Emma. I'm _____ the movie, *Y-Men 7* _____ my computer.

3 Emma: _____ is it?

4 Kyle: Don't ask. It's _____ _____ _____ I want to cry.

5 Emma: I'm sorry _____ _____ _____ .

6 Kyle: I'm so mad. The movie _____ said _____ was "_____ _____ _____ of the Year."

7 Emma: Well, you can't believe _____ _____ _____ _____ .

8 Kyle: They lied on the advertisement. I'm going to _____ _____ _____ _____ _____ .

9 Emma: _____ _____ , Kyle! They didn't really _____ _____ they used opinions, not facts.

10 Kyle: Huh? I'm _____ _____ _____ .

11 Emma: Opinions _____ _____ _____ like, "The desert is beautiful."

12 You can't say _____ it's true or not. But, facts _____ _____ _____ .

13 _____ _____ , "The Atacama Desert is in Chile," is a fact. You can _____ _____ _____ _____ _____ .

14 Kyle: Okay…. But what's _____ _____ movies?

15 Emma: _____ _____ . What's your favorite movie?

1 Emma: Kyle, 뭐 하고 있니?

2 Kyle: Emma. 나는 컴퓨터로 영화 "Y-Men 7"을 보고 있어.

3 Emma: 어때?

4 Kyle: 묻지 마. 너무 지루해서 울고 싶어.

5 Emma: 유감이야.

6 Klye: 난 정말 화가 나. 영화 광고에는 이것이 "올해의 가장 흥미진진한 영화"라고 쓰여 있었어.

7 Emma: 음, 넌 네가 읽는 것을 모두 믿을 수는 없어.

8 Kyle: 그들은 광고에 거짓말을 한 거야. 돈을 환불해 달라고 해야겠어.

9 Emma: 기다려, Kyle! 그들은 사실이 아닌 의견을 사용했기 때문에 꼭 거짓말을 한 것은 아니야.

10 Kyle: 뭐라고? 네 말을 이해하지 못하겠어.

11 Emma: 의견은 "사막은 아름다워."와 같이 사람들의 감정을 표현하는 것이야.

12 그것이 사실인지 아닌지 말할 수는 없어. 하지만 사실은 증명할 수 있어.

13 예를 들면, "아타카마 사막은 칠레에 있다."는 사실이야. 넌 그것을 지도에서 확인할 수 있어.

14 Kyle: 알겠어… 하지만 그게 영화와 무슨 관련이 있니?

15 Emma: 설명해 줄게. 네가 가장 좋아하는 영화가 뭐니?

16 Kyle: _____ *Forrest Gump*.

17 Emma: Okay. Let's _____ _____ _____ _____. What does it say?

18 Kyle: _____ _____, "Winner of 6 Academy Awards including Best Picture."

19 Emma: See? It _____ _____ _____ the *Y-Men 7* advertisement.

20 Do you see _____ _____?

21 Kyle: Not _____. The *Y-Men 7* ad _____ "Most Exciting Movie" and the *Forrest Gump* ad _____ "Best Picture."

22 _____ they _____ _____?

23 Emma: That's a great question, Kyle. When people use _____ _____ "best" or "most," they are _____ _____ _____.

24 But in the *Forrest Gump* ad, "Best Picture" is the award _____ _____ _____ _____.

25 We can check _____ _____ _____ _____ _____. That's a fact.

26 Kyle: Aha! _____ _____ _____ I'm only going to _____ ads _____ facts.

27 Emma: It's not _____ _____. Most ads _____ facts _____ opinions.

28 So you have to _____ _____ _____ _____ based on _____ of them.

29 Kyle: Got it! Emma, do you want _____ _____ the rest of *Y-Men 7* with me?

30 Emma: Thanks, but no thanks. Enjoy _____ _____ the movie!

---

16 Kyle: "Forrest Gump"야.

17 Emma: 좋아. 그 영화의 광고를 찾아보자. 뭐라고 쓰여 있니?

18 Kyle: "Best Picture를 포함하여 아카데미 6개 부문 수상작"이라고 쓰여 있어.

19 Emma: 알겠니? "Y-Men 7" 광고와는 달리 사실을 사용하고 있어.

20 차이를 알겠니?

21 Kyle: 잘 모르겠어. "Y-Men 7" 광고는 "Most Exciting Movie" 라고 쓰여 있고 "Forrest Gump" 광고는 "Best Picture"라고 쓰여 있잖아.

22 둘 다 의견 아니니?

23 Emma: 좋은 질문이야, Kyle. 사람들이 'best'나 'most'와 같은 말을 사용할 때, 그들은 대개 의견을 표현하는 거야.

24 하지만 "Forest Gump" 광고에서 "Best Picture"는 영화가 받은 상이야.

25 우리는 인터넷에서 그것을 확인할 수 있어. 그건 사실이야.

26 Kyle: 아하! 지금부터 사실로 이루어진 광고만 믿겠어.

27 Emma: 그렇게 간단하지는 않아. 대부분의 광고는 사실과 의견이 섞여 있어.

28 그러니 그 둘을 바탕으로 현명한 선택을 해야 해.

29 Kyle: 알겠어! Emma, "Y-Men 7"의 남은 부분을 나와 함께 볼래?

30 Emma: 고맙지만 사양할게. 영화의 남은 부분 잘 봐!

• 우리말을 참고하여 본문을 영작하시오.

1 Emma: Kyle, 뭐 하고 있니?

➡ _____

2 Kyle: Emma. 나는 컴퓨터로 영화 "Y-Men 7"을 보고 있어.

➡ _____

3 Emma: 어때?

➡ _____

4 Kyle: 묻지 마. 너무 지루해서 울고 싶어.

➡ _____

5 Emma: 유감이야.

➡ _____

6 Klye: 난 정말 화가 나. 영화 광고에는 이것이 "올해의 가장 흥미진진한 영화"라고 쓰여 있었어.

➡ _____

7 Emma: 음, 넌 네가 읽는 것을 모두 믿을 수는 없어.

➡ _____

8 Kyle: 그들은 광고에 거짓말을 한 거야. 돈을 환불해 달라고 해야겠어.

➡ _____

9 Emma: 기다려, Kyle! 그들은 사실이 아닌 의견을 사용했기 때문에 꼭 거짓말을 한 것은 아니야.

➡ _____

10 Kyle: 뭐라고? 네 말을 이해하지 못하겠어.

➡ _____

11 Emma: 의견은 "사막은 아름다워."와 같이 사람들의 감정을 표현하는 것이야.

➡ _____

12 그것이 사실인지 아닌지 말할 수는 없어. 하지만 사실은 증명할 수 있어.

➡ _____

13 예를 들면, "아타카마 사막은 칠레에 있다."는 사실이야. 넌 그것을 지도에서 확인할 수 있어.

➡ _____

14 Kyle: 알겠어…. 하지만 그게 영화와 무슨 관련이 있니?

➡ _____

15 Emma: 설명해 줄게. 네가 가장 좋아하는 영화가 뭐니?

➡ _____

16 Kyle: "Forest Gump"야.

➡ _____

17 Emma: 좋아. 그 영화의 광고를 찾아보자. 뭐라고 쓰여 있니?

➡ _____

18 Kyle: "Best Picture를 포함하여 아카데미 6개 부문 수상작"이라고 쓰여 있어.

➡ _____

19 Emma: 알겠니? "Y-Men 7" 광고와는 달리 사실을 사용하고 있어.

➡ _____

20 차이를 알겠니?

➡ _____

21 Kyle: 잘 모르겠어. "Y-Men 7" 광고는 "Most Exciting Movie"라고 쓰여 있고 "Forest Gump" 광고는 "Best Picture"라고 쓰여 있잖아.

➡ _____

22 둘 다 의견 아니니?

➡ _____

23 Emma: 좋은 질문이야, Kyle. 사람들이 'best'나 'most'와 같은 말을 사용할 때, 그들은 대개 의견을 표현하는 거야.

➡ _____

24 하지만 "Forest Gump" 광고에서 "Best Picture"는 영화가 받은 상이야.

➡ _____

25 우리는 인터넷에서 그것을 확인할 수 있어. 그건 사실이야.

➡ _____

26 Kyle: 아하! 지금부터 사실로 이루어진 광고만 믿겠어.

➡ _____

27 Emma: 그렇게 간단하지는 않아. 대부분의 광고는 사실과 의견이 섞여 있어.

➡ _____

28 그러니 그 둘을 바탕으로 현명한 선택을 해야 해.

➡ _____

29 Kyle: 알겠어! Emma, "Y-Men 7"의 남은 부분을 나와 함께 볼래?

➡ _____

30 Emma: 고맙지만 사양할게. 영화의 남은 부분 잘 봐!

➡ _____

[01~05] 다음 글을 읽고 물음에 답하시오.

Emma: What are you doing, Kyle?

Kyle: Oh, Emma. I'm watching the movie, *Y-Men 7* on my computer.

Emma: How is it?

Kyle: Don't ask. It's so boring that I want to cry.

Emma: I'm sorry to hear that.

Kyle: I'm so mad. The movie advertisement said it was "The Most Exciting Movie of the Year."

Emma: Well, you can't believe everything ___(A)___ you read.

Kyle: They lied on the advertisement. I'm going to ask for my money back.

Emma: (B)Hold on, Kyle! They didn't really lie because they used opinions, not facts.

01 빈칸 (A)에 들어갈 말로 적절한 것을 <u>모두</u> 고르시오.

① which   ② that   ③ what
④ whose   ⑤ who

02 다음 중 위 글의 내용과 일치하지 <u>않는</u> 것은?

① Kyle is watching *Y-Men 7*.
② Emma is wondering what Kyle is doing.
③ Kyle is satisfied with the movie.
④ Kyle wants to get his money back.
⑤ Kyle thinks that he was fooled by the movie advertisement.

서답형
03 다음과 같이 풀이되는 단어를 위 글에서 찾아 쓰시오.

> ideas or feelings about something.

➡ _____

서답형
04 Write the reason why Kyle wants to cry. Answer in English with the phrase 'It's because.'

➡ _____

05 다음 중 밑줄 친 (B)를 대신하여 쓰일 수 있는 것은?

① Go ahead   ② Wait
③ Let me see   ④ Watch out
⑤ Way to go

[06~09] 다음 글을 읽고 물음에 답하시오.

Kyle: Huh? I'm not following you.

Emma: Opinions express people's feelings like, "The desert is beautiful." You can't say that it's true or not. But, facts can be proven. ___(A)___, "The Atacama Desert is in Chile," is a fact. You can check (B) that on the map.

Kyle: Okay.... But what's the connection with movies?

Emma: Let me explain. What's your favorite movie?

Kyle: It's *Forrest Gump*.

Emma: Okay. Let's look for its advertisement. What does it say?

Kyle: It says, "Winner of 6 Academy Awards including Best Picture."

Emma: See? It uses facts unlike the *Y-Men 7* advertisement. Do you see the difference?

06 다음 중 빈칸 (A)에 들어갈 말로 가장 적절한 것은?

① However   ② Therefore
③ Also   ④ For example
⑤ Nevertheless

서답형

07 밑줄 친 (B)가 가리키는 것을 15자 이내의 우리말로 쓰시오.

➡ _____

08 다음 중 위 글을 읽고 답할 수 <u>없는</u> 질문은?

① What is opinion?

② Where is Atacama Desert?

③ What is Emma's favorite movie?

④ How many academy awards did *Forrest Gump* win?

⑤ What does *Forrest Gump* advertisement say?

09 According to the passage, which one is a fact?

① Jimmy is the kindest person I have ever met.

② I think the river is dangerous to swim in.

③ It seems that the butterfly is saying hello to me.

④ Mrs. Simpson looked upset today.

⑤ Barack Obama is the 44th president of the United States of America.

[10~15] 다음 글을 읽고 물음에 답하시오.

Kyle: Not exactly. The *Y-Men 7* ad says "Most Exciting Movie" and the *Forrest Gump* ad says "Best Picture." Aren't they both ①opinion?

Emma: That's a great question, Kyle. When people use words like "best" or "most," they are usually expressing opinions. But ②in the *Forrest Gump* ad, "Best Picture" is the award ③which the movie won. We can check that ④on the Internet. That's ___(A)___.

Kyle: Aha! (B)지금부터 I'm only going to trust ⑤ads with facts.

Emma: It's not that simple. Most ads mix facts with opinions. So you have to make a smart choice based on (C)both of them.

서답형

10 빈칸 (A)에 알맞은 말을 위 글에서 찾아 어법에 맞게 쓰시오.

➡ _____

11 밑줄 친 우리말 (B)를 영어로 바르게 옮긴 것은?

① For a long time　② For the time being

③ From now on　④ From time to time

⑤ Now and then

서답형

12 밑줄 친 (C)가 가리키는 것을 영어로 쓰시오.

➡ _____

13 ①~⑤ 중 어법상 바르지 <u>않은</u> 것은?

①　　②　　③　　④　　⑤

서답형

14 What do people usually use when they express their opinions? Answer in English with a full sentence.

➡ _____

_____

15 다음 중 위 글의 내용과 일치하지 <u>않는</u> 것은?

① There is a phrase "Most Exciting Movie" in the ad of *Y-Men 7*.

② *Forrest Gump* won the Best Picture award.

③ The ad of *Forrest Gump* used a fact.

④ There are many ads using only facts.

⑤ Kyle finally understands the difference between opinions and facts.

[16~20] 다음 글을 읽고 물음에 답하시오.

Emma: What are you doing, Kyle?

Kyle: Oh, Emma. I'm watching the movie, *Y-Men 7* on my computer.

Emma: (A)[What / How] is it?

Kyle: Don't ask. It's so (B)[boring / bored] that I want to cry.

Emma: I'm sorry ⓐto hear that.

Kyle: I'm so mad. The movie advertisement said it was "The Most Exciting Movie of the Year."

Emma: Well, you can't believe everything that you read.

Kyle: They lied on the advertisement. I'm going (C)[asking / to ask] for my money back.

Emma: Hold on, Kyle! They didn't really lie ___ⓑ___ they used opinions, not facts.

16 다음 중 밑줄 친 ⓐ와 쓰임이 같은 것은?

① David wants me to go with him to the theater.

② It is fun to spend time with you.

③ Julia made some cookies to give her friends.

④ There is a chance to win the race.

⑤ I am so happy to have such a nice teacher.

중요

17 다음 중 빈칸 ⓑ에 들어갈 말로 가장 적절한 것은?

① so   ② while   ③ and

④ because   ⑤ though

서답형

18 What is Kyle doing? Answer in English with a full sentence.

➡ _____

19 (A)~(C)에서 어법상 옳은 것을 바르게 짝지은 것은?

① What – boring – asking

② What – boring – to ask

③ What – bored – to ask

④ How – boring – to ask

⑤ How – bored – asking

서답형

20 According to the passage, what did the movie advertisement say about the movie?

➡ _____

_____

[21~25] 다음 글을 읽고 물음에 답하시오.

Kyle: Huh? I'm not following you.

Emma: Opinions express people's feelings like, "The desert is beautiful." ① You can't say that it's true or not. ② But, facts can (A)[prove / be proven]. ③ For example, "The Atacama Desert is in Chile," is a fact. ④

Kyle: Okay.... But what's the connection with movies? ⑤

Emma: Let me (B)[explain / to explain]. What's your favorite movie?

Kyle: It's *Forrest Gump*.

Emma: Okay. Let's look for its advertisement. What does it say?

Kyle: It says, "Winner of 6 Academy Awards (C)[including / included] Best Picture."

Emma: See? It uses facts unlike the *Y-Men 7* advertisement. Do you see the difference?

중요

21 ①~⑤ 중 주어진 문장이 들어가기에 가장 적절한 곳은?

You can check that on the map.

①   ②   ③   ④   ⑤

22 (A)~(C)에서 어법상 옳은 것을 바르게 짝지은 것은?

① be proven – explain – included
② be proven – explain – including
③ prove – to explain – included
④ prove – explain – including
⑤ prove – to explain – including

23 위 글의 내용을 참고하여 다음 빈칸에 알맞은 말을 쓰시오.

According to the passage, "She is the most beautiful baby I've ever seen," is _____. On the other hand, "Mountain Everest is the highest mountain in the world." is _____.

24 According to the passage, who says an opinion?

① Jane: King Sejong invented Hanguel.
② Tim: Canada is rich in natural resources.
③ Brad: The longest river in the world is the Nile in Egypt.
④ Zoe: Going to the beach alone is not safe.
⑤ Kelly: Tom's house is located near the river.

25 다음 중 위 글의 내용과 일치하지 <u>않는</u> 것은?

① People's feelings are expressed in opinions.
② Emma wants to know what Kyle's favorite movie is.
③ Emma is explaining the difference between opinions and facts.
④ The *Forrest Gump* ad uses facts.
⑤ *Forrest Gump* won seven Academy Awards.

[26~29] 다음 글을 읽고 물음에 답하시오.

Emma: Do you see the difference?
(A) That's a great question. When people use words like "best" or "most," they are usually expressing opinions. But in the *Forrest Gump* ad, "Best Picture" is the award which the movie won. We can check (a)that on the Internet. That's a fact.
(B) It's not that simple. Most ads mix facts ___ⓐ___ opinions. So you have to make a smart choice based on both of them.
(C) Aha! From now on I'm only going to trust ads ___ⓑ___ facts.
(D) Not exactly. The *Y-Men 7* ad says "Most Exciting Movie" and the *Forrest Gump* ad says "Best Picture." Aren't they both opinions?

26 자연스러운 대화가 되도록 (A)~(D)를 바르게 나열하시오.

➡ _____

27 다음 중 빈칸 ⓐ와 ⓑ에 공통으로 들어갈 말은?

① in   ② by   ③ with   ④ to   ⑤ at

28 밑줄 친 (a)가 가리키는 것을 우리말로 쓰시오.

➡ _____

29 위 글의 내용에 맞게 빈칸에 알맞은 말을 쓰시오.

We can find both _____ in most ads.

➡ _____

[01~05] 다음 글을 읽고 물음에 답하시오.

Emma: What are you doing, Kyle?

Kyle: Oh, Emma. I'm watching the movie, *Y-Men 7* on my computer.

Emma: How is it?

Kyle: Don't ask. (A)너무 지루해서 울고 싶어.

Emma: I'm sorry to hear that.

Kyle: I'm so mad. The movie advertisement said it was "The Most Exciting Movie of the Year."

Emma: Well, you can't believe everything that you read.

Kyle: They lied on the advertisement.
_____ (a)

Emma: Hold on, Kyle! (B)They didn't really lie because they used opinions, not facts.

중요
01 주어진 단어를 바르게 배열하여 빈칸 (a)에 들어갈 말을 쓰시오.

(back / am / to / I / ask / money / for / my / going)

➡ _____

02 밑줄 친 우리말 (A)를 영어로 쓰시오.

➡ _____

고난이도
03 주어진 단어를 이용하여 밑줄 친 (B)와 같은 의미의 문장을 쓰시오.

(not A but B / so)

➡ _____
_____

04 What is the title of the movie that Kyle is watching?

➡ _____

05 글의 내용에 맞게 빈칸에 알맞은 말을 쓰시오.

Unlike the movie advertisement, Kyle did not feel _____ while he was watching the movie.

[06~10] 다음 글을 읽고 물음에 답하시오.

Kyle: Huh? I'm not following you.

Emma: Opinions express people's feelings like, "The desert is beautiful." You can't say that it's true or not. But, facts can ___(A)___. For example, "(B)The Atacama Desert is in Chile," is a fact. You can check that on the map.

Kyle: Okay.... But what's the connection with movies?

Emma: Let me explain. What's your favorite movie?

Kyle: It's *Forrest Gump*.

Emma: Okay. Let's look for its advertisement. What does it say?

Kyle: It says, "Winner of 6 Academy Awards including Best Picture."

Emma: See? (C)It uses facts unlike the *Y-Men 7* advertisement. Do you see the difference?

06 주어진 단어를 빈칸 (A)에 어법에 맞게 쓰시오.

> prove

➡ _____

07 How can you know the underlined sentence (B) is a fact? Find the answer in the above passage.

➡ _____

08 다음 문장은 밑줄 친 문장 (C)를 읽고 알 수 있는 것이다. 빈칸에 알맞은 말을 쓰시오.

➡ The *Y-Men 7* ad _____.

09 위 글의 표현을 이용하여 다음 우리말을 영어로 쓰시오.

> 6개의 아카데미상을 수상한 그 영화를 보았니?

➡ _____

10 According to the passage, what is Kyle's favorite movie? Answer in English with a full sentence.

➡ _____

[11~14] 다음 글을 읽고 물음에 답하시오.

Kyle: Not exactly. The *Y-Men 7* ad says "Most Exciting Movie" and the *Forrest Gump* ad says "Best Picture." _____ (A)

Emma: That's a great question, Kyle. When people use words like "best" or "most," they are usually expressing opinions. But in the *Forrest Gump* ad, (B)"Best Picture" is the award which the movie won. We can check that on the Internet. That's a fact.

Kyle: Aha! From now on I'm only going to trust ads with facts.

Emma: It's not that simple. Most ads mix facts with opinions. So you have to make a smart choice based on both of them.

11 주어진 단어를 바르게 나열하여 빈칸 (A)에 알맞은 말을 쓰시오.

> (opinions / they / aren't / both)?

➡ _____

12 밑줄 친 문장 (B)를 두 문장으로 나누어 쓰시오.

➡ _____

13 주어진 어구를 바르게 배열하여 다음 우리말을 영어로 쓰시오.

> 'best'나 'most'와 같은 말을 사용하는 사람들은 대개 의견을 표현하는 중이다.
> (opinions / people / use / are / expressing / usually / 'best' or 'most' / who / like / words)

➡ _____
_____

14 위 글의 내용에 맞게 빈칸에 알맞은 말을 쓰시오.

> When we make a decision, we should _____ our choice on _____ _____.

Listen and Speak 2-C

A: How do you like your bicycle?
'~이 마음에 드니?' (만족하는지를 묻는 표현)

B: I'm not happy with it.
= the bicycle을 가리킨다.

A: Why not?
= Why are you not satisfied with it?

B: It's too heavy.

A: 자전거가 마음에 드니?
B: 마음에 들지 않아.
A: 왜?
B: 너무 무거워.

Think and Write

Harry Potter is a fantasy novel. It was written by J. K. Rowling. Harry Potter
인칭대명사(Harry Potter 지칭)

is the main character of the book. When Harry goes to magic school, his
주인공

adventures begin. I especially like the friendship of Harry and his friends. The

book was so interesting that I couldn't put it down. I strongly recommend it to
흥미를 유발할 때 현재분사 so+형용사/부사+that …: 너무 ~해서 …하다

everyone.

구문해설 • a fantasy novel: 공상 소설 • adventure: 모험 • especially: 특히
• friendship: 우정 • put A down: ~를 내려놓다 • recommend: 추천하다

"해리포터"는 공상 소설이다. 이 책은 J. K. Rowling에 의해 쓰였다. Harry Potter 는 이 책의 주인공이다. Harry가 마법 학교에 가면서 그의 모험은 시작된다. 나는 특히 Harry와 그의 친구들의 우정을 좋아한다. 이 책은 너무 재미있어서 나는 책을 놓을 수가 없었다. 나는 모두에게 이 책을 강력히 추천한다.

Project

Korean folk village

Facts: It is located in Yongin. There are Korean traditional houses. Visitors
~에 위치해 있다   ~이 있다 (뒤에 나오는 명사에 수의 일치)
can watch nongak and jultagi.

Opinions: It's a fun place in Yongin. Korean traditional houses are beautiful.

Nongak and jultagi will be exciting.
감정을 유발할 때 현재분사

구문해설 • folk village: 민속촌 • traditional: 전통적인 • exciting: 신나는

한국 민속촌

사실: 그것은 용인에 있습니다. 한국 전통 가옥이 있습니다. 방문객들은 농악과 줄타기를 볼 수 있습니다.

의견: 그곳은 용인에 있는 재미있는 장소입니다. 한국 전통 가옥들은 아름답습니다. 농악과 줄타기는 신이 날 것입니다.

01 다음 짝지어진 단어의 관계가 같도록 빈칸에 알맞은 말을 쓰시오.

> increase : decrease = empty : _____

02 다음 영영풀이가 가리키는 것을 고르시오.

> to say or write something that is not true

① explain   ② tell
③ present   ④ lie
⑤ express

03 다음 중 밑줄 친 부분의 뜻풀이가 바르지 <u>않은</u> 것은?

① I like this <u>pocket</u> on the back of the suitcase. 주머니
② I can <u>trust</u> her word. 신뢰하다
③ She answered <u>wisely</u>. 현명하게
④ This book is <u>worth</u> reading. 세계
⑤ The bag comes in <u>navy</u> and green. 남색

04 다음 주어진 우리말과 일치하도록 주어진 단어를 모두 배열하여 영작하시오.

(1) 선물이 마음에 드니?
(you / how / like / the / present / do)
➡ _____

(2) 그의 주장을 증명할 증거가 없다.
(no / his / evidence / is / to / claim / there / prove)
➡ _____

05 주어진 단어를 이용해서 다음 우리말에 맞게 빈칸에 알맞은 말을 쓰시오.

(1) 가격을 비교해 보고 선택하는 게 어때?
➡ Why don't you _____ after comparing the prices? (make)

(2) 나는 네가 다시 한 번 서류를 확인해야 할 것 같아.
➡ I think you should _____ the documents again. (out)

(3) 야외 시장은 사람들로 가득 차 있었다.
➡ The outdoor market was _____ people. (of)

06 다음 주어진 문장의 밑줄 친 lie와 같은 의미로 쓰인 것은?

> Why did you lie to me? I'm so disappointed with you.

① I want to go home and <u>lie</u> on the bed.
② <u>Lie</u> down here and take a rest.
③ I'm innocent because I didn't <u>lie</u> for a second.
④ My children usually <u>lie</u> on the right side when they sleep.
⑤ You can't <u>lie</u> on the floor.

07 다음 문장에 공통으로 들어갈 말을 고르시오.

> • This gallery is _____ a visit.
> • This movie is _____ watching.
> • This souvenir is _____ $100.

① worth   ② cost
③ price   ④ value
⑤ expense

Conversation

[08~09] 다음 대화를 읽고 물음에 답하시오.

Brian: (A)Can you recommend a good movie?

Emily: _____ (B) _____ I really liked it.

Brian: Oh, I haven't seen it yet.

Emily: It's the number one movie right now.

08 위 대화의 밑줄 친 (A)와 바꾸어 쓸 수 있는 것은?

① What do you think about a good movie?

② Would you recommend a good movie?

③ What is a good movie?

④ Do you want to see a good movie?

⑤ What should I do to find a good movie?

09 위 대화의 빈칸 (B)에 들어갈 말로 어색한 것은?

① Try *Star Wars*.

② How about watching *Star Wars*?

③ Why did you watch *Star Wars*?

④ What about watching *Star Wars*?

⑤ I recommend *Star Wars*.

[10~12] 다음 대화를 읽고 물음에 답하시오.

W: May I help you?

B: Yes. I'm looking for a backpack. Can you recommend one?

W: How about this red one? Red is the most popular color (A)these days.

B: My old backpack was red, so I want a different color.

W: How about this navy one? It has side pockets.

B: Oh, that looks good. I'll take it.

10 위 대화의 여자와 소년의 관계로 적절한 것은?

① doctor – patient ② clerk – customer

③ guide – tourist ④ teacher – student

⑤ writer – reader

11 위 대화의 밑줄 친 (A)와 바꾸어 쓸 수 있는 것은?

① those days ② nowadays

③ in the past ④ the day before

⑤ in the future

12 위 대화의 내용과 일치하지 <u>않는</u> 것은?

① 소년은 배낭을 찾고 있다.

② 요즘 빨간색이 가장 인기 있는 색이다.

③ 소년의 옛 배낭이 빨간색이었다.

④ 남색 배낭은 양옆에 주머니가 있다.

⑤ 소년은 주머니가 있는 빨간색 가방을 샀다.

[13~15] 다음 대화를 읽고 물음에 답하시오.

Jack: Hi, Suji. (A)경주 여행은 어땠니?
   (Gyeongju, trip, how, like)

Suji: I was very happy with it.

Jack: Where did you visit?

Suji: I visited Cheomseongdae. It was great.

Jack: Where else did you go?

Suji: Bulguksa. It was a wonderful place.

Jack: Sounds like the perfect trip.

Suji: Yeah, but walking up to Seokguram was difficult.

Jack: But I'm sure it was worth it.

13 위 대화의 밑줄 친 (A)의 우리말을 주어진 단어를 사용하여 영작하시오.

➡ _____

14 위 대화에서 다음 주어진 영영풀이가 나타내는 말을 찾아 쓰시오.

important, good or enjoyable enough for something

➡ _____

15 위 대화를 읽고 대답할 수 <u>없는</u> 질문은?

① Where did Suji travel?

② How did Suji like her trip to Gyeongju?

③ What did Suji think of Bulguksa?

④ What does Jack think about walking up to Seokguram?

⑤ How long did it take for Suji to walk up to Seokguram?

16 다음 짝지어진 대화가 <u>어색한</u> 것을 고르시오.

① A: Can you recommend a musical for me?

   B: How about *The Lion King*?

② A: How do you like your bicycle?

   B: I'm really happy with it.

③ A: Would you recommend a good movie?

   B: Why don't you try *Star Wars*?

④ A: How do you like your jacket?

   B: I'm not satisfied with it.

⑤ A: What do you like about your backpack?

   B: I like it so much.

Grammar

17 다음 중 주어진 문장의 밑줄 친 부분과 쓰임이 같은 것은?

> The health-care worker <u>that</u> I spoke to was helpful.

① Hudson said <u>that</u> he refused the job offer.

② It is true <u>that</u> I don't like your attitude.

③ Patrick woke up so late <u>that</u> he couldn't attend the meeting again.

④ The fact <u>that</u> you lied to the police officer doesn't change.

⑤ This is the same kind of watch <u>that</u> I lost.

18 주어진 문장과 같은 의미의 문장은?

> We postponed our trip because the weather was bad.

① The weather was bad enough that we postponed our trip.

② The weather was so bad that we postponed our trip.

③ Although the weather was bad, we postponed our trip.

④ Because we postponed our trip, the weather was bad.

⑤ The weather was too bad to postpone our trip.

19 다음 빈칸에 들어갈 말로 적절한 것을 <u>모두</u> 고르시오.

> The children _____ Mr. Smith adopted are from three different countries.

① who   ② that   ③ whose

④ which   ⑤ whom

20 주어진 문장과 같은 의미의 문장을 쓰시오.

> We went swimming because it was so hot yesterday. (so ~ that을 이용)

➡ _____

21 다음 중 빈칸에 들어갈 말로 적절한 것은?

> • She was so embarrassed that she wanted to run away and hide.
> = She wanted to run away and hide _____ she was embarrassed.

① although   ② because   ③ so

④ unless   ⑤ therefore

22 다음 중 의미가 나머지 넷과 <u>다른</u> 하나는?

① Maya is so afraid of flying that she can't travel by plane.

② Maya can't travel by plane because she is afraid of flying.

③ Maya is afraid of flying, so she can't travel by plane.

④ Maya is too afraid of flying to travel by plane.

⑤ Although Maya is afraid of flying, she travels by plane.

23 주어진 단어를 이용하여 다음 우리말을 영어로 쓰시오.

> 그 남자가 훔친 약은 그의 아들을 위한 것이었다.
> (drug)

➡ _____

24 다음 중 밑줄 친 부분이 생략 가능하지 <u>않은</u> 것은?

① The painting <u>which</u> you drew looks amazing.

② The car <u>that</u> Brian borrowed from his brother was dirty.

③ A girl <u>who</u> was called Puddle fell in love with my brother.

④ I ordered an expensive meal at the restaurant <u>which</u> Clark runs.

⑤ Joy saw a man looking into the car <u>which</u> Tom bought.

25 다음 두 문장을 하나의 문장으로 쓰시오.

> We eat the carrots. My grandfather grew them on the farm.

➡ _____

26 'so ~ that'을 이용하여 다음 두 문장을 한 문장으로 쓰시오.

> There are many leaves on a single tree. It is impossible to count them.

➡ _____

27 주어진 단어를 이용하여 다음 우리말을 영어로 쓰시오.

> 네가 지난주에 방문한 박물관에 관해 말해 줘.
> (tell / visit)

➡ _____

Reading

[28~30] 다음 글을 읽고 물음에 답하시오.

Emma: What are you doing, Kyle?

Kyle: Oh, Emma. I'm watching the movie, *Y-Men 7* on my computer.

Emma: How is it?

Kyle: Don't ask. (A)It's so boring that I want to cry.

Emma: I'm sorry to hear that.

Kyle: I'm so mad. The movie advertisement said it was "The Most Exciting Movie of the Year."

Emma: Well, you can't believe everything that you read.

Kyle: They lied on the advertisement. I'm going to ask for my money back.

Emma: Hold on, Kyle! They didn't really lie because they used opinions, not facts.

28 주어진 단어를 이용하여 다음 우리말을 영어로 쓰시오.

> Kyle이 선택한 영화는 광고에서 의견을 사용하였다. (chose / in the advertisement)

➡ _____

_____

29 다음 중 밑줄 친 (A)와 쓰임이 같은 것을 <u>모두</u> 고르시오.

① <u>It</u> is exciting to meet them this weekend.
② <u>It</u> is ten miles to Boston.
③ <u>It</u> will make our cake creamy.
④ <u>It</u> was windy and dark yesterday.
⑤ <u>It</u> means that they will quit as soon as possible.

30 다음 중 위 글을 읽고 답할 수 <u>없는</u> 질문은?

① What is Kyle doing?
② Why does Kyle want to cry?
③ How does Kyle feel about the movie?
④ Why does Kyle think they lied on the advertisement?
⑤ What does Emma think about Kyle?

[31~33] 다음 글을 읽고 물음에 답하시오.

> Kyle: Not exactly. The *Y-Men 7* ad says "Most Exciting Movie" and the *Forrest Gump* ad says "Best Picture." Aren't they both opinions?
>
> Emma: That's a great question, Kyle. When people use words like "best" or "most," they are usually expressing opinions. But in the *Forrest Gump* ad, "Best Picture" is the award ___(A)___ the movie won. We can check that on the Internet. That's a fact.

> Kyle: Aha! From now on I'm only going to trust ads with facts.
>
> Emma: (B)<u>It's not that simple.</u> Most ads mix facts with opinions. So you have to make a smart choice based on both of them.

31 다음 중 빈칸 (A)에 들어갈 말과 <u>다른</u> 하나는?

① I don't know _____ she is.
② The boys _____ you are looking at are my friends.
③ There are some flowers _____ Tom picked.
④ Many students _____ I teach are diligent.
⑤ A girl and a cat _____ are sitting together look happy.

32 다음은 좋은 영화를 고르기 위해 어떤 광고를 신뢰해야 하는지에 대한 조언이다. 올바른 조언을 한 사람은?

① Ben: Don't trust ads because they are full of lies.
② Amelia: Find ads which are full of facts.
③ Clark: Watch only movies that use opinions in their ads.
④ Molly: Choose a movie which only uses words like 'best' or 'most' in the ad.
⑤ Kevin: Check both facts and opinions and choose wisely.

33 Write the reason why Emma says like the underlined (B). Use the phrase "It's because."

➡ _____

01 출제율 90%

다음 영영풀이가 가리키는 것을 고르시오.

> to add something to something else

① devide
② prove
③ lift
④ advertise
⑤ mix

02 출제율 95%

다음 우리말에 맞게 빈칸에 알맞은 말을 쓰시오.

(1) 시간을 현명하게 써야 한다.
➡ You should spend your time _____.

(2) 좋은 식당을 추천해 줄래요?
➡ Can you _____ a good restaurant?

(3) 나는 강력하게 그의 의견에 동의한다.
➡ I _____ agree with his idea.

03 출제율 100%

다음 문장의 빈칸에 들어갈 말을 〈보기〉에서 골라 쓰시오.

┌─── 보기 ───┐
hold on / right now / look for / number one / worth it
└──────────┘

(1) Paris was the _____ destination for tourists.

(2) Would you help me _____ the information about Korean history?

(3) I'm working at the oil company _____.

(4) _____ for a moment. I'll bring my phone.

(5) I'm sure it'll _____.

04 출제율 90%

다음 주어진 문장에 이어지는 대화가 자연스럽게 이어지도록 순서대로 배열하시오.

> May I help you?

(A) How about this red one? Red is the most popular color these days.
(B) Oh, that looks good. I'll take it.
(C) My old backpack was red, so I want a different color.
(D) How about this navy one? It has side pockets.
(E) Yes. I'm looking for a backpack. Can you recommend one?

➡ _____

05 출제율 95%

다음 대화의 빈칸에 들어갈 말로 어색한 것은?

> A: How do you like your bicycle?
> B: I'm not satisfied with it.
> A: _____
> B: It's too heavy.

① What's wrong?
② Why not?
③ What's the problem?
④ What's the matter?
⑤ What do you like about it?

[06~08] 다음 대화를 읽고 물음에 답하시오.

Jack: Hi, Suji. (A)[What / How] did you like your trip to Gyeongju?

Suji: 여행은 매우 즐거웠어. (happy, it)

Jack: Where did you visit?

Suji: I visited Cheomseongdae. It was great.

Jack: Where else did you go?

Suji: Bulguksa. It was a wonderful place.

Jack: (B)[Sound / Sounds] like the perfect trip.

Suji: Yeah, but (C)[walk / walking] up to Seokguram was difficult.

Jack: But I'm sure it was worth it.

06 위 대화의 밑줄 친 우리말을 주어진 단어를 사용하여 영어로 쓰시오.

➡ _____

07 위 대화의 (A)~(C)에 들어갈 말로 적절한 것으로 짝지어진 것은?

	(A)	(B)	(C)
①	What	Sound	walk
②	What	Sounds	walking
③	How	Sounds	walk
④	How	Sounds	walking
⑤	How	Sound	walk

08 Check the places which Suji liked during the trip.

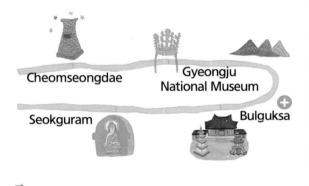

Cheomseongdae　　Gyeongju National Museum

Seokguram　　Bulguksa

➡ _____

09 다음 대화의 빈칸에 들어갈 말로 어색한 것은?

> **Bomi:** Jiho, can you recommend a musical for me?
> **Jiho:** How about *The Lion King*? _____
> **Bomi:** Okay. Sounds good.
> **Jiho:** I'm sure you'll like it.

① The story is exciting.
② The dancing is fantastic.
③ The music is so beautiful.
④ It is so popular these days.
⑤ I was so bored that I couldn't focus on it.

10 다음 대화의 내용과 일치하지 <u>않는</u> 것은?

> **Brian:** Mina, can you recommend a good pizza restaurant?
> **Mina:** Why don't you try Antonio's? It's my favorite.
> **Brian:** What do you like about it?
> **Mina:** The food is delicious. I recommend the bulgogi pizza.
> **Brian:** How are the prices?
> **Mina:** I think the prices are good, too.
> **Brian:** Sounds like a good restaurant. How do you like the service?
> **Mina:** It's a little slow on the weekends.
> **Brian:** Okay. I'll check it out. Thanks.
> **Mina:** No problem. Enjoy your meal!

① Brian is looking for a good pizza restaurant.
② Mina has eaten bulgogi pizza at Antonio's.
③ Mina thinks that the prices of Antonio's are resonable.
④ The service of Antonio's is a little slow on Saturdays and Sundays.
⑤ Brian is going to Antonio's to check whether the price is good or not.

11 다음 중 밑줄 친 부분의 쓰임이 <u>다른</u> 하나는?

① The girl <u>who</u> you invited didn't come.
② The man <u>who</u> gave me this ticket looks scary.
③ Can you tell me <u>who</u> they are?
④ The reporter <u>who</u> they hate wrote an article.
⑤ Tom is the boy <u>who</u> read lots of books.

12 다음 우리말을 영어로 바르게 옮긴 것은? 출제율 90%

> Jamie는 일을 너무 열심히 해서 병이 들었다.

① Jamie worked hardly to make himself sick.
② Jamie worked so that hard to become sick.
③ Jamie worked too hard to make himself sick.
④ Jamie worked so hard that he became sick.
⑤ Jamie worked so hardly that he became sick.

13 주어진 단어를 바르게 배열하여 다음 우리말을 영어로 쓰시오. 출제율 95%

> 네가 나에게서 빌려간 펜을 돌려줄래?
> (from / borrowed / the pen / me / can / you / back / give / you / me / that)

➡ _____
_____

14 다음 중 빈칸에 들어갈 말로 가장 적절한 것은? 출제율 100%

> That is the chair _____ your brother used to sit.

① which   ② on which   ③ who
④ on that   ⑤ that

15 다음 중 문장을 잘못 바꿔 쓴 것은? 출제율 90%

① Thomas is the man. You have to meet him.
= Thomas is the man you have to meet.
② This is the copy machine. Polly bought it.
= This is the copy machine that Polly bought.
③ Sally is too tired to do it.
= Sally is so tired that she can't do it.
④ Joe is looking at the candle. Maya made it.
= Joe is looking at the candle which Maya made.
⑤ Chris didn't know the man that his sister talked to.
= Chris didn't know the man to that his sister talked.

16 주어진 단어를 활용하여 다음 우리말을 영어로 쓰시오. 출제율 95%

> 그 역기는 너무 가벼워서 내가 들어 올릴 수 있었어. (barbell / lift)

➡ _____

[17~21] 다음 글을 읽고 물음에 답하시오.

Kyle: Huh? (A)I'm not following you.
Emma: Opinions express people's feelings like, "The desert is beautiful." You can't say (B)that it's true or not. But, facts can be proven. For example, "The Atacama Desert is in Chile," is a fact. You can check that on the map.
Kyle: Okay.... But what's the connection with movies?
Emma: Let me explain. What's your favorite movie?
Kyle: It's *Forrest Gump*.

Emma: Okay. Let's look for its advertisement. What does it say?

Kyle: It says, "Winner of 6 Academy Awards including Best Picture."

Emma: See? It uses facts unlike the *Y-Men 7* advertisement. Do you see the difference?

Kyle: Not exactly. The *Y-Men 7* ad says "Most Exciting Movie" and the *Forrest Gump* ad says "Best Picture." Aren't they both opinions?

✏ 출제율 95%

17 다음 중 밑줄 친 (A) 대신에 쓸 수 있는 것은?

① I can't go after you.
② I can't understand you.
③ You are following me.
④ I need to follow up something.
⑤ It is hard to catch up with you.

✏ 출제율 100%

18 다음 중 밑줄 친 (B)와 쓰임이 다른 것은?

① He thinks that his friends are nice.
② Do you know the fact that the movie is bad?
③ It is true that she bought two tickets.
④ He is the boy that you want to see.
⑤ They said that I had to deal with the problem.

✏ 출제율 90%

19 글의 내용에 맞게 빈칸에 알맞은 말을 쓰시오.

> Unlike _____, _____ cannot be proven.

✏ 출제율 85%

20 What are they mainly talking about? Answer in English with a full sentence.

➡ _____

_____

✏ 출제율 95%

21 다음 중 의견에 해당하는 것은?

① Bulguksa is located in Gyeongju.
② The Han River is not as long as the Nile River.
③ Watching movies is interesting.
④ Bill Gates founded Microsoft.
⑤ Mother Teresa was born in 1910.

[22~24] 다음 글을 읽고 물음에 답하시오.

> *Charlotte's Web* is a children's novel. It was written by E. B. White. A little pig named Wilbur is the main character of the book. When Wilbur is in danger, his friend Charlotte helps him out. I especially like the friendship of Wilbur and Charlotte. _____(A)_____ I strongly recommend it to everyone.

✏ 출제율 90%

22 주어진 어구를 바르게 배열하여 빈칸 (A)에 들어갈 말을 쓰시오.

> (touching / many times / the book / that / I / so / read / was / it)

➡ _____

✏ 출제율 95%

23 다음 중 위 글을 읽고 답할 수 없는 질문은?

① When did Charlotte help Wilbur?
② Who wrote the novel?
③ What is the name of the main character?
④ Who is Wilbur's friend?
⑤ How many friends does Wilbur have?

✏ 출제율 90%

24 다음 두 문장을 하나의 문장으로 쓰시오.

> *Charlotte's Web* is a children's novel. E. B. White wrote the book.

➡ _____

_____

[01~03] 다음 대화를 읽고 물음에 답하시오.

> Brian: Mina, can you recommend a good pizza restaurant?
> Mina: Why don't you try Antonio's? It's my favorite.
> Brian: What do you like about it?
> Mina: The food is delicious. I recommend the bulgogi pizza.
> Brian: How are the prices?
> Mina: I think the prices are good, too.
> Brian: Sounds like a good restaurant. How do you like the service?
> Mina: It's a little slow on the weekends.
> Brian: Okay. I'll check it out. Thanks.
> Mina: No problem. Enjoy your meal!

01 What is Mina's favorite restaurant?

➡ _____

02  Which food does Mina recommend?

➡ _____

03 What does Mina think about the service?

➡ _____

04 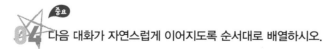 다음 대화가 자연스럽게 이어지도록 순서대로 배열하시오.

> (A) What do you like most about it?
> (B) Yes, I did. I'm really happy with it.
> (C) Tom, you got a new smartphone.
> (D) I love the camera. It takes great pictures.

➡ _____

05 다음 두 문장을 하나의 문장으로 쓰시오.

> I can't find the cup. My husband likes to use it.

➡ _____

06 지시에 맞게 주어진 문장과 같은 의미의 문장을 쓰시오. 각각 The wind를 주어로 시작할 것.

> The wind was strong, so it blew my hat off my head.

(1) because를 이용하여

➡ _____
_____

(2) so ~ that을 이용하여

➡ _____
_____

07 두 문장이 같은 의미가 되도록 빈칸에 알맞은 말을 쓰시오.

> • Peter fell in love with a woman. She left him a few weeks ago.
> = The woman _____ a few weeks ago.

➡ _____
_____

08 다음 우리말에 맞게 빈칸에 알맞은 말을 쓰시오.

> The cookies _____ was _____ I ate all of them.
> 네가 구운 쿠키가 너무 맛있어서 내가 모두 먹어 버렸어.

09 주어진 단어를 활용하여 다음 우리말을 영어로 쓰시오.

> 그 보석은 너무 귀해서 값을 매길 수가 없다.
> (jewel / precious / that / priceless)

➡ _____

[10~13] 다음 글을 읽고 물음에 답하시오.

> Kyle: Huh? I'm not following you.
>
> Emma: Opinions express people's feelings like, "The desert is beautiful." You can't say that it's true or not. But, facts can be proven. For example, "The Atacama Desert is in Chile," is a fact. You can check that on the map.
>
> Kyle: Okay.... But what's the connection with movies?
>
> Emma: Let me explain. What's your favorite movie?
>
> Kyle: It's *Forrest Gump*.
>
> Emma: Okay. Let's look for its advertisement. What does it say?
>
> Kyle: It says, "Winner of 6 Academy Awards including Best Picture."
>
> Emma: See? It uses facts unlike the *Y-Men 7* advertisement. Do you see the difference?

10 What does the advertisement say about *Forrest Gump*?

➡ _____
_____

⭐ 중요
11 What is Emma using to explain the difference between facts and opinions? Answer in English.

➡ _____

12 According to the passage, what is the difference between facts and opinions? Answer in Korean.

➡ _____

⭐ 중요
13 글의 내용에 맞게 빈칸에 알맞은 말을 쓰시오.

> There are many _____ that we can't trust in the ads. We need an ad which has many _____.

[14~15] 다음 글을 읽고 물음에 답하시오.

> *Harry Potter* is a fantasy novel. It was written by J. K. Rowling. Harry Potter is the main character of the book. When Harry goes to magic school, his adventures begin. I especially like the friendship of Harry and his friends. (A)그 책은 아주 재미있어서 나는 책을 놓을 수가 없었다. I strongly recommend it to everyone.

14 밑줄 친 우리말 (A)를 영어로 쓰시오.

➡ _____
_____

15 What is the genre of the book, *Harry Potter*?

➡ _____

01 다음 대화의 내용과 일치하도록 Mina의 소개문을 완성하시오.

> Brian: Mina, can you recommend a good pizza restaurant?
> Mina: Why don't you try Antonio's? It's my favorite.
> Brian: What do you like about it?
> Mina: The food is delicious. I recommend the bulgogi pizza.
> Brian: How are the prices?
> Mina: I think the prices are good, too.
> Brian: Sounds like a good restaurant. How do you like the service?
> Mina: It's a little slow on the weekends.
> Brian: Okay. I'll check it out. Thanks.
> Mina: No problem. Enjoy your meal!

> I'll introduce my favorite restaurant, Antonio's. It is a good pizza restaurant. I recommend (A)_____, which is so delicious. The (B)_____ are reasonable. If you visit there on the weekends, the service can be (C)_____. How about trying Antonio's?

02 'so ~ that' 구문을 이용하여 다음 두 문장을 하나의 문장으로 써 보시오.

> Tom was busy. He couldn't answer the phone.
> The waves were high. We couldn't swim in the sea.

(1) _____

(2) _____

03 한국 민속촌에 관한 다음 글을 읽고 Facts와 Opinions를 구별하시오.

> I want to introduce Korean folk village. It is located in Yongin. It's a fun place in Yongin. There are Korean traditional houses. They are beautiful. Visitors can watch nongak and jultagi. Nongak and jultagi are very exciting to see.

Facts	Opinions
_____	_____
_____	_____

단원별 모의고사

[01~03] 다음 대화를 읽고 물음에 답하시오.

Jack: Hi, Suji. How did you like your trip to Gyeongju?

Suji: I was very happy with it.

Jack: Where did you visit?

Suji: I visited Cheomseongdae. It was great.

Jack: Where else did you go?

Suji: Bulguksa. It was a wonderful place.

Jack: _____ (A) _____

Suji: Yeah, but walking up to Seokguram was difficult.

Jack: But I'm sure it was worth it.

01 위 대화의 빈칸 (A)에 들어갈 말로 <u>어색한</u> 것은?

① That sounds great.

② Sounds like the perfect trip.

③ You seem to enjoy it a lot.

④ You seem to like it so much.

⑤ I'm sorry to hear that.

02 위 대화에서 알 수 있는 Suji의 심경으로 적절한 것은?

① disappointed   ② satisfied

③ nervous   ④ gloomy

⑤ upset

03 How was it to walk up to Seokguram for Suji?

➡ _____

[04~06] 다음 대화를 읽고 물음에 답하시오.

W: May I help you?

B: Yes. I'm looking for a backpack. Can you ____(A)____ one?

W: How about this red one? Red is the most popular color these days.

B: My old backpack was red, so I want a different color.

W: _____(B)_____ It has side pockets.

B: Oh, that looks good. I'll take it.

04 위 대화의 빈칸 (A)에 들어갈 수 있는 단어를 고르시오.

① watch   ② guess

③ recommend   ④ advise

⑤ introduce

05 위 대화의 빈칸 (B)에 들어갈 말로 <u>어색한</u> 것은?

① How about this navy one?

② I recommend this navy one.

③ What about this navy one?

④ Why don't you choose this navy one?

⑤ How was this navy one?

06 위 대화의 내용과 일치하도록 소년의 일기의 빈칸을 완성하시오.

Mon, Nov 4th, 2019

I was excited because I bought the new backpack. I used to wear the (A)_____ color backpack, so I wanted to buy (B)_____. The clerk recommended (C)_____, which had (D)_____. I liked it a lot and bought it. I'm looking forward to wearing the new backpack tomorrow.

[07~09] 다음 대화를 읽고 물음에 답하시오.

Sue: Tom, you got a new smartphone.
Tom: Yes, I did. I'm really happy with it.
Sue: What do you like most about it?
Tom: I love the camera. It takes great pictures.

07 What are Tom and Sue talking about?

➡ _____

08 How does Tom like his new smartphone?

➡ _____

09 What does Tom like most about his smartphone?

➡ _____

[10~11] 다음 대화를 읽고 물음에 답하시오.

Brian: Mina, can you recommend a good pizza restaurant?
Mina: Why don't you try Antonio's? It's my ⓐfavorite.
Brian: What do you like about it?
Mina: The food is delicious. I recommend the bulgogi pizza.
Brian: How are the prices?
Mina: I think the prices are good, too.
Brian: ⓑSounds like a good restaurant. How do you like the service?
Mina: It's ⓒa little slow on the weekends.
Brian: Okay. I'll ⓓcheck out it. Thanks.
Mina: No problem. ⓔEnjoy your meal!

10 위 대화의 밑줄 친 ⓐ~ⓔ 중 어법상 어색한 것을 찾아 바르게 고치시오.

➡ _____

11 위 대화를 읽고 대답할 수 없는 질문은?

① What is Mina's favorite restaurant?
② What food did Mina recommend Brian to try at Antonio's?
③ How was the price of Antonio's?
④ When was the service of Antonio's slow?
⑤ How much was the bulgogi pizza at Antonio's?

12 다음 우리말에 맞게 주어진 단어를 사용하여 영작하시오.

(1) 버터를 설탕과 함께 섞으세요. (mix)
➡ _____

(2) Jack이 의자를 들어 올렸다. (lifted)
➡ _____

(3) 너는 진실을 말하고 있니? (telling)
➡ _____

13 다음 중 의미가 다른 하나는?

① It was so fine that we went out.
② We went out because of the fine weather.
③ It was fine, so we went out.
④ It was too fine for us to go out.
⑤ As it was fine, we went out.

14 다음 중 쓰임이 다른 하나는?

① The doll that Rose carries around all the time is made by her mother.
② I know the fact that she doesn't trust anyone.
③ The vase that the boy broke was not expensive.
④ The paper that Danny tore into pieces was an important document.
⑤ Who is the woman that Lisa is talking to?

15 주어진 단어를 활용하여 다음 우리말을 영어로 쓰시오.

> 그의 연설은 너무 유명해서 모두가 그것에 관해 알았다. (speech / that)

➡ _____

_____

16 다음 중 어법상 바르지 <u>않은</u> 것은?

① Are these the keys you lost the other day?
② Is there anything that I can do for you?
③ The dog is so smart that everyone loves him.
④ What is the name of the movie that you are going to see?
⑤ The women whom I work with in the office is friendly.

17 주어진 문장과 같은 의미의 문장을 아홉 단어로 이루어진 한 문장으로 쓰시오.

> My mouth is frozen because it is so cold.

➡ _____

[18~23] 다음 글을 읽고 물음에 답하시오.

Emma: What are you doing, Kyle?
Kyle: ① _____
Emma: ② _____
Kyle: ③ _____
Emma: ④ _____
Kyle: I'm so mad. The movie advertisement said that it was "The Most Exciting Movie of the Year."
Emma: Well, you can't believe everything that you read.
Kyle: They lied on the advertisement. I'm going to ask for my money back.

Emma: Hold ___ⓐ___, Kyle! They didn't really ⓑlie because they used opinions, not facts.
Kyle: Huh? (A)I'm not following you.
Emma: Opinions express people's feelings like, "The desert is beautiful." You can't say (B)that it's true or not. But, facts can be ⓒproven. For example, "The Atacama Desert is in Chile," is a fact. You can check that on the map.
Kyle: Okay.... But what's the (C)connection with movies?
Emma: Let me explain. What's ⓓyour favorite movie?
Kyle: It's *Forrest Gump*.
Emma: Okay. Let's ⓔlook for its advertisement. What does (D)it say?
Kyle: It says, "Winner of 6 Academy Awards (E)including Best Picture."
Emma: See? It uses facts ⓕlike the *Y-Men 7* advertisement. Do you see the difference?

18 자연스러운 대화가 되도록 ①~④에 들어갈 말을 바르게 나열한 것은?

> ⓐ How is it?
> ⓑ I'm sorry to hear that.
> ⓒ Oh, Emma. I'm watching the movie, *Y-Men 7* on my computer.
> ⓓ Don't ask. It's so boring that I want to cry.

① ⓑ – ⓐ – ⓓ – ⓒ   ② ⓑ – ⓓ – ⓒ – ⓐ
③ ⓒ – ⓐ – ⓓ – ⓑ   ④ ⓒ – ⓑ – ⓐ – ⓓ
⑤ ⓓ – ⓑ – ⓐ – ⓒ

19 빈칸 ⓐ에 들어갈 말로 가장 적절한 것은?

① in   ② at   ③ by   ④ on   ⑤ out

20 다음 중 위 글의 내용과 일치하는 것은?

① It is hard to prove facts.
② Ads always tell lies about their products.
③ We had better believe everything that we read.
④ It is not allowed to use opinions in ads.
⑤ People who advertise products use not only facts but also opinions.

21 다음 중 (A)~(E)에 관한 설명으로 바르지 않은 것은?

① (A): 'I can't understand you.'로 바꾸어 쓸 수 있다.
② (B): 접속사로 동사 say의 목적어가 되는 명사절을 이끌고 있다.
③ (C): the way in which two things are related to each other로 풀이되는 말이다.
④ (D): "Forest Gump"를 가리키는 대명사이다.
⑤ (E): '~을 포함하여'라는 의미의 전치사이다.

22 밑줄 친 ⓑ~ⓕ 중 내용상 어색한 것을 골라 바르게 고치시오.

➡ _____

23 글의 내용에 맞게 빈칸에 알맞은 말을 쓰시오.

> According to the passage, if something can be proven, it is a _____. However, if it is hard to say something is true or not, you can say it is _____ _____.

[24~25] 다음 글을 읽고 물음에 답하시오.

> *Charlotte's Web* is a children's novel. It was written by E. B. White. A little pig named Wilbur is the main character of the book. When Wilbur is in danger, his friend Charlotte helps him out. I especially like the friendship of Wilbur and Charlotte. The book was so touching that I read it many times. I strongly recommend it to everyone.

24 Which is NOT true about the passage?

① The writer of the book is E. B. White.
② Wilbur is the name of the main character.
③ Wilbur and Charlotte are friends.
④ Charlotte ignores Wilbur when he is in danger.
⑤ The writer read the book many times.

25 위 글의 표현을 이용하여 다음 우리말을 영어로 쓰시오.

> 내가 읽은 책은 너무 감동적이어서 나는 그것을 너에게 추천하고 싶어.

➡ The book _____
  I want to _____.

Be like Sherlock!

 의사소통 기능

- 도움 요청하기

  A: Can you help me mop the floor?

  B: No problem.

- 추측하기

  A: I guess you're playing the piano.

  B: You're right.

언어 형식

- something+형용사

  Is there **something wrong**?

- 간접의문문

  Could you tell me **when this happened**?

Words & Expressions

Key Words

- **afraid** [əfréid] 형 걱정하는, 두려워하는
- **anymore** [ènimɔ́ːr] 부 이제는, 지금은, 더 이상
- **anyway** [éniwèi] 부 어차피
- **broken** [bróukən] 형 깨진, 부서진
- **bronze** [brɑnz] 명 청동
- **call** [kɔːl] 동 전화를 걸다, 부르다
- **carry** [kǽri] 동 나르다, 옮기다
- **clue** [kluː] 명 단서, 실마리
- **crime** [kraim] 명 범죄
- **dangerous** [déindʒərəs] 형 위험한
- **detective** [ditéktiv] 명 탐정
- **else** [els] 부 또 다른
- **favor** [féivər] 명 호의, 친절, 부탁
- **feather** [féðər] 명 깃털
- **flash** [flæʃ] 명 섬광, 번쩍임
- **footprint** [fútprìnt] 명 발자국
- **handprint** [hǽndprint] 명 손자국
- **horror** [hɔ́ːrər] 명 공포
- **inside** [ìnsáid] 전 ~ 안에
- **leave** [liːv] 동 ~을 두고 가다
- **lightning** [láitniŋ] 명 번개
- **lose** [luːz] 동 잃어버리다

- **mop** [mɑp] 동 대걸레로 닦다
- **playground** [pléigràund] 명 운동장
- **poem** [póuəm] 명 시
- **post** [poust] 동 게시하다, 공고하다
- **principal** [prínsəpəl] 명 교장
- **real** [ríːəl] 형 진짜의, 실제의
- **refrigerator** [rifrídʒərèitər] 명 냉장고
- **rush** [rʌʃ] 동 (급히) 움직이다, 서두르다
- **silver** [sílvər] 명 은
- **steal** [stiːl] 동 훔치다
- **strange** [streindʒ] 형 이상한
- **stranger** [stréindʒər] 명 낯선 사람, 모르는 사람
- **suddenly** [sʌ́dnli] 부 갑자기
- **talent** [tǽlənt] 명 재능
- **talent show** 장기 자랑 대회
- **text** [tekst] 동 문자 메시지를 보내다 명 문자
- **thief** [θiːf] 명 도둑
- **thirsty** [θɔ́ːrsti] 형 목마른
- **thunder** [θʌ́ndər] 명 천둥
- **treasure** [tréʒər] 명 보물
- **water** [wɔ́ːtər] 동 물을 주다
- **wonder** [wʌ́ndər] 동 궁금해 하다

Key Expressions

- **a few** 몇몇의, 조금의
- **ask ~ a favor** ~에게 부탁을 하다
- **at the moment** 그 순간에, 그때에
- **bring ~ back** ~을 돌려주다
- **do ~ a favor** ~의 부탁을 들어주다
- **get into trouble** 곤경에 빠지다
- **look for** ~을 찾다
- **make one's round** 순찰을 돌다

- **not ~ anymore** 더 이상 ~ 않다
- **on the way home** 집에 가는[오는] 길에
- **right now** 지금, 곧, 당장
- **run across** ~을 가로질러[건너서] 뛰다
- **rush over** 달려가다
- **take care of** ~을 돌보다
- **wash the dishes** 설거지하다
- **win first place** 일등을 하다

Word Power

※ 서로 반대되는 뜻을 가진 어휘

- □ **inside** ~ 안에 ↔ **outside** ~ 밖에
- □ **low** 낮은 ↔ **high** 높은
- □ **safe** 안전한 ↔ **dangerous** 위험한
- □ **completely** 완전히 ↔ **partially** 부분적으로
- □ **ask** 묻다 ↔ **answer** 대답하다
- □ **leave** 떠나다 ↔ **arrive** 도착하다
- □ **find** 찾다 ↔ **lose** 잃어버리다
- □ **catch** 잡다 ↔ **run away** 도망가다

※ 수사 관련 어휘

- □ **crime** 범죄
- □ **clue** 단서
- □ **investigation** 조사, 수사
- □ **detective** 탐정
- □ **suspect** 용의자
- □ **judge** 판사
- □ **witness** 증인
- □ **victim** 피해자

English Dictionary

- □ **anyway** 어쨌든
  → in any case
  어떤 경우에든

- □ **bronze** 청동
  → a yellowish-brown metal containing copper and tin
  구리와 주석을 포함한 황갈색의 금속

- □ **clue** 단서, 실마리
  → something that helps a person find something
  누군가가 무언가를 찾도록 도와주는 어떤 것

- □ **crime** 범죄
  → activities that involve breaking the law
  법을 어기는 것을 포함하는 행동들

- □ **detective** 탐정
  → a person whose job is to find information about something or someone
  무언가 또는 누군가에 관한 정보를 찾는 것이 직업인 사람

- □ **else** 또 다른
  → in addition to something already mentioned
  이미 언급된 무언가에 더하여

- □ **flash** 섬광, 번쩍임
  → a bright light that shines for a short time
  짧은 시간 동안 빛나는 밝은 빛

- □ **footprint** 발자국
  → a mark left by a foot or shoe
  발 또는 신발에 의해 남겨진 자국

- □ **horror** 공포
  → a strong feeling of shock and fear
  충격과 두려움의 강한 느낌

- □ **lightning** 번개
  → a powerful flash of light in the sky and usually followed by thunder
  보통 천둥이 뒤따라오는 하늘의 강력한 빛의 번쩍임

- □ **mop** 대걸레로 닦다
  → to clean the floor with a mop
  대걸레로 바닥을 닦다

- □ **principal** 교장
  → the person in charge of a school
  학교를 담당하고 있는 사람

- □ **rush** (급히) 행동하다
  → to move or do something very quickly
  매우 빠르게 무언가를 하거나 움직이다

- □ **steal** 훔치다
  → to take something that does not belong to you in a wrong way
  잘못된 방식으로 당신에게 속하지 않은 무언가를 취하다

- □ **talent** 재능
  → a natural and special ability to do something well
  무언가를 잘하는 타고난, 특별한 능력

- □ **thief** 도둑
  → someone who steals things from another person
  다른 사람으로부터 무언가를 훔치는 사람

서답형

01 다음 짝지어진 단어의 관계가 같도록 빈칸에 알맞은 말을 쓰시오.

> top : bottom = _____ : outside

02 다음 영영풀이가 가리키는 것을 고르시오.

> a natural and special ability to do something well

① feather　　② talent
③ footprint　　④ text
⑤ treasure

중요

03 다음 중 밑줄 친 부분의 뜻풀이가 바르지 <u>않은</u> 것은?

① This small school has just three teachers and one <u>principal</u>. 교장
② <u>Lightning</u> struck a big tree. 가벼운
③ There is something <u>strange</u> in the sky. 이상한
④ <u>Suddenly</u> the power went out. 갑자기
⑤ The <u>thief</u> stole the computer equipment. 도둑

04 다음 주어진 문장의 밑줄 친 post와 같은 의미로 쓰인 것은?

> What did you <u>post</u> on the bulletin board?

① There was a lot of <u>post</u> this morning.
② I want to <u>post</u> the advertisement on the websites.
③ Has the <u>post</u> come yet?
④ I was waiting for the next <u>post</u> with my friends.
⑤ I sent some presents to my cousins by <u>post</u>.

중요

05 다음 문장에 공통으로 들어갈 말을 고르시오.

> • Emma is really good at paraphrasing the _____.
> • I needed Brian's help, so I sent a _____ to ask him a favor.
> • He memorized the whole _____ of the speech.
> • I'll _____ you before I drop by your office.
>
> *paraphrase: 바꿔 쓰다

① book　　② text
③ call　　④ article
⑤ poem

서답형

06 다음 우리말에 맞게 빈칸에 알맞은 말을 쓰시오.

(1) 나는 오늘 식물에 물을 주지 않았다.
　➡ I didn't _____ the plant today.
(2) 도둑이 내 지갑을 가져갔다.
　➡ A _____ took my purse.
(3) 나는 음악적 재능이 없다.
　➡ I have no musical _____.
(4) 나는 토요일에 내 사촌들을 돌볼 것이다.
　➡ I'll _____ my cousins on Saturday.
(5) 나는 집에 오는 길에 Jane을 만났다.
　➡ I met Jane _____.
(6) 그는 밤에 순찰을 돌고 있었다.
　➡ He was making _____ at night.

01 다음 짝지어진 단어의 관계가 같도록 빈칸에 알맞은 말을 쓰시오.

> leave : arrive = find : _____

02 다음 문장의 빈칸에 들어갈 말을 〈보기〉에서 골라 쓰시오.

> ┌─ 보기 ─
> afraid / refrigerator / carry / poem / clue / thunder

(1) What did you put in the _____?

(2) I can't sleep because of the _____.

(3) We need a _____ to catch the thief.

(4) I'm _____ of singing in front of the audience.

(5) In English class, we studied rhyme on the _____.

(6) Can you help me _____ these heavy boxes?

03 다음 우리말에 맞게 빈칸에 알맞은 말을 쓰시오.

(1) 이상한 소음이 그녀를 깨웠다.
　➡ A _____ noise woke her up.

(2) 그는 갑자기 그가 해야 할 일을 깨달았다.
　➡ He _____ realized what he had to do.

(3) 선생님은 학생들의 시험 성적을 게시판에 게시하시지 않을 것이다.
　➡ The teacher won't _____ the students' exam grades on the board.

04 다음 우리말과 일치하도록 주어진 어구를 모두 배열하여 영작하시오.

(1) 그의 인생은 더 이상 행복하지 않았다.
(happy / his / anymore / not / was / life)
➡ _____

(2) 우리는 곤경에 처할 때, 이겨내기 위해 노력해야 한다. (종속절로 시작할 것.)
(we / a trouble / we / to / overcome / into / try / should / when / get)
➡ _____
_____

(3) 그는 장기 자랑 대회에서 1등을 하였다.
(show / first / the talent / in / he / won / place)
➡ _____

05 다음 주어진 단어를 사용하여 우리말을 영작하시오.

(1) 범죄율이 증가하고 있다. (rate, rise)
➡ _____

(2) 그는 춤추는 재능을 보였다. (talent, for)
➡ _____

(3) 그녀의 개는 천둥을 두려워한다. (afraid)
➡ _____

(4) 바닥을 닦아 줄 수 있나요? (could, mop)
➡ _____

(5) 그녀는 그 문제를 해결하기 위해 탐정을 고용했다. (hire)
➡ _____

(6) 그녀의 가방이 깃털만큼 가볍다. (as)
➡ _____

Conversation

교과서

1 도움 요청하기

A Can you help me mop the floor? 바닥 닦는 것 좀 도와줄래?
B No problem. 좋아.

■ "Can you ~?"는 상대방에게 도움을 요청할 때 사용할 수 있는 표현이다. "Can you help me mop the floor?"와 같이 도움이 필요한 사항을 구체적으로 말하며 도움을 요청할 수 있다. 도움 요청을 승낙할 경우에는 "Sure.", "Of course.", "No problem." 등으로 답하고, 거절할 경우에는 "Sorry, I can't." 또는 "I'm afraid I can't."로 답하고 도울 수 없는 이유를 덧붙여 말할 수 있다.

도움 요청하기

- Can I ask you a favor? 부탁 좀 드려도 될까요?
- Can you do me a favor? 부탁 좀 들어 주실래요?
- Can you give me a hand? 좀 도와주시겠어요?
- Can you help me out, please? 좀 도와주실 수 있으세요?
- I have a favor to ask. 부탁하고 싶은 것이 있어.
- I need your help. 나 네 도움이 필요해.
- Please help me (to) ~. 나 좀 도와주세요.
- Would you mind helping me (to) ~? 나를 좀 도와주시겠어요?

도움 요청을 수락하거나 거절하는 표현

- 수락: Sure. / No problem. / Of course.
- 거절: I'm afraid not. / I don't think I can do that.

핵심 Check

1. 다음 주어진 우리말과 일치하도록 빈칸을 완성하시오.

(1) **A:** Can you do me a _____? (부탁 좀 들어줄래?)
   B: Sure. What is it? (물론이지. 무엇인데?)
   A: _____ _____ _____ _____ carry these books?
      (이 책들을 나르는 것을 도와줄래?)

(2) **A:** I have a _____ to ask. (부탁하고 싶은 게 있어.)
   B: _____ _____ _____? (무엇인데?)
   A: Can you help me _____ this notice on the bulletin board?
      (게시판에 이 공지를 붙이는 것을 도와줄래?)
   B: I'm _____ I can't. (미안하지만 못할 것 같아.)

② 추측하기

> **A** I guess you're playing the piano. 나는 네가 피아노를 치고 있는 거 같아.
> **B** You're right. 맞아.

■ "I guess ~."는 어떤 것을 추측하여 말할 때 사용하는 표현으로, "I guess" 뒤에 자신이 추측하는 내용을 말한다.

추측하기

- I think the dog took your sock. 나는 그 개가 네 양말을 가져갔다고 생각해.
- Maybe it will snow tonight. 아마도 오늘밤 눈이 올 것 같다.
- I suppose prices will go up. 추측컨대 물가가 오를 것 같다.
- It's difficult to say, but I think the Korean team will win the game.
  말하긴 어렵지만 내 생각에는 한국 팀이 경기를 이길 것 같아.

핵심 Check

2. 다음 주어진 우리말과 일치하도록 빈칸을 완성하시오.

(1) **A:** _____ what I'm doing. (내가 무엇을 하고 있는지 추측해 봐.)

   B: _____ _____ you're fishing. (네가 낚시하고 있는 것 같아.)

   A: You're right. (맞아.)

(2) **A:** I guess you're going up a ladder. (네가 사다리를 올라가는 것 같아.)

   B: You're _____. Guess again. (틀렸어. 다시 추측해 봐.)

(3) **A:** _____ it will grow even bigger. (아마도 이게 더 크게 자랄 것 같아.)

   B: I think so, too. (나도 그렇게 생각해.)

Listen and Speak 1-B

Narae: Tony, can you do me a favor?

Tony: Sure. What is it, Narae?

Narae: Can you ❶take care of my dog this weekend? My family is going to visit my grandmother in Busan.

Tony: Oh, ❷I'm sorry but I can't. My mom doesn't like dogs.

Narae: Oh, what should I do?

Tony: ❸Why don't you ask Sumin? Her family loves dogs.

Narae: Okay. I'll call ❹her right now.

Narae: Tony야, 부탁 하나 해도 될까?

Tony: 물론이지. 뭔데, 나래야?

Narae: 이번 주말에 내 개를 돌 봐 줄 수 있니? 우리 가 족은 부산에 계신 할머 니를 방문할 예정이야.

Tony: 오, 미안하지만 안 돼. 엄 마가 개를 좋아하지 않으 셔.

Narae: 오, 어떻게 해야 하지?

Tony: 수민이에게 물어보는 게 어때? 그녀의 가족은 개 를 정말 좋아해.

Narae: 알겠어. 지금 당장 그녀 에게 전화해야겠다.

❶ take care of: ~을 돌보다
❷ 부탁을 거절하는 표현이다.
❸ Why don't you ~? = How about ~? = What about ~?: ~하는 게 어때?
❹ her는 Sumin을 가리킨다.

Check(√) True or False

(1) Narae is going to visit Busan this weekend. T ☐ F ☐

(2) Tony is going to help Narae this weekend. T ☐ F ☐

Listen and Speak 2-B

G: Good morning, classmates! Nine months ❶have passed so fast, and we are almost ❷at the end of this school year. We all had a wonderful year. I guess ❸only a few of us will be in the same class next year. Don't be a stranger. Say hello when we see ❹each other, okay? Thank you.

G: 좋은 아침이야, 학급 친구들 아! 9개월은 아주 빨리 지나갔 고, 우리는 이번 학년의 거의 막바지에 있어. 우리 모두는 멋진 한 해를 보냈어. 우리 중 극소수가 내년에 같은 반이 될 거라고 생각해. 모르는 사람처 럼 지내지 말자. 서로 만나면 인사말을 건네자. 알겠지? 고 마워.

❶ 과거부터 지금까지 이어지는 것을 나타내기 위해 현재완료 시제가 사용되었다.
❷ at the end of: ~의 끝에
❸ only a few: 극소수의, few: 거의 없는
❹ each other: 서로

Check(√) True or False

(3) The girl asks her classmates not to be strangers next year. T ☐ F ☐

(4) The girl felt bored in this school year. T ☐ F ☐

Listen and Speak 1-A

Emily: Jinsu, can I ask you a favor?

Jinsu: Sure. What is it?

Emily: Can you help me ❶wash the dishes?

Jinsu: ❷No problem.

❶ wash the dishes: 설거지하다
❷ 도움 요청을 수락하는 표현으로 Sure. 또는 Of course.로 바꾸어 쓸 수 있다.

Listen and Speak 1-C

A: ❶Can you do me a favor?

B: Sure. What is it?

A: Can you help me ❷mop the floor?

B: No problem. / ❸Sorry, I can't.

❶ 상대방에게 도움을 요청할 때 사용하는 표현으로 Can I ask you a favor?와 바꿔 쓸 수 있다.
❷ mop: 대걸레로 닦다
❸ 도움 요청에 거절하는 표현으로 I'm afraid I can't.로 바꿔 쓸 수 있다.

Listen and Speak 2-A

Brian: Did you see my baseball glove?

Jane: Yes, I saw ❶it under the table.

Brian: Really? It's not ❷there anymore.

Jane: Then I guess Spot took ❶it.

Brian: Oh, there ❸he is. You bad dog, Spot!

❶ it은 Brian's baseball glove를 가리킨다.
❷ there는 under the table을 가리킨다.
❸ he는 Spot을 가리킨다.

Listen and Speak 2-C

A: ❶Guess what I'm doing.

B: ❷I guess you're playing the piano.

A: You're wrong. Guess again.

B: I guess you're ❸working on the computer.

A: That's right.

❶ 자신의 동작에 대해 상대방의 추측을 유도하는 표현이다.
❷ I guess (that)+주어+동사 ~.는 어떤 것을 추측하여 말할 때 사용하는 표현이다.
❸ work on the computer: 컴퓨터로 일하다

Real Life Talk – Step 1

Brian: Mom, I can't find my smartphone. Can you help me find ❶it?

Mom: Are you sure you lost ❶it ❷inside the house?

Brian: Yes. I just ❸texted my friend a few minutes ago.

Mom: Where were you ❹at the time?

Brian: In the kitchen. I was making a sandwich.

Mom: Then I guess you left ❶it somewhere in the kitchen.

Brian: I already checked the kitchen, Mom.

Mom: Well, let's check ❺it again. Oh, here it is. Inside the refrigerator.

Brian: Thanks, Mom. You are the greatest!

Mom: You're welcome, honey.

❶ it은 Brian's smartphone을 가리킨다.
❷ inside: ~ 안에 ↔ outside: ~ 밖에
❸ text: 문자 메시지를 보내다
❹ at the time: 그때
❺ it은 the kitchen을 가리킨다.

Real Life Talk – Step 2

A: Can you help me find my baseball glove?

B: Okay. Where did you see it last?

A: On the bench.

B: ❶I guess a dog took your baseball glove. I can see its ❷footprints on the bench.

❶ 추측을 나타내는 표현이다.
❷ footprint: 발자국

Conversation **65**

● 다음 우리말과 일치하도록 빈칸에 알맞은 말을 쓰시오.

Listen and Speak 1-A

Emily: Jinsu, can I ask you a _____?

Jinsu: Sure. What is it?

Emily: Can you help me _____ _____ _____?

Jinsu: No problem.

Emily: 진수야, 부탁 하나 해도 될까?
Jinsu: 물론이지. 뭔데?
Emily: 설거지하는 것 좀 도와줄래?
Jinsu: 좋아.

Listen and Speak 1-B

Narae: Tony, can you do me a favor?

Tony: Sure. What is it, Narae?

Narae: Can you _____ _____ _____ my dog this weekend? My family is going to visit my grandmother in Busan.

Tony: Oh, _____ _____ _____ _____ _____. My mom doesn't like dogs.

Narae: Oh, _____ _____ _____ _____?

Tony: _____ _____ _____ ask Sumin? Her family loves dogs.

Narae: Okay. I'll call her _____ _____.

Narae: Tony야, 부탁 하나 해도 될까?
Tony: 물론이지. 뭔데, 나래야?
Narae: 이번 주말에 내 개를 돌봐 줄 수 있니? 우리 가족은 부산에 계신 할머니를 방문할 예정이야.
Tony: 오, 미안하지만 안 돼. 엄마께서 개를 좋아하지 않으셔.
Narae: 오, 어떻게 해야 하지?
Tony: 수민이에게 물어보는 게 어때? 그녀의 가족은 개를 정말 좋아해.
Narae: 알겠어. 지금 당장 그녀에게 전화해야겠다.

Listen and Speak 1-C

A: Can you _____ _____ _____ _____?

B: Sure. What is it?

A: Can you _____ _____ _____ the floor?

B: No _____. / Sorry, I _____.

A: 부탁 하나 해도 될까?
B: 물론이지. 뭔데?
A: 바닥 닦는 것을 도와줄래?
B: 좋아. / 미안하지만 못해.

Listen and Speak 2-A

Brian: Did you see my baseball glove?

Jane: Yes, I saw it _____ _____ _____.

Brian: Really? It's not there _____.

Jane: Then I _____ Spot took it.

Brian: Oh, there _____ _____. You bad dog, Spot!

Brian: 내 야구 글러브 보았니?
Jane: 그래, 탁자 아래에서 봤어.
Brian: 정말? 더 이상 그곳에 없어.
Jane: 그럼 Spot이 가져간 것 같구나.
Brian: 오, 저기 있네. 이런 나쁜 개, Spot!

Listen and Speak 2-B

G: Good morning, classmates! Nine months _____ _____ so fast, and we are almost _____ _____ _____ _____ this school year. We all had a _____ _____. I guess only _____ _____ of us will be in the same class next year. Don't be a _____. Say hello when we see _____ _____, okay? Thank you.

Listen and Speak 2-C

A: Guess _____ _____ _____.

B: _____ _____ you're playing the piano.

A: You're _____. Guess again.

B: I guess you're _____ _____ the computer.

A: That's _____.

Real Life Talk - Step 1

Brian: Mom, I can't find my smartphone. _____ _____ _____ _____ find it?

Mom: Are you sure you lost it _____ the house?

Brian: Yes. I just _____ my friend a few minutes ago.

Mom: _____ _____ you at the time?

Brian: In the kitchen. I _____ _____ a sandwich.

Mom: Then I guess you left it _____ in the kitchen.

Brian: I already _____ the kitchen, Mom.

Mom: Well, _____ _____ _____ _____ _____. Oh, here _____ _____. Inside the _____.

Brian: Thanks, Mom. You are the greatest!

Mom: You're _____, honey.

Real Life Talk - Step 2

A: Can you _____ _____ _____ my baseball glove?

B: Okay. Where _____ you _____ it _____?

A: On the bench.

B: I _____ a dog _____ your baseball glove. I can _____ _____ _____ on the bench.

G: 좋은 아침이야, 학급 친구들아! 9개월은 아주 빨리 지나갔고, 우리는 이번 학년의 거의 막바지에 있어. 우리 모두는 멋진 한 해를 보냈어. 우리 중 극소수가 내년에 같은 반이 될 거라고 생각해. 모르는 사람처럼 지내지 말자. 서로 만나면 인사말을 건네자. 알겠지? 고마워.

A: 내가 무엇을 하고 있는지 맞혀 봐.
B: 너는 피아노를 치고 있는 것 같아.
A: 틀렸어. 다시 맞혀 봐.
B: 너는 컴퓨터로 일하고 있는 것 같아.
A: 맞아.

Brian: 엄마, 제 스마트폰을 찾을 수가 없어요. 제가 그것을 찾는 걸 도와주시겠어요?
Mom: 집 안에서 잃어버린 것이 확실하니?
Brian: 네. 불과 몇 분 전에 친구에게 문자 메시지를 보냈어요.
Mom: 너는 그때 어디에 있었니?
Brian: 부엌에요. 샌드위치를 만들고 있었어요.
Mom: 그럼 네가 부엌 어딘가에 놓은 것 같구나.
Brian: 이미 부엌은 확인했어요, 엄마.
Mom: 음, 다시 확인해 보자. 오, 여기 있구나. 냉장고 안에 있어.
Brian: 고마워요, 엄마. 엄마는 최고예요!
Mom: 천만에, 애야.

A: 내 야구 글러브를 찾는 것을 도와줄래?
B: 응. 그것을 어디에서 마지막으로 봤니?
A: 벤치 위에서.
B: 개가 네 야구 글러브를 가져간 것 같아. 벤치 위에 발자국을 볼 수 있어.

[01~02] 다음 대화를 읽고 물음에 답하시오.

Emily: Jinsu, (A)부탁 하나 해도 될까?
Jinsu: Sure. What is it?
Emily: Can you help me wash the dishes?
Jinsu: ＿＿＿＿＿＿(B)＿＿＿＿＿＿

01 위 대화의 밑줄 친 (A)의 우리말을 주어진 단어를 모두 배열하여 영작하시오.

┌─ 보기 ┤
ask / I / favor / a / you / can
└

➡ ＿＿＿＿＿＿＿＿＿＿＿＿＿＿＿＿＿

02 위 대화의 빈칸 (B)에 들어갈 말로 나머지 넷과 의도가 다른 것은?

① Of course.
② No problem.
③ I'll give you a hand.
④ Sure.
⑤ I'm afraid I can't.

[03~04] 다음 대화를 읽고 물음에 답하시오.

Brian: Did you see my baseball glove?
Jane: Yes, I saw it under the table.
Brian: Really? (A)It's not there anymore.
Jane: (B)Then I guess Spot took it.
Brian: Oh, there he is. You bad dog, Spot!

03 위 대화의 밑줄 친 (A)가 가리키는 것을 영어로 쓰시오.

➡ ＿＿＿＿＿＿＿＿＿＿＿＿＿＿＿＿＿

04 위 대화의 밑줄 친 (B)의 의도로 적절한 것은?

① 확신 표현하기   ② 제안하기
③ 추측하기   ④ 계획 말하기
⑤ 도움 요청하기

[01~03] 다음 대화를 읽고 물음에 답하시오.

> Narae: Tony, can you do me a favor?
> Tony: Sure. What is it, Narae?
> Narae: Can you take care of my dog this weekend? My family is going to visit my grandmother in Busan.
> Tony: Oh, (A)I'm sorry but I can't. My mom doesn't like dogs.
> Narae: Oh, what should I do?
> Tony: (B)Why don't you ask Sumin? Her family loves dogs.
> Narae: Okay. I'll call her right now.

01 위 대화의 밑줄 친 (A)와 바꾸어 쓸 수 있는 것은?

① I'm afraid I can't.   ② All right.
③ No problem.   ④ Of course.
⑤ Sounds good.

02 중요
위 대화의 밑줄 친 (B)와 바꾸어 쓸 수 없는 것은? (2개)

① How about asking Sumin?
② I think you can ask Sumin.
③ I can ask Sumin.
④ What about asking Sumin?
⑤ How did you ask Sumin?

03 위 대화의 내용과 일치하지 않는 것은?

① Narae는 주말에 가족들과 함께 부산에 갈 것이다.
② Narae는 Tony에게 그녀의 개를 돌봐 줄 것을 요청하였다.
③ Tony의 엄마는 개를 좋아하지 않는다.
④ Sumin의 가족은 개를 아주 좋아한다.
⑤ Narae는 Tony에게 개를 맡긴 후 부산에 갈 것이다.

서답형
04 다음 대화가 자연스럽게 이어지도록 순서대로 배열하시오.

> (A) Really? It's not there anymore.
> (B) Oh, there he is. You bad dog, Spot!
> (C) Yes, I saw it under the table.
> (D) Then I guess Spot took it.
> (E) Did you see my baseball glove?

➡ _____

[05~06] 다음 대화를 읽고 물음에 답하시오.

> Amy: Can you help me find my baseball glove?
> Jack: Okay. Where did you see it last?
> Amy: On the bench.
> Jack: (A)개가 네 야구 글러브를 가져간 것 같구나.(guess, took) I can see its footprints on the bench.

서답형
05 위 대화의 밑줄 친 (A)의 우리말을 주어진 단어를 이용하여 영작하시오.

➡ _____

06 중요
위 대화의 내용과 일치하지 않는 것은?

① Amy needs help to find her baseball glove.
② Amy saw her baseball glove on the bench last.
③ Jack thinks that a dog took Amy's baseball glove.
④ Jack saw a dog running away with a baseball glove.
⑤ Jack finds a dog's footprints on the bench.

[07~09] 다음 대화를 읽고 물음에 답하시오.

Brian: Mom, I can't find my smartphone. Can you help me ⓐfinding it?

Mom: Are you sure you lost it inside the house?

Brian: Yes. I just ⓑtexted my friend a few minutes ago.

Mom: Where were you at the time?

Brian: In the kitchen. I ⓒwas making a sandwich.

Mom: Then I guess you left it ⓓsomewhere in the kitchen.

Brian: I already checked the kitchen, Mom.

Mom: Well, let's check ⓔit again. Oh, here it is. Inside the refrigerator.

Brian: Thanks, Mom. You are the greatest!

Mom: You're welcome, honey.

서답형

07 위 대화의 밑줄 친 ⓐ~ⓔ 중 어법상 어색한 것을 찾아 바르게 고치시오.

➡ _____

08 위 대화를 읽고 대답할 수 없는 질문은?

① What is Brian looking for?
② What does Brian ask his mom to do?
③ What was Brian doing in the kitchen?
④ Why did Brian text to his friend?
⑤ Where did his mom find the smartphone?

중요

09 위 대화에서 나타난 Brian의 심경 변화로 적절한 것은?

① happy → worried
② lonely → irritated
③ confused → pleased
④ satisfied → dissatisfied
⑤ nervous → upset

[10~12] 다음 글을 읽고 물음에 답하시오.

Sujin: Good morning, classmates! Nine months have (A)[passed / passing] so fast, and we are almost at the end of this school year. We all had a wonderful year. I guess only (B)[a little / a few] of us will be in the same class next year. Don't be a stranger. Say hello when we see (C)[each other / other], okay? Thank you.

서답형

10 위 글에서 주어진 영영풀이가 가리키는 말을 찾아 쓰시오.

people who are in the same class as you at school or college

➡ _____

중요

11 위 글의 (A)~(C)에 들어갈 말로 바르게 짝지어진 것은?

	(A)	(B)	(C)
①	passed	a little	each other
②	passed	a few	each other
③	passed	a few	other
④	passing	a few	other
⑤	passing	a little	other

12 위 글의 내용과 일치하지 <u>않는</u> 것은?

① 9개월이 아주 빨리 지나갔다.
② 수진과 학급 친구들은 이번 학년의 거의 막바지에 있다.
③ 수진은 학급 친구들에게 모르는 사람처럼 지내지 말 것을 당부하였다.
④ 수진은 학급 친구들에게 학급이 달라져도 서로 만나면 인사말을 할 것을 요청하였다.
⑤ 수진과 학급 친구들은 대부분 내년에 같은 반이 될 것이다.

[01~02] 다음 글을 읽고 물음에 답하시오.

> Sujin: Good morning, classmates! Nine months have passed so fast, and we are almost at the end of this school year. We all had a wonderful year. (A)우리 중 극소수만이 내년에 같은 반이 될 거라고 생각해. Don't be a stranger. Say hello when we see each other, okay? Thank you.

01 위 글에서 주어진 영영풀이에 해당하는 말을 찾아 쓰시오.

> a person that you do not know

➡ _____

 02 위 글의 밑줄 친 (A)의 우리말을 〈보기〉에 주어진 어구를 모두 배열하여 영작하시오.

> ┤ 보기 ├
> in / next / guess / I / a few of / us / be / will / the same / year / only / class

➡ _____
_____

[03~05] 다음 대화를 읽고 물음에 답하시오.

> Brian: Mom, I can't find my smartphone. (A)제가 그것을 찾는 것을 도와주시겠어요? (help, can)
> Mom: Are you sure you lost it inside the house?
> Brian: Yes. I just texted my friend a few minutes ago.
> Mom: Where were you at the time?
> Brian: In the kitchen. I was making a sandwich.
> Mom: Then I guess you left it somewhere in the kitchen.

> Brian: I already checked the kitchen, Mom.
> Mom: Well, let's check it again. Oh, here it is. Inside the refrigerator.
> Brian: Thanks, Mom. You are the greatest!
> Mom: You're welcome, honey.

03 위 대화의 밑줄 친 (A)의 우리말을 주어진 단어를 사용하여 영작하시오.

➡ _____

 04 Where did Brian use his smartphone last?

➡ _____

05 Where was Brian's smartphone?

➡ _____

[06~07] 다음 대화를 읽고 물음에 답하시오.

> Amy: Can you help me find my baseball glove?
> Jack: Okay. Where did you see it last?
> Amy: On the bench.
> Jack: I guess a dog took your baseball glove. I can see its ___(A)___ s on the bench.

06 위 대화의 빈칸 (A)에 다음 주어진 영영풀이가 나타내는 말을 쓰시오.

> a mark left by a foot or shoe

➡ _____

07 Why does Jack think a dog took Amy's baseball glove?

➡ _____

Grammar

1 something+형용사

> • She has **something cute**. 그녀는 귀여운 무언가를 가지고 있다.
> • I know **someone dependable**. 나는 의지할 만한 누군가를 알아요.

■ '-body, -thing, -one'으로 끝나는 부정대명사는 형용사가 뒤에서 수식한다. 이러한 대명사에는 somebody, something, someone, anybody, anything, anyone, nobody, nothing, no one 등이 있다.

- I need **something exciting**. 나는 신나는 무언가가 필요해.
- Do you have **anything long**? 길쭉한 무언가를 가지고 있니?
- Catherine did **something terrible**. Catherine은 무언가 끔찍한 일을 저질렀다.
- Didn't you bring **anything small**? 어떤 작은 것을 가지고 오지 않았니?

■ 위의 대명사를 to부정사와 형용사가 동시에 수식할 때 어순은 '대명사+형용사+to부정사'이다.

- Is there **someone brave** to tell the truth? 그 사실을 말할 용감한 누군가가 있나요?
- They want **something valuable** to have. 그들은 가지기에 귀중한 어떤 것을 원해요.
- He knew **nothing important** to tell. 그는 말하기에 중요한 것을 아무것도 몰랐다.

핵심 Check

1. 다음 우리말과 일치하도록 빈칸에 알맞은 말을 쓰시오.
   (1) 그는 어떤 시끄러운 소리를 들었다.
      ➡ He heard _____ _____.
   (2) 그의 차에 무슨 문제가 있어.
      ➡ There is _____ _____ with his car.
   (3) 음식에 이상한 것이 있다.
      ➡ There is _____ _____ in the food.

② 간접의문문

> • I don't know **what she is doing**. 나는 그녀가 무엇을 하고 있는지 몰라요.
> • Tell me **why he came late**. 그가 왜 늦게 왔는지 말해 줘.

■ 간접의문문은 명사절을 이끌며 주어, 목적어, 보어 역할을 한다. 의문사가 있는 간접의문문은 '의문사+주어+동사' 어순으로 쓰인다. 직접의문문인 '의문사+동사+주어 ~?'의 어순과 혼동하지 않도록 유의한다.

- Where is she going? 〈직접의문문〉

  Can you tell me **where she is going**? 〈간접의문문〉 그녀가 어디에 가고 있는지 말해 줄 수 있니?
- Ted didn't know **how she broke in his house**. Ted는 어떻게 그녀가 그의 집에 침입했는지 몰랐다.
- Do you remember **when she went out**? 그녀가 언제 나갔는지 기억하니?

■ 다음과 같이 의문사가 주어 역할을 하는 경우가 있다. 이때에는 '의문사+동사'의 어순이 된다.

- June doesn't know **who built the house**. June은 누가 그 집을 지었는지 모른다.

■ 의문사가 없는 경우 간접의문문의 어순은 'if/whether+주어+동사'로 쓴다.

- Can you tell me? + Do you know her?

  → Can you tell me **if[whether] you know her**? 네가 그녀를 아는지 말해 줄래?
- I wonder **whether they came to the party in time**. 나는 그들이 제때에 그 파티에 왔는지 궁금해.
- Branda tried to guess **if they needed her help**.
  Branda는 그들이 그녀의 도움을 필요로 하는지 추측하려고 애썼다.

핵심 Check

2. 다음 우리말과 일치하도록 빈칸에 알맞은 말을 쓰시오.

(1) 나는 그 영화가 언제 시작하는지 몰라.

➡ I don't know ＿＿＿＿ ＿＿＿＿ ＿＿＿＿ ＿＿＿＿.

(2) 그가 무엇을 먹었는지 말해 줘.

➡ Tell me ＿＿＿＿ ＿＿＿＿ ＿＿＿＿.

(3) 그 시계가 얼마인지 아니?

➡ Do you know ＿＿＿＿ ＿＿＿＿ ＿＿＿＿ ＿＿＿＿?

01 다음 문장에서 어법상 <u>어색한</u> 부분을 바르게 고쳐 쓰시오.

(1) Is there nice anyone like you?

_____ ➡ _____

(2) Can you tell me where can I find the church?

_____ ➡ _____

(3) Tell me something to see pretty in your class.

_____ ➡ _____

(4) May I ask that you are a student?

_____ ➡ _____

02 다음 빈칸에 괄호 안의 단어를 바르게 배열하시오.

(1) Do you know _____? (is / she / who)
(2) I don't understand _____. (angry / her / what / made)
(3) Is there _____? (on / comfortable / to / sit / something)
(4) Can you tell me _____? (is / old / how / she)
(5) Is _____? (cold / there / something)

03 주어진 단어를 바르게 배열하여 다음 우리말을 영어로 쓰시오.

(1) sweet: 달콤한

(1) 달콤한 무언가를 먹고 싶어. (sweet / I / eat / to / want / something)

➡ _____

(2) 이것보다 더 큰 무언가를 가지고 있니? (this / have / you / than / anything / do / bigger)

➡ _____

(3) Jason은 엄마가 그를 어떻게 찾았는지 모른다. (him / know / his mom / doesn't / found / Jason / how)

➡ _____

(4) 우리는 그들이 언제 올지 몰라요. (come / we / when / they / will / don't / know)

➡ _____

01 다음 우리말을 영어로 옮길 때 다섯 번째로 오는 단어는?

> 나는 다채롭고 아름다운 무언가를 보고 싶어.

① to   ② colorful   ③ and
④ see   ⑤ something

02 다음 중 빈칸에 들어갈 말로 가장 적절한 것은?

> Can you tell me _____?

① when are you going there
② who called you last night
③ where do they want to meet
④ how will you keep the promise
⑤ what does she choose to eat

03 다음 빈칸에 들어갈 말이 바르게 짝지어진 것은?

> • Is there _____?
> • I wonder _____.

① something excited – what are they
② something excite – whether they do
③ something do – what do they do
④ anything exciting – what they are
⑤ anything doing – if they do

04 주어진 단어를 바르게 배열하여 다음 우리말을 영어로 쓰시오.

> 그녀에게는 함께 대화할 친절한 사람이 없어.
> (with / anyone / have / she / kind / talk /
> doesn't / to)

➡ _____

05 다음 빈칸에 들어갈 말로 적절하지 <u>않은</u> 것은?

> Daisy knows someone _____.

① friendly   ② lovely   ③ lonely
④ lively   ⑤ politely

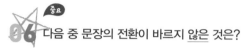
06 다음 중 문장의 전환이 바르지 <u>않은</u> 것은?

① 그가 언제 숙제를 했는지 궁금해.
   → I wonder when he did his homework.
② 나는 귀중한 무언가를 원해요.
   → I want something precious.
③ 그가 그것을 좋아하는지 물어봐도 될까?
   → May I ask him whether he likes it?
④ 누가 그녀를 봤는지 아니?
   → Do you know who she saw?
⑤ 저기에 작은 무언가가 있어.
   → There is something small there.

07 다음 중 빈칸에 들어갈 말로 적절한 것을 <u>모두</u> 고르시오.

> David wanted to know _____ Julia
> went home.

① if   ② who   ③ which
④ whether   ⑤ what

08 다음 빈칸에 알맞은 말을 쓰시오.

> 우리가 언제 만날지 기억나지 않아.
> I can't remember _____ _____
> _____ _____ _____.

09 다음 중 어법상 바르지 <u>않은</u> 것은?

① They don't know if Molly will take part in the race.
② Jimmy has something big.
③ I remember how they made the cake.
④ Do you know why he stopped his car?
⑤ I have something to talk about fun.

10 다음 중 대화의 빈칸에 들어갈 말로 가장 적절한 것은?

A: Can you tell me _____?
B: Go straight one block and turn left.

① when I go out to have dinner
② how can I get to the bakery
③ why you want to go there
④ how I can get to the police office
⑤ how long one block is

11 다음 중 우리말을 영어로 바르게 옮긴 것은?

누가 그 공을 찼는지 나는 알고 싶어.

① I want to know who the ball kicked.
② I want to know who did you kick the ball.
③ I want to know who kicked the ball.
④ I want to know whom you kicked the ball.
⑤ I want to know how you kicked the ball.

서답형
12 주어진 단어를 활용하여 다음 우리말을 영어로 쓰시오.

처리해야 할 중요한 무언가가 있어.
(there / deal with)

➡ _____

13 다음 중 빈칸에 들어갈 말이 바르게 짝지어진 것은?

• I'm looking for something _____.
• Remember what _____.

① fresh to eat – is he saying to you
② fresh to eat – he said to you
③ fresh to eat – does he say to you
④ eat fresh to – he said to you
⑤ eat to fresh – did he say to you

14 다음 두 문장을 하나의 문장으로 바르게 옮기지 <u>않은</u> 것은?

① Tell me. Why did you leave me?
   → Tell me why you left me.
② I wonder. What made you so happy?
   → I wonder what made you so happy.
③ Can I ask you? Are you mad at me?
   → Can I ask you if you are mad at me?
④ I don't know. Who helped you?
   → I don't know who you helped.
⑤ Do you remember? What's his name?
   → Do you remember what his name is?

15 다음 빈칸에 들어갈 수 <u>없는</u> 것은?

I want someone _____ right now.

① reliable   ② fun   ③ cute
④ to talk to   ⑤ care

서답형
16 주어진 단어를 바르게 배열하여 다음 우리말을 영어로 쓰시오.

나는 그가 지금 누구와 이야기하고 있는지 궁금해. (wonder / with / I / talking / is / he / who / now)

➡ _____

17 다음 중 주어진 문장의 밑줄 친 부분과 쓰임이 같은 것은?

> You didn't tell me <u>who</u> gave this file for the meeting.

① The boy <u>who</u> plays the piano looks handsome.
② There are many people <u>who</u> want to participate in the marathon.
③ Let me guess <u>who</u> will help us to prepare the meal.
④ Can you tell me about the woman <u>who</u> is swimming in our pool?
⑤ We ran with the employees <u>who</u> donated their blood.

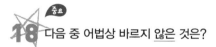

18 다음 중 어법상 바르지 <u>않은</u> 것은?

> A: ①Is there ②something wrong?
> B: Yes, there ③is. Someone ④stole my money. I think I know ⑤who is he.

① ② ③ ④ ⑤

서답형

19 주어진 단어를 활용하여 다음 우리말을 영어로 쓰시오.

> 언제 이게 발생했는지 말해 주겠니?
> (could / happen)

➡ _____

서답형

20 다음 두 문장을 하나의 문장으로 쓰시오.

> • Do you know?
> • Who brought this T-shirt?

➡ _____

---

21 다음 빈칸에 들어갈 말로 가장 적절한 것은?

> Tell me. Is he going to sing the song?
> = Tell me _____ he is going to sing the song.

① that   ② why   ③ if
④ how   ⑤ when

22 다음 중 우리말을 영어로 바르게 옮기지 <u>않은</u> 것은?

① 새로운 것은 없습니다.
  → There is nothing new.
② 누가 그 꽃을 꺾었는지 아니?
  → Do you know who picked the flower?
③ 우리는 무거운 것은 필요 없어요.
  → We don't need heavy anything.
④ 왜 울고 있는지 물어봐도 될까?
  → Can I ask you why you are crying?
⑤ 누가 문을 두드렸는지는 중요하지 않아.
  → Who knocked the door doesn't matter.

23 여덟 개의 단어를 이용하여 다음 우리말을 영어로 쓸 때 다섯 번째와 여섯 번째 오는 단어를 바르게 짝지은 것은?

> 그는 다른 사람들을 위해 뭔가 좋은 일을 하려고 애쓴다.

① to – do
② do – something
③ something – good
④ good – for
⑤ for – others

서답형

24 다음 대화의 빈칸에 알맞은 말을 쓰시오.

> A: We have a medical experiment, so we need _____ _____ _____ _____.
> B: Oh, I know someone like that. Mr. Han is very strong and healthy.

01 주어진 단어를 활용하여 다음 우리말을 영어로 쓰시오.

> 나는 믿을 만한 누군가가 필요해. (reliable)

➡ _____

02 다음 두 문장을 하나의 문장으로 쓰시오.

(1) Do you know? How does she bake these cookies?

➡ _____

(2) I'll ask Jason. Where does he live?

➡ _____

(3) Do you remember? What is Brad's last name?

➡ _____

(4) I wonder. Will they go abroad to study English?

➡ _____
_____

(5) Can you tell me? Is she going to run or walk?

➡ _____
_____

(6) I don't understand. What did they want to do?

➡ _____

(7) I want to know. Who made the decision last night?

➡ _____

03 다음 우리말을 영어로 쓰시오.

> 그가 몇 살인지 알려 줘. (let / know)

➡ _____

04 다음 대화의 빈칸에 알맞은 말을 쓰시오.

> A: I can't remember _____ home.
> B: You came home at 10 p.m.

➡ _____

05 주어진 단어를 활용하여 다음 우리말을 영어로 쓰시오.

> A: 나는 어제 파티에서 흥미로운 어떤 사람을 만났어. (someone / at a party)
> B: 그가 누구였는지 내게 말해 줘. (tell)

➡ A: _____
   B: _____

06 주어진 어구를 바르게 배열하여 다음 우리말을 영어로 쓰시오.

> Mike는 존경받을 만한 용감한 누군가를 만나길 원했다.
> (to be admired / wanted / Mike / brave / meet / to / someone)

➡ _____
_____

07 주어진 단어를 활용하여 다음 대화를 완성하시오.

> A: I'd like to know _____.(what / about)
> B: The story is about a princess and seven dwarfs.

➡ _____

08 빈칸에 알맞은 단어를 넣어 다음 대화를 완성하시오.

> A: Look! I found _____ _____.
> B: It looks really strange. Do you know what _____ _____?
> A: I have no idea.

09 중요 다음 빈칸에 공통으로 들어갈 알맞은 말을 쓰시오.

> • I will drive the car _____ you lend me yours.
> • Did they tell you _____ they had lunch together?

10 주어진 단어를 활용하여 다음 우리말을 8단어로 이루어진 한 문장의 영어로 쓰시오.

> 나는 이 트리를 장식할 다채로운 무언가가 필요해.
> (colorful / decorate / something)
>
> ➡ _____

11 고난이도 다음 대화를 영어로 쓰시오. 한 칸에 하나의 단어만 쓰시오.

> A: 나는 그가 무엇을 원하는지 모르겠어.
> (_____ _____ _____ _____ _____ _____.)
> B: 그는 다른 무언가를 원해. (_____ _____ _____ _____.)

12 주어진 단어를 활용하여 다음 우리말을 영어로 쓰시오.

> 이 단어가 무엇을 의미하는지 아니?
> (mean)
>
> ➡ _____

13 중요 대화의 빈칸에 알맞은 말을 세 단어로 쓰시오.

> A: It's so hot. I want _____ _____ _____. Do you have any?
> B: Oh, yes. I have a bottle of water.

14 다음 문장에서 어법상 바르지 않은 것을 바르게 고쳐 쓰시오.

> I don't remember where did I put my purse yesterday.
>
> ➡ _____
> _____

15 고난이도 다음 그림에 맞게 대화 내용을 완성하시오. 주어진 단어를 활용하시오.

> A: I wonder _____ _____ _____ watching.
> B: They are watching _____ _____ in the theater.

> (surprising / what / something)

Reading

The Missing Gold!

Mr. Reese, the principal, ran across the wet playground.
콤마로 연결된 동격 관계

"Shirley! Shirley! I need your help!"

Shirley was an eighth grade student at Bakersville Middle School.
eight의 서수
She was also the best detective in the whole town.

"Is there something wrong?" asked Shirley.
–thing으로 끝나는 부정대명사는 형용사가 뒤에서 수식

"Someone has stolen the gold medal for the talent show!"
결과 용법의 현재완료

Mr. Reese took Shirley to the scene of the crime. There was a case
take A to B: A를 B로 데려가다
with a broken window. The silver and bronze medals were still there.
~이 있는   *= in the case*

But the gold medal was missing. There was a poem in its place.
없어진, 실종된(형용사)

Tomorrow is the talent show.

Where did the gold medal go?

Look high and low.
구석구석 살펴라
You can't catch me. You're too slow.

Shirley asked, "Could you tell me when this happened?"
간접의문문: 의문사+주어+동사

"A little after nine last night. I was making my rounds when I heard a
9시 조금 지나서   *make one's rounds: 순찰을 돌다, 순찰하다*
scream. I rushed over and found Jocelyn and the case like this."
이와 같은 (모습의)

"I wonder who else was here last night."
간접의문문: 의문사+주어+동사(동사 wonder의 목적어로 쓰임)

"Sylvia and Harry. They were also practicing for the talent show. I'll

call them to my office."
call A to B A를 B로 부르다

principal 교장
run across ~을 가로질러 뛰다
detective 탐정
steal 훔치다
talent show 장기 자랑 대회
scene 현장
crime 범죄
broken 깨진, 부서진
silver 은
bronze 동
thief 도둑
else 또 다른

📎 **확인문제**

● 다음 문장이 본문의 내용과 일치하면 T, 일치하지 <u>않으면</u> F를 쓰시오.

1   The ground was wet when Mr. Reese ran across it. ☐

2   Shirley went to the scene of the crime alone. ☐

3   The thief stole the medal without breaking anything. ☐

4   Mr. Reese knew who was at the school last night. ☐

Jocelyn was a ninth grade student with short curly red hair.

"I was practicing my song and I became thirsty. I stepped outside the classroom to get some water. It was completely dark. Suddenly, there was a loud sound of thunder. I think the thief broke the window at that moment. Lightning followed right after and it became bright for a second or two. Then I saw someone running away from the case."

"Did you see the thief's face?"

"No, I only saw the thief's back. But the thief had short hair."

Next was an eighth grade student, Sylvia. She was tall with long black hair. She said, "I was reading my poem aloud in the classroom. I heard a scream and went outside. There was a girl next to the case. With the flash from the lightning, it was like a horror movie. I got scared so I ran straight home."

"Did you hear the window break?"

"No, the thunder was too loud. Well, I didn't do it. I was going to win first place anyway."

Harry, a seventh grader, had short blonde hair. He said, "Hey, you got the wrong guy. I was practicing my dance moves. I went home a little before nine. I didn't take one step outside the classroom until then."

"Did you hear anything strange?"

"How could I? My music was really loud."

"Did you see anyone on the way home?"

"No, I heard someone singing really badly, but I didn't see anyone."

Shirley said, "I don't need to hear anymore." Then she turned to the thief.

"Why don't you bring the medal back before you get into some real trouble?"

단어	뜻
curly	곱슬머리의
completely	완전히
suddenly	갑자기
thunder	천둥
thief	도둑
at that moment	그 순간에, 그 때에
lightning	번개
flash	섬광, 번쩍임
horror	공포
win first place	일등을 하다, 우승하다
anyway	어쨌든, 어차피
strange	이상한
on the way home	집에 가는[오는] 길에
not ~ anymore	더 이상 ~ 않다
get into trouble	곤경에 빠지다
real	진짜의, 실제의

📎 **확인문제**

● 다음 문장이 본문의 내용과 일치하면 T, 일치하지 않으면 F를 쓰시오.

1 Jocelyn knew nothing about the thief. ☐

2 Harry heard someone sing poorly on the way home. ☐

3 Shirley found out who had stolen the medal. ☐

● 우리말을 참고하여 빈칸에 알맞은 말을 쓰시오.

1 Mr. Reese, the principal, _____ _____ the wet playground.

2 "Shirley! Shirley! I _____ your _____!"

3 Shirley was an _____ _____ student at Bakersville Middle School.

4 She was also _____ _____ _____ in the whole town.

5 "Is there _____ _____?" asked Shirley.

6 "Someone _____ _____ the gold medal _____ the talent show!"

7 Mr. Reese _____ Shirley _____ the _____ of the crime.

8 There _____ a case with a _____ window.

9 The silver and bronze medals _____ _____ _____.

10 But the gold medal was _____. There was _____ _____ in _____ _____.

11 Tomorrow is the talent show. _____ _____ the gold medal _____?

12 Look _____ _____ _____. You can't catch me. You're _____ slow.

13 Shirley asked, "Could you tell me _____ _____ _____?"

14 "A little _____ nine last night. I was _____ _____ _____ when I heard a scream. I _____ _____ and found Jocelyn and the case like this."

15 "I wonder _____ _____ _____ _____ last night."

16 "Sylvia and Harry. They were also _____ for the talent show. I'll _____ _____ to my office."

17 Jocelyn was a _____ _____ student with short _____ red hair.

1 Reese 교장은 젖은 운동장을 달려왔다.

2 "Shirley! Shirley! 네 도움이 필요하구나!"

3 Shirley는 Bakersville 중학교의 8학년 학생이었다.

4 그녀는 또한 그 마을 최고의 탐정이었다.

5 "무슨 일이 있나요?" Shirley가 물었다.

6 "누군가 장기 자랑 대회 금메달을 훔쳐갔어!"

7 Reese 교장은 Shirley를 범죄 현장으로 데려갔다.

8 유리창이 깨진 진열장이 있었다.

9 은메달과 동메달은 그곳에 그대로 있었다.

10 하지만 금메달은 사라졌다. 그 자리에는 시가 있었다.

11 내일은 장기 자랑 대회다. 금메달은 어디로 갔을까?

12 구석구석 찾아라. 당신은 나를 잡을 수 없어. 당신은 너무 느려.

13 Shirley는 "언제 이 사건이 일어났는지 말씀해 주시겠어요?"라고 물었다.

14 "어젯밤 9시가 조금 넘은 후에. 내가 순찰을 돌고 있었을 때 비명 소리가 들렸어. 나는 달려가서 Jocelyn과 이 상태인 진열장을 발견했지."

15 "어젯밤에 또 다른 누가 여기 있었는지 궁금해요."

16 "Sylvia와 Harry가 있었어. 그 두 사람 또한 장기 자랑을 위해 연습 중이었어. 내가 그들을 내 사무실로 부르마."

17 Jocelyn은 빨간색 짧은 곱슬머리를 가진 9학년 학생이었다.

18 "I was _____ my song and I became _____. I _____ _____ the classroom _____ _____ some water. _____ was _____ dark. _____, there was a loud sound of _____. I think the thief _____ the window at that moment. _____ _____ right after and it became bright for a second or two. Then I saw someone _____ _____ from the case."

19 "Did you see the thief's _____?"

20 "No, I only saw the thief's _____. But the thief had _____ hair."

21 Next was an _____ _____ student, Sylvia. She was tall _____ _____ _____ hair.

22 She said, "I was _____ my poem _____ in the classroom. I heard a scream and went outside. There was a girl _____ _____ the case. With the _____ from the lightning, it was _____ _____ _____ _____ _____. I got _____ so I ran straight home."

23 "Did you _____ the window _____?"

24 "No, the thunder was _____ _____. Well, I didn't do it. I _____ _____ _____ _____ first place anyway."

25 Harry, a seventh grader, had _____ _____ hair.

26 He said, "Hey, you got the _____ guy. I was practicing my dance _____. I went home _____ _____ _____ nine. I didn't _____ one step _____ the classroom _____ then."

27 "Did you hear _____ _____?"

28 "_____ _____ I? My music was really loud."

29 "Did you see anyone _____ _____ _____ _____ _____?"

30 "No, I heard someone _____ really badly, but I didn't see anyone."

31 Shirley said, "I don't need _____ _____ _____." Then she _____ _____ the thief.

32 "Why don't you _____ _____ before you get into some real trouble?"

---

18 "저는 제 노래를 연습하고 있었는데 목이 말랐어요. 저는 물을 가지러 교실 밖으로 나갔어요. 완전히 어두웠어요. 갑자기, 커다란 천둥소리가 났어요. 저는 도둑이 그 순간에 유리창을 깼다고 생각해요. 번개가 바로 뒤따랐고 1~2초 정도 밝아졌어요. 그때 저는 누군가가 진열장에서 도망치는 걸 봤어요."

19 "도둑의 얼굴을 봤나요?"

20 "아니요, 도둑의 뒷모습만 봤어요. 하지만 그 도둑은 짧은 머리였어요."

21 다음은 8학년 학생인 Sylvia였다. 그녀는 긴 검은색 머리에 키가 컸다.

22 그녀는 말했다. "저는 교실에서 큰 소리로 제 시를 낭송하고 있었어요. 비명 소리를 듣고 밖으로 나갔어요. 진열장 옆에 한 소녀가 있었어요. 번개의 번쩍임과 어우러져 그것은 공포 영화 같았어요. 저는 겁이 나서 곧장 집으로 달려갔어요."

23 "창이 깨지는 소리를 들었나요?"

24 "아니요, 천둥소리가 너무 컸어요. 음, 제가 그런 게 아니에요. 저는 어쨌든 1등을 할 거였으니까요."

25 7학년인 Harry는 짧은 금발을 가지고 있었다.

26 그는 말했다. "이봐요, 사람을 잘못 짚었어요. 저는 제 춤 동작을 연습하고 있었어요. 저는 9시 조금 전에 집에 갔어요. 저는 그때까지 교실 밖으로 한 발자국도 나가지 않았어요."

27 "이상한 소리라도 들었나요?"

28 "제가 어떻게 듣겠어요? 제 음악 소리가 정말 컸어요."

29 "집에 가는 길에 누군가를 보았나요?"

30 "아니요, 누군가가 노래를 정말 끔찍하게 부르는 소리는 들었지만 누구도 보진 못했어요."

31 Shirley는 "더 이상 들을 필요는 없겠네요."라고 말했다. 그러고 나서 그녀는 도둑을 향했다.

32 "정말 곤경에 빠지기 전에 금메달을 돌려주는 게 어때요?"

● 우리말을 참고하여 본문을 영작하시오.

1 Reese 교장은 젖은 운동장을 달려왔다.
➡ _____

2 "Shirley! Shirley! 네 도움이 필요하구나!"
➡ _____

3 Shirley는 Bakersville 중학교의 8학년 학생이었다.
➡ _____

4 그녀는 또한 그 마을 최고의 탐정이었다.
➡ _____

5 "무슨 일이 있나요?" Shirley가 물었다.
➡ _____

6 "누군가 장기 자랑 대회 금메달을 훔쳐갔어!"
➡ _____

7 Reese 교장은 Shirley를 범죄 현장으로 데려갔다.
➡ _____

8 유리창이 깨진 진열장이 있었다.
➡ _____

9 은메달과 동메달은 그곳에 그대로 있었다.
➡ _____

10 하지만 금메달은 사라졌다. 그 자리에는 시가 있었다.
➡ _____

11 내일은 장기 자랑 대회다. 금메달은 어디로 갔을까?
➡ _____

12 구석구석 찾아라. 당신은 나를 잡을 수 없어. 당신은 너무 느려.
➡ _____

13 Shirley는 "언제 이 사건이 일어났는지 말씀해 주시겠어요?"라고 물었다.
➡ _____

14 "어젯밤 9시가 조금 넘은 후에. 내가 순찰을 돌고 있었을 때 비명 소리가 들렸어. 나는 달려가서 Jocelyn과 이 상태인 진열장을 발견했지."
➡ _____
_____

15 "어젯밤에 또 다른 누가 여기 있었는지 궁금해요."
➡ _____

16 "Sylvia와 Harry가 있었어. 그 두 사람 또한 장기 자랑을 위해 연습 중이었어. 내가 그들을 내 사무실로 부르마."
➡ _____

17 Jocelyn은 빨간색 짧은 곱슬머리를 가진 9학년 학생이었다.
➡ _____

18 "저는 제 노래를 연습하고 있었는데 목이 말랐어요. 저는 물을 가지러 교실 밖으로 나갔어요. 완전히 어두웠어요. 갑자기, 커다란 천둥소리가 났어요. 저는 도둑이 그 순간에 유리창을 깼다고 생각해요. 번개가 바로 뒤따랐고 1~2초 정도 밝아졌어요. 그때 저는 누군가가 진열장에서 도망치는 걸 봤어요."

➡ _____

_____

_____

19 "도둑의 얼굴을 봤나요?"

➡ _____

20 "아니요, 도둑의 뒷모습만 봤어요. 하지만 그 도둑은 짧은 머리였어요."

➡ _____

21 다음은 8학년 학생인 Sylvia였다. 그녀는 긴 검은색 머리에 키가 컸다.

➡ _____

22 그녀는 말했다. "저는 교실에서 큰 소리로 제 시를 낭송하고 있었어요. 비명 소리를 듣고 밖으로 나갔어요. 진열장 옆에 한 소녀가 있었어요. 번개의 번쩍임과 어우러져 그것은 공포 영화 같았어요. 저는 겁이 나서 곧장 집으로 달려갔어요."

➡ _____

_____

_____

23 "창이 깨지는 소리를 들었나요?"

➡ _____

24 "아니요, 천둥소리가 너무 컸어요. 음, 제가 그런 게 아니에요. 저는 어쨌든 1등을 할 거였으니까요."

➡ _____

25 7학년인 Harry는 짧은 금발을 가지고 있었다.

➡ _____

26 그는 말했다. "이봐요, 사람을 잘못 짚었어요. 저는 제 춤 동작을 연습하고 있었어요. 저는 9시 조금 전에 집에 갔어요. 저는 그때까지 교실 밖으로 한 발자국도 나가지 않았어요."

➡ _____

_____

27 "이상한 소리라도 들었나요?"

➡ _____

28 "제가 어떻게 듣겠어요? 제 음악 소리가 정말 컸어요."

➡ _____

29 "집에 가는 길에 누군가를 보았나요?"

➡ _____

30 "아니요, 누군가가 노래를 정말 끔찍하게 부르는 소리는 들었지만 누구도 보진 못했어요."

➡ _____

31 Shirley는 "더 이상 들을 필요는 없겠네요."라고 말했다. 그러고 나서 그녀는 도둑을 향했다.

➡ _____

32 "정말 곤경에 빠지기 전에 금메달을 돌려주는 게 어때요?"

➡ _____

[01~04] 다음 글을 읽고 물음에 답하시오.

Mr. Reese, the principal, ①ran across the wet playground.

"Shirley! Shirley! I need your help!"

Shirley was an eighth grade student at Bakersville Middle School. She was also the best detective in the whole town.

"Is there something wrong?" asked Shirley.

"Someone has stolen the gold medal for the talent show!"

Mr. Reese ②took Shirley to ③the scene of the crime. There was ④a case with a broken window. The silver and bronze medals were still (A)there. But the gold medal was missing. There was a poem in its place.

Tomorrow is the talent show.
Where did the gold medal go?
⑤Look high and low.
You can't catch me. You're too slow.

01 다음 중 위 글에서 찾아볼 수 없는 것은?

① a man who ran across the playground
② a case with a gold medal
③ a poem written by someone
④ a case with a silver and bronze medals
⑤ a man and a girl going to the scene of the crime

서답형
02 밑줄 친 (A)가 의미하는 것을 영어로 쓰시오.

➡ _____

03 ①~⑤ 중 단어의 의미풀이가 바르지 않은 것은?

① 가로질러 뛰었다   ② 데려갔다
③ 범죄의 현장   ④ 사건
⑤ 구석구석 찾아라

서답형
04 다음 물음에 세 단어로 이루어진 한 문장의 영어로 답하시오.

> Q: What happened to the gold medal for the talent show?

➡ _____

[05~08] 다음 글을 읽고 물음에 답하시오.

Shirley asked, "Could you tell me when this happened?"

"A little after nine last night. I was making my rounds when I heard a scream. I rushed over and found Jocelyn and the case like this."

"I wonder who else was here last night."

"Sylvia and Harry. They were also practicing for the talent show. I'll call ⓐthem to my office."

Jocelyn was a ninth grade student with short curly red hair.

"I was practicing my song and I became thirsty. I stepped outside the classroom to get some water. ⓑIt was completely dark. Suddenly, there was a loud sound of thunder. I think the thief broke the window at that moment. Lightning followed right after and it became bright for a second or two. Then I saw someone running away from the case."

"Did you see the thief's face?"

"No, I only saw the thief's back. But the thief had short hair."

서답형
05 밑줄 친 ⓐ가 가리키는 것을 영어로 쓰시오.

➡ _____

06 Which one is <u>NOT</u> true about Jocelyn?

① She had short curly hair.

② She became thirsty while practicing.

③ She drank water in the classroom.

④ She heard a sound of thunder.

⑤ She practiced songs for the talent show.

07 다음 중 밑줄 친 ⓑ와 쓰임이 같은 것은?

① It was my mistake to bring you here.

② It was cloudy and windy.

③ It climbs a tree by itself.

④ It is true that she stole my money.

⑤ It belongs to my brother.

서답형

08 According to the passage, what did Jocelyn know about the thief? Answer in English with a full sentence.

➡ _____

[09~13] 다음 글을 읽고 물음에 답하시오.

Next was an eighth grade student, Sylvia. She was tall with long black hair. She said, "I was ①reading my poem aloud in the classroom. I heard a scream and went outside. There was a girl next to the case. With ②the flash from the lightning, it was like a horror movie. I got ③scared so I ran straight home."

"Did you hear the window break?"

"No, the thunder was too loud. Well, I didn't do it. I was going to win first place anyway."

Harry, a seventh grader, had short blonde hair. He said, "Hey, you got the ④wrong guy. I was practicing my dance moves. I went home a little before nine. I didn't take one step outside the classroom until then."

"Did you hear anything strange?"

"How could I? My music was really ⑤quiet."

"Did you see anyone on the way home?"

"No, I heard someone singing really badly, but I didn't see anyone."

Shirley said, "I don't need to hear anymore." Then she turned to the ___(A)___.

"Why don't you bring the medal back before you get into some real trouble?"

서답형

09 다음과 같이 풀이되는 단어를 빈칸 (A)에 쓰시오.

> a person who steals something from another person

➡ _____

서답형

10 ①~⑤ 중 글의 흐름상 어색한 것은?

①   ②   ③   ④   ⑤

서답형

11 위 글의 내용에 맞게 빈칸에 알맞은 말을 쓰시오.

> Shirley: I wonder _____ .
>
> Harry: No, I just heard someone singing badly.

➡ _____

서답형

12 Write the reason why Sylvia didn't hear the window break.

➡ It was because _____ .

13 다음 중 위 글을 읽고 답할 수 <u>없는</u> 질문은?

① Where was Sylvia reading her poem?

② Why did Sylvia go outside?

③ Why did Sylvia see a horror movie?

④ What was Harry doing?

⑤ When did Harry go home?

[14~17] 다음 글을 읽고 물음에 답하시오.

Mr. Reese, the principal, ran across the wet playground.

"Shirley! Shirley! I need your help!"

Shirley was an eighth grade student at Bakersville Middle School. She was also the best detective in the whole town.

"Is there something wrong?" asked Shirley.

"Someone has stolen the gold medal for the talent show!"

Mr. Reese took Shirley to the scene of the crime. There was a case with a broken window. The silver and bronze medals were still there. But the gold medal was missing. There was a poem in its place.

Tomorrow is the talent show.
Where did the gold medal go?
Look high and low.
You can't catch me. You're too slow.

Shirley asked, "Could you tell me _____(A)_____?"

"A little after nine last night. I was making my rounds when I heard a scream. I rushed over and found Jocelyn and the case like this."

"I wonder who else was here last night."

"Sylvia and Harry. They were also practicing for the talent show. I'll call them to my office."

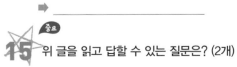

14 단어 this를 이용하여 빈칸 (A)에 들어갈 알맞은 말을 3단어로 쓰시오.

➡ _____

15 위 글을 읽고 답할 수 있는 질문은? (2개)

① When did Mr. Reese find Shirley?

② Where does Shirley live?

③ How many case did Shirley solve?

④ When did the medal disappear?

⑤ When is the talent show?

16 Choose what we can know from the poem. (2개)

① The gold medal was placed somewhere high.

② The talent show was going to be held the next day.

③ The person who wrote it wondered who took the medal.

④ The thief wrote the poem.

⑤ The person who wrote it wanted someone to catch him or her.

서답형

17 위 글의 내용에 맞게 빈칸에 알맞은 말을 쓰시오.

The thief took only _____.

[18~22] 다음 글을 읽고 물음에 답하시오.

Jocelyn was a ninth grade student with short curly red hair.

"I was practicing my song and I became thirsty. ① I stepped outside the classroom to get some water. ② It was completely dark. ③ Suddenly, there was a loud sound of thunder. ④ I think the thief broke the window at that moment. Lightning followed right after and it became bright for a second or two. ⑤"

"Did you see the thief's face?" asked Shirley.

"No, I only saw the thief's back. But the thief had short hair."

Next was an eighth grade student, Sylvia. She was tall with long black hair. She said, "I was reading my poem aloud in the classroom. I heard a scream and went outside. There was a girl next to the case. With the flash from the lightning, it was like a horror movie. I got scared so I ran straight home."

"Did you hear the window break?" asked Shirley.

"No, the thunder was too loud. Well, I didn't do it. I was going to win first place anyway."

18 ①~⑤ 중 주어진 문장이 들어가기에 가장 적절한 곳은?

> Then I saw someone running away from the case.

①   ②   ③   ④   ⑤

19 Sylvia가 교실 밖을 나와 느낀 감정으로 가장 적절한 것은?

① interested   ② happy   ③ sad
④ frightened   ⑤ bored

20 Which one is NOT true about the passage?

① Shirley wondered if Jocelyn saw the thief's face.
② Sylvia was an eighth grade student.
③ Sylvia was reading a poem when there was thunder.
④ Sylvia saw a girl beside the case.
⑤ The sound of the thunder was very loud.

21 According to the passage, why did Jocelyn step outside the classroom? Answer in English with a full sentence.

➡ _____

22 다음 물음에 완전한 문장의 영어로 답하시오.

> Q: What did Sylvia look like?

➡ _____

[23~25] 다음 글을 읽고 물음에 답하시오.

Harry, a seventh grader, had short blonde hair. He said, "Hey, you got the wrong guy. I was practicing my dance moves. I went home a little before nine. I didn't take one step outside the classroom until then."

"Did you hear (A)[strange anything / anything strange]?"

"ⓐHow could I? My music was really loud."

"Did you see anyone on the way home?"

"No, I heard someone (B)[singing / to sing] really badly, but I didn't see anyone."

Shirley said, "I don't need to hear anymore." Then she turned to the thief.

"Why don't you (C)[bring / bringing] the medal back before you get into some real trouble?"

23 (A)~(C)에서 어법상 옳은 것을 바르게 짝지은 것은?

① anything strange – to sing – to bring
② anything strange – singing – bring
③ strange anything – singing – to bring
④ strange anything – singing – bring
⑤ strange anything – to sing – to bring

24 밑줄 친 ⓐ의 의미로 가장 적절한 것은?

① It was my fault.
② I heard someone talk.
③ It was impossible.
④ I could hear something.
⑤ I couldn't practice well.

25 What was Harry doing in the classroom? Answer in English with a full sentence.

➡ _____

[01~04] 다음 글을 읽고 물음에 답하시오.

Mr. Reese, the principal, ran across the wet playground.

"Shirley! Shirley! I need your help!"

Shirley was an eighth grade student at Bakersville Middle School. She was also the best detective in the whole town.

"_____(A)_____" asked Shirley.

"Someone has stolen the gold medal for the talent show!"

Mr. Reese took Shirley to the scene of the crime. There was a case with a broken window. The silver and bronze medals were still there. But the gold medal was missing. There was a poem in its place.

Tomorrow is the talent show.
Where did the gold medal go?
Look high and low.
You can't catch me. You're too slow.

01 주어진 단어를 바르게 배열하여 빈칸 (A)에 알맞은 말을 쓰시오.

(wrong / there / something / is)?

➡ _____

02 위 글의 등장인물에 대한 정보를 완성하시오.

• Mr. Reese: the _____ of Bakersville Middle School.
• Shirley: an _____ grade student / the _____ _____ in the town

03 Where were silver and bronze medals for the talent show? Answer in English with six words.

➡ _____

04 다음은 Shirley의 일기 중 일부이다. 빈칸에 알맞은 말을 쓰시오.

When I was walking, I heard someone _____ my name. It was _____. He said somebody _____ _____ _____ _____ for the talent show. I went to the scene of the crime with him. I saw the window of the case _____. There was a _____ instead of _____ _____ _____.

[05~07] 다음 글을 읽고 물음에 답하시오.

Shirley asked, "Could you tell me when this happened?"

"A little after nine last night. I was making my rounds when I heard a scream. I rushed over and found Jocelyn and the case like this."

"I wonder who else was here last night."

"Sylvia and Harry. They were also practicing for the talent show. I'll call them to my office."

Jocelyn was a ninth grade student with short curly red hair.

"I was practicing my song and I became thirsty. I stepped outside the classroom to get some water. It was completely dark. Suddenly, there was a loud sound of thunder. I think the thief broke the window (A)at that moment. Lightning followed right after and it became bright for a second or two. Then I saw someone running away from the case."

"Did you see the thief's face?"

"No, I only saw the thief's back. But the thief had short hair."

05 밑줄 친 (A)가 의미하는 것을 10자 이내의 우리말로 쓰시오.

➡ _____

06 위 글의 내용에 맞게 빈칸에 알맞은 말을 쓰시오.

> Shirley: I'd like to ask _____ _____ _____ when you heard a scream.
> Mr. Reese: I was making my rounds when I heard a scream.

07 Who was in the school at the time of the accident? Answer in English with a full sentence.

➡ _____

_____

[08~13] 다음 글을 읽고 물음에 답하시오.

Next was an eighth grade student, Sylvia. She was tall with long black hair. She said, "I was reading my poem aloud in the classroom. I heard a scream and went outside. There was a girl next to the case. With the flash from the lightning, it was like a horror movie. I got scared so I ran straight home."

"Did you hear the window break?"

"No, the thunder was too loud. Well, I didn't do it. I was going to win first place anyway."

Harry, a seventh grader, had short blonde hair. He said, "Hey, you got the wrong guy. I was practicing my dance moves. I went home a little before nine. I didn't take one step outside the classroom until then."

"Did you hear anything strange?"

"How could I? My music was really loud."

"Did you see anyone on the way home?"

"No, I heard someone singing really badly, but I didn't see anyone."

Shirley said, "I don't need to hear anymore." Then she turned to the thief.

"Why don't you bring the medal back before you get into some real trouble?"

08 Write the reason why Harry couldn't hear anything strange. Use the phrase 'It was because.'

➡ _____

09 What did Sylvia see when she went outside? Answer in English with a full sentence.

➡ _____

10 According to the passage, why did Sylvia run straight home?

➡ _____

11 According to what Sylvia said, what made the crime scene look like a horror movie? Answer in English with six words.

➡ _____

12 다음 중 글의 내용과 일치하지 않는 것 두 개를 찾아 바르게 고치시오.

> Sylvia was tall. She was reading her poem for the talent show. She heard a scream and went home. She heard someone breaking the window.

➡ _____ , _____

13 주어진 단어를 활용하여 Shirley가 한 말을 영어로 쓰시오.

> 나는 누가 금메달을 훔쳤는지 알아냈어.
> (find out)

➡ _____

해석

Think and Write

When Rapunzel was a baby, a witch put her in a tall tower. Rapunzel grew up in the tower. She had long hair. The witch used it to climb up the tower. The witch always said, "The world outside is very dangerous." One day, a prince
to부정사의 부사적 용법 중 목적(~하기 위해서)
heard Rapunzel singing beautifully. He said, "Come down. The world outside
지각동사+목적어+Ving
is wonderful." Rapunzel said, "I don't know who is telling the truth." Rapunzel
간접의문문(의문대명사+동사)
was confused. Finally, she made up her mind. She cut her hair and came down from the tower. When she faced the world for the first time, she couldn't
처음으로
believe her eyes. "What a beautiful world!"
'S+V'가 생략된 감탄문

구문해설 · put someone in ~: …을 ~에 가두다 · grow up: 자라다 · climb up: ~을 오르다
· wonderful: 아름다운 · confused: 혼란스러운 · make up one's mind: 결심하다
· face: ~에 직면하다, 마주하다

Rapunzel이 아기였을 때, 한 마녀가 그녀를 높은 탑에 가뒀다. Rapunzel은 그 탑에서 자랐다. 그녀는 긴 머리카락을 가지고 있었다. 마녀는 탑을 올라가기 위해 그 머리카락을 이용했다. 마녀는 항상 "바깥세상은 매우 위험해."라고 말했다. 어느 날, 한 왕자가 Rapunzel이 노래를 아름답게 부르고 있는 것을 들었다. 그는 "내려와요. 바깥세상은 멋져요."라고 말했다. Rapunzel은 "누가 사실을 말하고 있는지 모르겠어."라고 말했다. Rapunzel은 혼란스러웠다. 마침내, 그녀는 결심했다. 그녀는 머리카락을 자르고 탑에서 내려왔다. 그녀가 처음으로 세상과 마주했을 때, 그녀는 자신의 눈을 믿을 수 없었다. "정말 아름다운 세상이야!"

Project

To the treasure hunters,

Hello. We have hidden our treasure in the classroom. It is something delicious.
현재완료 *부정대명사는 형용사가 뒤에서 수식*
Do you want to know where it is? Then follow the steps. First, look for a plant
간접의문문(의문사+주어+동사)
near the window. Look under the plant. You'll find a key. Second, pick up the
~ 아래를 보아라
key and walk to the back of the classroom. You'll see the lockers. The treasure is in the third locker from the left. It is locked, so use the key to open it. Got
왼쪽에서부터 *= The third locker* *부사적 용법(목적)*
it? Help yourself.

From Group 5

구문해설 · hide(hid–hidden): 숨기다 · delicious: 맛있는 · step: 단계 · pick up: 주워들다
· locker: 사물함 · treasure: 보물 · Got it?: 알겠니?

보물 사냥꾼들에게,

안녕. 우리는 교실에 우리 보물을 숨겼어. 그것은 맛있는 것이야. 그것이 어디에 있는지 알고 싶니? 그러면 다음 단계를 따라 봐. 우선, 창문 옆에 있는 식물을 찾아. 그 식물 아래를 봐. 너는 열쇠 하나를 찾을 거야. 두 번째, 그 열쇠를 들고 교실 뒤쪽으로 걸어가. 너는 사물함을 볼 거야. 보물은 왼쪽에서 세 번째 사물함 안에 있어. 그것은 잠겼으니 그것을 열기 위해 열쇠를 사용해. 알겠지? 많이 먹으렴.

Check Up

A: Can you do me a favor?
상대방에게 도움을 요청하는 표현(=Can I ask you a favor?)
B: Sure. What is it?
도움 요청에 승낙하는 표현(=Of course. = No problem.)
A: Can you help me blow up these balloons?

B: No problem.
상대방의 요청에 승낙하는 표현

구문해설 · blow up: (입으로) 불다

A: 부탁 하나 해도 될까?
B: 물론이지. 뭔데?
A: 이 풍선들을 부는 것 좀 도와줄 수 있니?
B: 좋아.

01 다음 짝지어진 단어의 관계가 같도록 빈칸에 알맞은 말을 쓰시오.

hand : foot = handprint : _____

02 다음 중 밑줄 친 부분의 뜻풀이가 바르지 않은 것은?

① This information is a valuable clue. 단서
② The boy's eyes were wide with horror. 공포
③ He left his footprints on the sand. 발자국
④ The city can be a dangerous place to live in. 위험한
⑤ Can I ask you a favor? 맛, 풍미

03 다음 주어진 문장의 밑줄 친 principal과 다른 의미로 쓰인 것은?

Mr. Kim, the principal, ran across the wet playground.

① I talked about my career with the principal for an hour.
② Bad weather is one of the principal causes to cancel the event.
③ My grandfather used to work at the elementary school as a principal.
④ The principal usually manages the teachers and the students.
⑤ I met the principal on the way home tonight.

04 다음 문장의 빈칸에 들어갈 말을 〈보기〉에서 골라 쓰시오.

보기
broken / footprint / thirsty / detective

(1) I felt so _____ after running the playground.
(2) Do you know what a _____ does to find the thief?
(3) He found the _____ which could be a clue.
(4) Don't touch the _____ window with your hand.

05 다음 주어진 문장에 공통으로 들어갈 말을 고르시오.

• You have to _____ the gate and show your ID card.
• I believe that my son will _____ the test.
• Would you _____ me the bread and knife?
• Time _____(e)s so fast.

① cross
② pass
③ steal
④ water
⑤ lose

06 다음 우리말을 주어진 단어를 이용하여 영작하시오.

(1) 그녀는 내게 은목걸이를 주었다. (necklace) (6 words)
➡ _____

(2) 제가 당신 방으로 당신 짐을 옮겨드릴게요. (carry, luggage) (7 words)
➡ _____

(3) 이 이야기는 하늘을 나는 마녀에 관한 것이다. (who, witch) (11 words)
➡ _____

Conversation

[07~08] 다음 대화를 읽고 물음에 답하시오.

Emily: (A)Can I ask you a favor?
Jinsu: Sure. What is it?
Emily: _____(B)
Jinsu: No problem.

07 위 대화의 밑줄 친 (A)와 바꾸어 쓸 수 없는 것은?

① Can you do me a favor?
② Can you give me a hand?
③ Can you help me out?
④ Would you mind helping me?
⑤ How can I help you?

08 위 대화의 빈칸 (B)에 들어갈 말을 <보기>에 주어진 단어를 모두 배열하여 영작하시오.

보기
you / the / dishes / me / wash / help / can

➡ _____

09 다음 짝지어진 대화가 어색한 것을 고르시오.

① A: Guess what I'm doing.
  B: I guess you're going up a ladder.
② A: Can you guess what I'm doing?
  B: Hmm.... I think you're flying a kite.
③ A: I think you're working on the computer.
  B: You're wrong. Guess again.
④ A: I guess you're fishing.
  B: That's right.
⑤ A: I guess you're playing the piano.
  B: That's too bad.

[10~12] 다음 대화를 읽고 물음에 답하시오.

Narae: Tony, ⓐcan you do me a favor? (hand)
Tony: (A) Sure. What is it, Narae?
Narae: (B) My family is going to visit my grandmother in Busan.
Tony: (C) Oh, I'm sorry but I can't. My mom doesn't like dogs.
Narae: (D) Oh, what should I do?
Tony: (E) Why don't you ask Sumin? Her family loves dogs.
Narae: Okay. I'll call her right now.

10 위 대화의 (A)~(E) 중 주어진 문장이 들어가기에 적절한 곳은?

Can you take care of my dog this weekend?

① (A) ② (B) ③ (C) ④ (D) ⑤ (E)

11 위 대화의 밑줄 친 ⓐ와 의미가 같도록 주어진 단어를 사용하여 다시 쓰시오.

➡ _____

12 위 대화를 읽고 대답할 수 없는 질문은?

① What is Narae going to do this weekend?
② Where does Narae's grandmother live?
③ What is Narae asking Tony to do?
④ Why can't Tony help Narae?
⑤ How does Narae take care of her dog?

[13~14] 다음 글을 읽고 물음에 답하시오.

Sujin: Good morning, classmates! Nine months have passed so fast, and we are almost at the end of this school year. We all had a wonderful year. I guess only a few of us will be in the same class next year. Don't be a stranger. Say hello when we see each other, okay? Thank you.

13 When is Sujin making this speech?

➡ _____

14 What is Sujin asking her classmates to do?

➡ _____

_____

[15~16] 다음 대화를 읽고 물음에 답하시오.

Brian: Mom, I can't find my smartphone. Can you help me find ⓐit?

Mom: Are you sure you lost ⓑit inside the house?

Brian: Yes. I just texted my friend a few minutes ago.

Mom: Where were you at the time?

Brian: In the kitchen. I was making a sandwich.

Mom: Then I guess you left ⓒit somewhere in the kitchen.

Brian: I already checked the kitchen, Mom.

Mom: Well, let's check ⓓit again. Oh, here ⓔit is. Inside the refrigerator.

Brian: Thanks, Mom. You are the greatest!

Mom: You're welcome, honey.

15 위 대화의 ⓐ~ⓔ 중 가리키는 대상이 나머지 넷과 다른 것은?

① ⓐ   ② ⓑ   ③ ⓒ   ④ ⓓ   ⑤ ⓔ

16 위 대화의 내용과 일치하지 않는 것은?

① Brian은 스마트폰을 찾고 있다.

② Brian은 몇 분 전에 친구에게 문자 메시지를 보냈다.

③ 엄마는 Brian이 부엌 어딘가에 핸드폰을 놓은 것 같다고 추측하였다.

④ 엄마는 부엌에서 Brian을 위해 샌드위치를 만들고 있었다.

⑤ 엄마는 냉장고 안에서 Brian의 스마트폰을 찾았다.

Grammar

17 다음 중 빈칸에 들어갈 말로 알맞지 <u>않은</u> 것은?

I'd like to know _____.

① who you met an hour ago

② who made you this skirt

③ who your purse found

④ who invited you to the party

⑤ who you want to talk to

18 다음 우리말을 영어로 옮길 때 다섯 번째와 여섯 번째로 오는 단어를 바르게 묶은 것은?

나는 내 생일 파티에 신나는 무엇인가를 하고 싶다.

① do – something

② something – exciting

③ exciting – for

④ for – my

⑤ my – birthday

19 다음 우리말을 영어로 바르게 옮긴 것은?

누가 너를 그 파티에 초대했는지 말해 줄래?

① Can you tell me who you will invite to the party?

② Can you tell me whom you invited to the party?

③ Can you tell me who invite to the party?

④ Can you tell me who invited you to the party?

⑤ Can you tell me who is going to invite you?

20 다음 두 문장을 하나의 문장으로 쓰시오.

Do you know? What color is her bag?

➡ _____

21 빈칸에 들어갈 말로 가장 적절한 것은?

> I have _____.

① to tell you important something
② something to tell you important
③ to you something important tell
④ you to tell you something important
⑤ something important to tell you

22 다음 중 어법상 옳은 것을 바르게 짝지은 것은?

> • Let's decide what [should we do / we should do].
> • I have something [to do interesting / interesting to do].
> • They will ask [that / if] you live alone.

① should we do – to do interesting – that
② should we do – interesting to do – that
③ should we do – interesting to do – if
④ we should do – interesting to do – if
⑤ we should do – to do interesting – if

23 다음 중 어법상 바르지 <u>않은</u> 것은?

① There is something wrong with this computer.
② I want to have something cute.
③ I don't know what Tim took to the party.
④ Patrick wondered whether they would agree with his idea.
⑤ There is nothing to keep precious.

24 주어진 단어를 활용하여 다음 우리말을 7 단어로 이루어진 한 문장의 영어로 쓰시오.

> 그녀는 자기 엄마를 위해 특별한 것을 샀다.
> (special / for)

➡ _____

25 빈칸에 들어갈 말로 가장 적절한 것은?

> A: Why did she come late?
> B: I don't know _____. But she said she was sorry for being late.

① why she hates me
② why she was sorry
③ why she came late
④ why she comes lately
⑤ why she was coming

26 주어진 단어를 바르게 배열하여 다음 우리말을 영어로 쓰시오.

> 나는 기댈 만한 믿음직한 누군가가 필요해.
> (need, I, depend, trustful, to, someone, on)

➡ _____

Reading

[27~28] 다음 글을 읽고 물음에 답하시오.

Mr. Reese, the principal, ran across the wet playground.
"Shirley! Shirley! I need your help!"
Shirley was an eighth grade student at Bakersville Middle School. She was also the best detective in the whole town.
"Is there something wrong?" asked Shirley.
"Someone has stolen the gold medal for the talent show!"
Mr. Reese took Shirley to (A)the scene of the crime. There was a case with a broken window. The silver and bronze medals were still there. But the gold medal was missing. There was a poem in its place.

Tomorrow is the talent show.
Where did the gold medal go?
Look high and low.
You can't catch me. You're too slow.

Shirley asked, "Could you tell me when this happened?"

"A little after nine last night. I was making my rounds when I heard a scream. I rushed over and found Jocelyn and the case like this."

"I wonder who else was here last night."

"Sylvia and Harry. They were also practicing for the talent show. I'll call them to my office."

27 Which one is NOT true about the underlined (A)?

① There was a case whose window was broken.

② The gold medal was missing.

③ Mr. Reese was the first man that arrived at the crime scene.

④ The thief didn't take the other medals.

⑤ The thief left a poem.

28 위 글의 내용과 일치하지 <u>않는</u> 것은?

① The playground was wet.

② Mr. Reese ran across the playground, calling Shirley's name.

③ Shirley wondered when the accident happened.

④ Mr. Reese wasn't at school when the accident happened.

⑤ Mr. Reese knew who was at school last night.

[29~31] 다음 글을 읽고 물음에 답하시오.

When Rapunzel was a baby, a witch put her in a tall tower. Rapunzel grew up in the tower. She had long hair.

(A) He said, "Come down. The world outside is wonderful. Rapunzel said, "I don't know who is telling the truth." Rapunzel was confused.

(B) The witch used it to climb up the tower. The witch always said, "The world outside is very dangerous." One day, a prince heard Rapunzel singing beautifully.

(C) Finally, she made up her mind. She cut her hair and came down from the tower. When she faced the world for the first time, she couldn't believe her eyes. "What a beautiful world!"

29 자연스러운 글이 되도록 (A)~(C)를 바르게 배열한 것은?

① (A) – (C) – (B)   ② (B) – (A) – (C)
③ (B) – (C) – (A)   ④ (C) – (A) – (B)
⑤ (C) – (B) – (A)

30 What did Rapunzel do before she came down from the tower? Answer in English with four words.

➡ _____

31 다음 중 위 글을 읽고 답할 수 <u>없는</u> 질문은?

① Who put Rapunzel in a tall tower?

② Where did Rapunzel grow up?

③ Why did Rapunzel feel confused?

④ How did the witch climb up the tower?

⑤ What did Rapunzel use to come down from the tower?

출제율 90%

01 다음 영영풀이가 가리키는 것을 고르시오.

> a yellowish-brown metal containing copper and tin

① gold   ② silver   ③ bronze
④ diamond   ⑤ glass

출제율 100%

02 다음 대화가 자연스럽게 이어지도록 순서대로 배열하시오.

> (A) No problem.
> (B) Sure. What is it?
> (C) Jinsu, can I ask you a favor?
> (D) Can you help me wash the dishes?

➡ _____

[03~04] 다음 대화를 읽고 물음에 답하시오.

> Brian: Mom, I can't find my smartphone. Can you help me find it?
> Mom: (A) Are you sure you lost it inside the house?
> Brian: (B) Yes. I just texted my friend a few minutes ago.
> Mom: (C) Where were you at the time?
> Brian: (D) I was making a sandwich.
> Mom: (E) Then I guess you left it somewhere in the kitchen.
> Brian: I already checked the kitchen, Mom.
> Mom: Well, let's check it again. Oh, here it is. Inside the refrigerator.
> Brian: Thanks, Mom. You are the greatest!
> Mom: You're welcome, honey.

출제율 90%

03 위 대화의 (A)~(E) 중 주어진 문장이 들어가기에 적절한 곳은?

> In the kitchen.

① (A)   ② (B)   ③ (C)   ④ (D)   ⑤ (E)

출제율 95%

04 위 대화의 내용과 일치하는 것은?

① Brian and his mom were making a sandwich.
② His mom texted Brian a few minutes ago.
③ Brian helped his mom find her smartphone.
④ Brian is sure that he left his smartphone in the kitchen.
⑤ Brian's smartphone was discovered in the refrigerator.

[05~06] 다음 대화를 읽고 물음에 답하시오.

> Narae: Tony, can you do me a favor?
> Tony: Sure. What is it, Narae?
> Narae: (A)이번 주말에 내 개를 돌봐 줄 수 있니? (can, take) My family is going to visit my grandmother in Busan.
> Tony: Oh, I'm sorry but I can't. My mom doesn't like dogs.
> Narae: _____ (B) _____
> Tony: Why don't you ask Sumin? Her family loves dogs.
> Narae: Okay. I'll call her right now.

출제율 90%

05 위 대화의 밑줄 친 (A)의 우리말을 주어진 단어를 이용하여 영작하시오.

➡ _____

출제율 95%

06 위 대화의 빈칸 (A)에 들어갈 말로 적절한 것을 모두 고르시오.

① I don't know what to do.
② What can I do for you?
③ Oh, what should I do?
④ Can you give me a hand?
⑤ Would you help me out?

[07~08] 다음 글을 읽고 물음에 답하시오.

Sujin: Good morning, classmates! ①Nine months have passed so fast, and we are almost at the end of this school year. ② We all had a wonderful year. ③I guess only a few of us will be in the same class next year. Don't be a stranger. ④You should learn how to turn the stranger into your friends. ⑤Say hello when we see each other, okay? Thank you.

출제율 95%

07 다음 ①~⑤ 중 글의 흐름상 어색한 것을 고르시오.

①   ②   ③   ④   ⑤

출제율 100%

08 위 대화를 읽고 대답할 수 없는 것은?

① Who are the listeners?
② When is Sujin making this speech?
③ How many months have passed after this school year began?
④ What is Sujin asking her classmates to do?
⑤ What should Sujin do whenever she meets strangers?

[09~10] 다음 대화를 읽고 물음에 답하시오.

Emily: Jinsu, can I ask you a favor?
Jinsu: Sure. What is it?
Emily: (A)Can you help me wash the dishes? (give)
Jinsu: No problem.

출제율 90%

09 What does Emily ask Jinsu to do?

➡ _____

출제율 90%

10 위 대화의 밑줄 친 (A)와 같은 의미가 되도록 주어진 단어를 이용하여 바꿔 쓰시오.

➡ _____

출제율 100%

11 다음 빈칸에 들어갈 말로 적절하지 않은 것은?

| _____ who the man is? |

① Does she know
② Can you tell me
③ Do they remember
④ Does it happen
⑤ Do you want to know

출제율 95%

12 다음 대화의 빈칸에 알맞은 말로 가장 적절한 것은?

A: I wonder _____.
B: It was James. He found the flag.

① who bought the flag
② how James found the flag
③ who found the flag
④ when James brought the flag
⑤ where James found the flag

출제율 90%

13 다음 우리말을 영어로 바르게 옮긴 것은?

당신과 함께 논의할 중요한 것이 있습니다.

① There are some important things to discuss.
② There are important something to discuss with you.
③ There is something important to discuss about you.
④ There is something important to discuss with you.
⑤ There is something discuss with you important.

14 출제율 90%
다음 중 어법상 올바른 문장은?

① Tell me who the ball kicked.
② They need old someone.
③ Ask her that she likes to eat pizza with us.
④ Did they say what would he want from you?
⑤ Judy wants something powerful.

15 출제율 85%
다음 대화의 빈칸에 알맞은 말을 쓰시오.

A: It's very cold. I want something _____ _____ _____.
B: Here, you can wear my coat. It will make you warm.

16 출제율 90%
다음 두 문장을 하나의 문장으로 쓰시오.

• Please ask him.
• What time can he pick me up?

➡ _____

17 출제율 95%
다음 대화의 빈칸에 알맞은 말을 쓰시오.

A: Do you know _____?
B: Yes. My grandfather built it.

➡ _____

[18~20] 다음 글을 읽고 물음에 답하시오.

When Rapunzel was a baby, a witch put her in a tall tower. Rapunzel grew up in the tower. She had long hair. The witch used it to climb up the tower. The witch always said, "The world outside is very dangerous." One day, a prince heard Rapunzel singing beautifully. He said, "Come down. The world outside is wonderful. Rapunzel said, "I don't know (A)누가 사실을 말하고 있는지." Rapunzel was confused. ____(B)____, she made up her mind. She cut her hair and came down from the tower. When she faced the world for the first time, she couldn't believe her eyes. "What a beautiful world!"

18 출제율 90%
밑줄 친 우리말 (A)를 영어로 쓰시오.

➡ _____

19 출제율 100%
빈칸 (B)에 들어갈 말로 가장 적절한 것은?

① For example   ② Therefore
③ Moreover   ④ Finally
⑤ In addition

20 출제율 95%
다음 중 위 글의 내용과 일치하지 않는 것은?

① Rapunzel grew up in the tall tower because of the witch.
② The witch had long hair.
③ The prince told Rapunzel that the world outside was wonderful.
④ The prince wanted Rapunzel to come down.
⑤ Rapunzel felt the world outside was beautiful.

[21~25] 다음 글을 읽고 물음에 답하시오.

Jocelyn was a ninth grade student with short curly red hair.

"I was practicing my song and I became thirsty.

(A) I think the thief broke the window at that moment. Lightning followed right after and it became bright for a second or two.

(B) Suddenly, there was a loud sound of thunder.

(C) I stepped outside the classroom to get some water. It was completely dark.

(D) Then I saw someone running away from the case."

"Did you see the thief's face?"

"No, I only saw the thief's back. But the thief had short hair."

Next ①was an eighth grade student, Sylvia. She was tall with long black hair. She said, "I was reading my poem ②aloud in the classroom. I heard a scream and went outside. There was a girl ③next to the case. With the flash from the lightning, it was like a horror movie. I got scared ④so I ran straight home."

"Did you hear the window ⑤to break?"

"No, the thunder was too loud. Well, I didn't do it. I was going to win first place anyway."

21 자연스러운 내용이 되도록 (A)~(D)를 바르게 배열하시오.

➡ _____

22 ①~⑤ 중 어법상 바르지 않은 것은?

①   ②   ③   ④   ⑤

23 다음 중 위 글의 내용을 바르게 이해한 사람은?

① Jacky: Jocelyn must be really scared to see the thief's face.

② Polly: I think Sylvia is the thief. Because she had short hair.

③ Jason: Jocelyn is the same grade student as Sylvia.

④ Teo: Sylvia is confident enough to think that she is going to win.

⑤ Christine: Jocelyn saw the thief when he broke the case. He must be really scared.

24 위 글의 내용에 맞게 빈칸에 알맞은 말을 쓰시오.

The gold medal was stolen. Shirley wanted to find out _____ _____ it, so she talked with some students who were at school when the accident happened. Jocelyn was _____ _____ _____ and Sylvia was _____ _____ _____ in the classroom.

25 다음 중 위 글을 읽고 답할 수 없는 것은?

① What does Jocelyn look like?

② What was Sylvia doing in the classroom?

③ How long did it became bright when lightning stroke?

④ Why did Sylvia go outside?

⑤ What time did Sylvia heard a scream?

[01~03] 다음 대화를 읽고 물음에 답하시오.

> Narae: Tony, can you do me a favor?
> Tony: Sure. What is it, Narae?
> Narae: Can you take care of my dog this weekend? My family is going to visit my grandmother in Busan.
> Tony: Oh, I'm sorry but I can't. My mom doesn't like dogs.
> Narae: Oh, what should I do?
> Tony: Why don't you ask Sumin? Her family loves dogs.
> Narae: Okay. I'll call her right now.

01 What does Narae ask Tony to do?

➡ _____

_____

02 Who doesn't like dogs?

➡ _____

03 Why does Tony recommend Narae to ask Sumin?

➡ _____

04 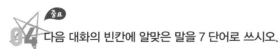다음 대화의 빈칸에 알맞은 말을 7 단어로 쓰시오.

> A: I want to ask _____.
> B: Donna says she was satisfied with your service.
> A: That's good to know. Thank you.

➡ _____

05 주어진 단어를 활용하여 다음 우리말을 영어로 쓰시오.

> 나는 그녀가 둥근 어떤 것을 가지고 있는지 궁금해요. (wonder / something)

➡ _____

06 주어진 단어를 바르게 배열하여 다음 우리말을 영어로 쓰시오.

> 나는 그것이 영어로 뭐라고 불리는지 기억할 수 없어.
> (in / English / what / called / remember / is / it / can't / I)

➡ _____

07 다음 대화의 빈칸에 알맞은 말을 쓰시오.

> A: Do you want something?
> B: Yes, I want _____ _____ _____ _____.
> A: Then, how about eating ice cream? It is really sweet.

08 다음 두 문장을 하나의 문장으로 쓰시오.

> • I really don't understand.
> • Why is she crying?

➡ _____

When Rapunzel was a baby, a witch put her in a tall tower. Rapunzel grew up in the tower. She had long hair. The witch used it to climb up the tower. The witch always said, "The world outside is very dangerous." One day, a prince heard Rapunzel singing beautifully. He said, "Come down. The world outside is wonderful. Rapunzel said, "I don't know who is telling the truth." Rapunzel was confused. Finally, she made up her mind. She cut her hair and came down from the tower. When she faced the world for the first time, (A)she couldn't believe her eyes. "What a beautiful world!"

09 What did the witch use in order to climb up the tower? Answer in English with a full sentence.

➡ _____

10 주어진 어구를 바르게 배열하여 밑줄 친 (A)의 이유를 설명하시오.

> (what the witch said / because / unlike / beautiful / outside / the world / was)

➡ _____

_____

[11~15] 다음 글을 읽고 물음에 답하시오.

Mr. Reese, the principal, ran across the wet playground.

"Shirley! Shirley! I need your help!"

Shirley was an eighth grade student at Bakersville Middle School. She was also the best detective in the whole town.

"Is there something wrong?" asked Shirley.

"Someone has stolen the gold medal for the talent show!"

Mr. Reese took Shirley to the scene of the crime. There was a case with a broken window. The silver and bronze medals were still there. But the gold medal was missing. There was a poem in (A)its place.

Shirley asked, "Could you tell me when this happened?"

"A little after nine last night. I was making my rounds when I heard a scream. I rushed over and found Jocelyn and the case like this."

11 When and where did the accident happen? Answer in English with a full sentence.

➡ _____

_____

12 What did Mr. Reese find when he rushed over?

➡ _____

_____

13 Where did Mr. Reese take Shirley?

➡ _____

14 Who is Mr. Reese? Answer in English with a full sentence.

➡ _____

15 밑줄 친 (A)its가 지칭하는 것을 위 글에서 찾아 쓰시오.

➡ _____

01 다음 대화를 읽고 대화의 내용과 일치하도록 Narea의 일기를 완성하시오.

Narae: Tony, can you do me a favor?

Tony: Sure. What is it, Narae?

Narae: Can you take care of my dog this weekend? My family is going to visit my grandmother in Busan.

Tony: Oh, I'm sorry but I can't. My mom doesn't like dogs.

Narae: Oh, what should I do?

Tony: Why don't you ask Sumin? Her family loves dogs.

Narae: Okay. I'll call her right now.

Today, I was worried about my dog, Pony. I will visit my grandmother this weekend, so I had to find someone who can (A)_____ my dog. At first, I asked Tony to look after my dog. Unfortunately, he can't help me because (B)_____.
I didn't know what to do. Then, Tony recommended Sumin because (C)_____.
I made a call to Sumin and asked her a favor. She said she could help me during this weekend. I was happy and really appreciated her.

---

02 다음 두 사람의 대화를 읽고 빈칸에 알맞은 말을 쓰시오.

David: Who is your favorite actor?

Alison: My favorite actor is Tom Cruz.

David: When was he born?

Alison: He was born in 1962.

David: Is he married?

Alison: Yes, he was.

I talked with David about my favorite actor. David wondered _____,
so I answered it was Tom Cruz. Then, he wanted me to tell him _____.
I told him that Tom Cruz was born in 1962. David also would like to know
_____, so I answered, "Yes, he was."

단원별 모의고사

01 다음 영영풀이가 가리키는 것을 고르시오.

> someone who steals things from another person

① detective   ② thief
③ lawyer   ④ policeman
⑤ judge

02 다음 문장의 빈칸에 들어갈 말을 〈보기〉에서 골라 알맞은 형태로 쓰시오.

> ┌ 보기 ┐
> bring back / at the moment / rush over / run across / win first place

(1) I wanted to _____, so I did my best.

(2) I was so nervous that I couldn't say anything _____.

(3) I saw my brother _____ here.

(4) I felt so thirsty after _____ the road.

(5) I need to _____ this book _____ by 12 o'clock.

03 다음 문장에 공통으로 들어갈 말을 고르시오.

> • You should not use the _____ of a camera in the museum.
> • That _____ means danger.
> • A red light on the screen will _____ when you touch it.
> • I saw a _____ of lightning in the dark.

① flash   ② light   ③ call
④ clue   ⑤ favor

04 다음 우리말과 일치하도록 주어진 단어를 모두 배열하여 영작하시오.

(1) 도둑이 어제 금메달을 훔쳐갔다.
(stole / the / medal / yesterday / gold / a thief)

➡ _____

(2) 이 풍선들을 부는 것을 도와주시겠어요?
(balloons / me / blow / can / these / you / help / up)

➡ _____

(3) 우리 장기 자랑 사진 좀 보내 줄래?
(talent / you / me / some / of / show / pictures / will / send / our)

➡ _____
_____

[05~07] 다음 대화를 읽고 물음에 답하시오.

> Brian: Did you see my baseball glove?
> Jane: Yes, I saw it under the table.
> Brian: Really? It's not there anymore.
> Jane: Then (A)I guess Spot took it.
> Brian: Oh, there he is. You bad dog, Spot!

05 위 대화의 밑줄 친 (A)와 바꾸어 쓸 수 있는 것을 모두 고르시오.

① I doubt that Spot took it.
② I think Spot took it.
③ I'm wondering if Spot took it.
④ Maybe Spot took it.
⑤ I don't know whether Spot took it.

06 What was Brian looking for?

➡ _____

07 Who took Brian's baseball glove?

➡ _____

08 다음 대화가 자연스럽게 이어지도록 순서대로 배열하시오.

> (A) Okay. Where did you see it last?
>
> (B) On the bench.
>
> (C) Can you help me find my baseball glove?
>
> (D) I guess a dog took your baseball glove. I can see its footprints on the bench.

➡ _____

09 다음 짝지어진 대화가 <u>어색한</u> 것을 고르시오.

① A: Can you help me mop the floor?
　 B: Of course.

② A: Can you do me a favor?
　 B: Sure. What is it?

③ A: Can you help me clean the board?
　 B: I'm afraid I can't.

④ A: Would you mind helping me carry these books?
　 B: No problem.

⑤ A: Can you give me a hand?
　 B: You should wash your hands first.

[10~11] 다음 대화를 읽고 물음에 답하시오.

> Brian: Mom, I can't find my smartphone. Can you help me find it?
>
> Mom: Are you sure you (A)[lost / losing] it inside the house?
>
> Brian: Yes. I just (B)[texted / texting] my friend a few minutes ago.

Mom: Where were you at the time?

Brian: In the kitchen. I was making a sandwich.

Mom: Then I guess you left it (C)[anywhere / somewhere] in the kitchen.

Brian: I already checked the kitchen, Mom.

Mom: Well, let's check it again. Oh, here it is. Inside the refrigerator.

Brian: Thanks, Mom. You are the greatest!

Mom: You're welcome, honey.

10 위 대화의 괄호 (A)~(C)에 들어갈 말로 알맞은 것끼리 짝지어진 것은?

	(A)	(B)	(C)
①	lost	texted	anywhere
②	lost	texting	somewhere
③	lost	texted	somewhere
④	losing	texting	somewhere
⑤	losing	texted	anywhere

11 위 대화의 내용과 일치하도록 빈칸을 완성하시오.

> Brian felt confused when he couldn't find _____(A)_____. He asked his mother to help find it. Brian was sure that it must be inside _____(B)_____ because he just texted his friend a few minutes ago. He was making _____(C)_____ in the kitchen, so his mom checked the kitchen again. Finally, his mom found it inside _____(D)_____.

➡ (A) _____ (B) _____
　 (C) _____ (D) _____

12 다음 중 우리말을 영어로 <u>잘못</u> 옮긴 것은?

① Clair는 공원에서 무엇인가 차가운 것을 마셨다.
  → Clair drank something cold at the park.
② 그가 내일 몇 시에 올지 알려줘.
  → Let me know what time he will come tomorrow.
③ 그 학교가 여기에서 얼마나 먼지 아니?
  → Do you know how the school is far from here?
④ 해야 할 즐거운 것이 있어.
  → There is something pleasant to do.
⑤ 누가 너에게 그 편지를 보냈는지 나는 몰라.
  → I don't know who sent you the letter.

13 빈칸에 알맞은 말로 가장 적절한 것은?

> I want to ask this. Are you married?
> = I want to ask _____.

① when are you married
② that you are married
③ whether you are married
④ who you are married
⑤ if you will marry or not

14 다음 중 어법상 바르지 <u>않은</u> 것은?

① I want to see something touching.
② They need someone reliable to be with.
③ Do you understand what I'm saying?
④ Tell her when does she have to move out.
⑤ Polly had nothing precious.

15 주어진 단어를 활용하여 다음 우리말을 영어로 쓰시오.

> 그가 어디에 있는지 내게 말해 줄 수 있니?
> (can / tell)

➡ _____

16 다음 우리말에 맞게 빈칸에 알맞은 말을 쓰시오.

> 그 과학자는 중요한 무언가를 발견했다.
> The scientist found _____ _____.

[17~20] 다음 글을 읽고 물음에 답하시오.

Mr. Reese, the principal, ran across the wet playground.

"Shirley! Shirley! I need your help!"

Shirley was an eighth grade student at Bakersville Middle School. She was also the best detective in the whole town.

"Is there something wrong?" asked Shirley.

"Someone has stolen the gold medal for the talent show!"

Mr. Reese took Shirley to the scene of the crime. There was a case with a broken window. The silver and bronze medals were still there. But the gold medal was missing. There was a poem in its place.

Shirley asked Mr. Reese, "Could you tell me __ⓐ__ this happened?"

"A little after nine last night. I was making my rounds __ⓑ__ I heard a scream. I rushed over and found Jocelyn and the case like this."

"_____ⓒ_____"

"Sylvia and Harry. They were also practicing for the talent show. I'll call them to my office."

Jocelyn was a ninth grade student with short curly red hair.

"I was practicing my song and I became thirsty. I stepped outside the classroom (A) to get some water. It was completely dark. Suddenly, there was a loud sound of thunder. I think the thief broke the window at that moment. Lightning followed right after and it became bright for a second or two. Then I saw someone running away from the case."

"Did you see the thief's face?"

"No, I only saw the thief's back. But the thief had short hair."

17 빈칸 ⓐ와 ⓑ에 공통으로 들어갈 말로 가장 적절한 것은?

① how　　　② when　　　③ why
④ who　　　⑤ where

18 다음 중 빈칸 ⓒ에 들어갈 말로 가장 적절한 것은?

① I'd like to know how the case was broken.
② I wonder when you saw her.
③ Can you tell me who else was here last night?
④ Tell me who broke the case.
⑤ Do you know who saw the thief?

19 다음 중 밑줄 친 (A)와 쓰임이 같은 것은?

① They wanted to make *bibimbap*.
② You must listen to many songs to make your own song.
③ It is important to keep your friends' secret.
④ Is there something comfortable to wear?
⑤ To exercise regularly is essential.

20 According to what Jocelyn said, what did she see when there was lightning?

➡ _____

[21~23] 다음 글을 읽고 물음에 답하시오.

　Next was an eighth grade student, Sylvia. She was tall with long black hair. She said, "I was reading my poem aloud in the classroom. I heard a scream and went outside. There was a girl next to the case. With the flash from the lightning, it was like a horror movie. I got scared so I ran straight home."
　"Did you hear the window broken?"
　"No, the thunder was too loud. Well, I didn't do it. I was going to win first place anyway."
　Harry, a seventh grader, had short blonde hair. He said, "Hey, you got the wrong guy. I was practicing my dance moves. I went home a little before nine. I didn't take one step outside the classroom until then."
　"Did you hear anything strange?"
　"How could I? My music was really loud."
　"Did you see anyone on the way home?"
　"No, I heard someone singing really badly, but I didn't see anyone."

21 When did Harry go home? Answer in English with a full sentence.

➡ _____

22 위 글에서 어법상 어색한 것을 하나 찾아 전체 문장을 어법에 맞게 다시 쓰시오.

➡ _____

23 다음 중 위 글을 읽고 답할 수 없는 것은?

① Why did Sylvia go straight home?
② Why did Sylvia get scared?
③ What was Harry going to do for the talent show?
④ What did Harry hear on the way home?
⑤ Who won the first place?

Special

Frindle

Words & Expressions

Key Words

- **agree** [əgríː] 동 동의하다
- **article** [áːrtikl] 명 (신문의) 기사
- **bark** [bɑːrk] 동 (개가) 짖다
- **borrow** [bárou] 형 빌리다
- **classmate** [klǽsmèit] 명 급우, 반 친구
- **cool** [kuːl] 형 멋진
- **cover** [kávər] 동 보도하다, 덮다
- **cute** [kjuːt] 형 귀여운
- **date** [deit] 동 날짜를 적다 명 날짜
- **decide** [disáid] 동 결정하다
- **dictionary** [díkʃənèri] 명 사전
- **entire** [intáiər] 형 전체의, 온
- **envelope** [énvəlòup] 명 봉투
- **excited** [iksáitid] 형 신이 난
- **extra** [ékstrə] 형 여분의, 추가의
- **funny** [fáni] 형 재미있는
- **grade** [greid] 명 학년
- **graduate** [grǽdʒuèit, -it] 동 졸업하다

- **inside** [ìnsáid] 부 안에, 내부에
- **local** [lóukəl] 형 지역의, 지방의
- **mean** [miːn] 동 의미하다
- **meaning** [míːniŋ] 명 의미
- **nearby** [nìərbái] 형 인근의, 가까이의
- **package** [pǽkidʒ] 명 소포
- **perfectly** [pə́ːrfiktli] 부 완벽하게
- **pleased** [pliːzd] 형 기쁜, 기뻐하는
- **punish** [pániʃ] 동 처벌하다, 벌주다
- **quickly** [kwíkli] 부 재빨리, 빠르게
- **receive** [risíːv] 동 받다
- **reporter** [ripɔ́ːrtər] 명 기자
- **satisfied** [sǽtisfàid] 형 만족하는
- **signature** [sígnətʃər] 명 서명
- **situation** [sìtʃuéiʃən] 명 상황
- **spread** [spred] 동 퍼지다, 확산되다
- **vocabulary** [voukǽbjulèri] 명 어휘
- **war** [wɔːr] 명 전쟁

Key Expressions

- **be excited about** ~에 신이 나다
- **be famous for** ~로 유명하다
- **be over** ~이 끝나다
- **be worried about** ~에 대해 걱정하다
- **by the time** 그때까지, ~할 때까지
- **find out about** ~에 대해 알게 되다
- **have no choice** 선택의 여지가 없다, 대안이 없다

- **hold up** 쥐다, 잡다
- **look up** (사전 등에서) 찾아보다
- **more and more** 더욱 더, 갈수록 더
- **on the way home** 집으로 가는 길에
- **out of hand** 손을 쓸 수 없는
- **take out** ~을 꺼내다
- **turn+나이** ~ 살이 되다

Word Power

※ 서로 반대되는 뜻을 가진 어휘

□ **agree** 동의하다 ↔ **disagree** 반대하다

□ **cover** 덮다 ↔ **uncover** 덮개를 벗기다

□ **excited** 신이 난 ↔ **boring** 지루한

□ **quickly** 재빨리 ↔ **slowly** 천천히

□ **pleased** 기쁜 ↔ **unpleased** 기뻐하지 않는, 불쾌한

□ **satisfied** 만족한 ↔ **dissatisfied** 만족스럽지 않은

□ **borrow** 빌리다 ↔ **lend** 빌려주다

□ **entire** 전체의 ↔ **partial** 부분적인

□ **inside** 안에 ↔ **outside** 밖에

□ **receive** 받다 ↔ **give** 주다

□ **hate** 미워하다 ↔ **like** 좋아하다

□ **more and more** 점점 더 ↔ **less and less** 점점 적게[덜]

English Dictionary

□ **agree** 동의하다
→ to have the same opinion as somebody
누군가와 같은 의견을 갖다

□ **borrow** 빌리다
→ to take and use something that belongs to somebody else, and return it to them at a later time
다른 누군가에게 속한 무언가를 가져다가 사용하고 나중에 그것을 그들에게 돌려주다

□ **classmate** 급우
→ a person who is or was in the same class as you at school or college
학교 또는 대학에서 당신과 같은 학급에 있거나 있었던 사람

□ **dictionary** 사전
→ a book that gives a list of the words of a language in alphabetical order and explains what they mean, or gives a word for them in a foreign language
알파벳 순서로 한 언어의 단어들의 목록을 제공하고 그들이 의미하는 것을 설명하거나 그것들에 대해 외국어에 있는 단어를 제공하는 책

□ **entire** 전체의
→ including everything, everyone or every part
모든 것, 모든 사람 또는 모든 부분을 포함하는

□ **envelope** 봉투
→ a flat paper container used for sending letters in
편지를 보내기 위해 사용되는 납작한 종이 용기

□ **extra** 여분의
→ more than is usual, expected, or than exists already
보통 기대되는 것 이상의 또는 이미 존재하는 것 이상의

□ **graduate** 졸업하다
→ to complete a course in education
교육에서 한 과정을 완료하다

□ **package** 소포
→ a box, bag, etc. in which things are wrapped or packed
물건들이 포장되거나 채워 넣어지는 상자, 가방 등

□ **punish** 처벌하다
→ to make somebody suffer because they have broken the law or done something wrong
누군가가 법을 어기거나 무언가를 잘못했기 때문에 고통을 주다

□ **reporter** 기자
→ a person who collects and reports news for newspapers, radio or television
신문, 라디오 또는 텔레비전에 뉴스를 모아 보도하는 사람

□ **signature** 서명
→ your name as you usually write it, for example at the end of a letter
예를 들어 편지 끝에 당신이 보통 쓰는 당신의 이름

□ **situation** 상황
→ all the circumstances and things that are happening at a particular time and in a particular place
특정 시간과 특정 장소에서 일어나는 모든 주위의 사정

□ **vocabulary** 어휘
→ all the words that a person knows or uses
한 사람이 알거나 사용하는 모든 단어들

Frindle

Nick Allen <u>was excited about</u> starting fifth grade, but he <u>was worried</u>
~에 신났다 ~에 대해 걱정했다
<u>about</u> one thing — Mrs. Granger's English class. Mrs. Granger
one thing과 동격
<u>was famous for</u> her difficult vocabulary lessons.
~으로 유명했다

In the first class, Mrs. Granger said, "Everyone should have a good
dictionary. You can <u>look up</u> the meanings of new words in <u>it</u>."
~을 찾다 a good dictionary

"Mrs. Granger? Who decides the meanings of words? I mean, who
decided <u>that</u> 'dog' means an animal <u>that</u> barks?" Nick asked.
명사절 접속사 주격 관계대명사

"You did, Nick. You, me, and the entire town and country. We all
agreed. That <u>gives the word its meaning</u>."
give+간접목적어+직접목적어

Nick wasn't satisfied. "When did I agree?" he said to <u>himself</u>.
재귀대명사(주어와 목적어가 같을 때 목적어로 재귀대명사 사용)

<u>On the way home</u>, he <u>decided to</u> test Mrs. Granger's idea. He <u>took</u>
집으로 가는 길에 to부정사를 목적어로 취하는 동사 ~을 꺼냈다
<u>out</u> a pen and said, "From today, this is a *frindle*."

The next day, he <u>asked</u> five friends <u>to use</u> the word *frindle*. During
to부정사를 목적격보어로 취하는 동사
class, Nick said, "Mrs. Granger, I forgot my *frindle* today." His friend,
John, held up a pen and said, "I have an extra *frindle*. Do you want to
borrow my *frindle*?" Mrs. Granger was not pleased. She said, "Your
new word is cute, but it already has a perfectly good name — a pen."

Nick's classmates <u>found this funny</u> and <u>began</u> to use the word more
find+목적어+목적격보어 to부정사와 동명사 모두를 목적어로 취할 수 있음
and more. In just three days, it became the cool word at school.

vocabulary: 어휘
dictionary: 사전
bark: 짖다
entire: 전체의, 온
satisfied: 만족하는
extra: 여분의
borrow: 빌리다

확인문제

● 다음 문장이 본문의 내용과 일치하면 T, 일치하지 <u>않으면</u> F를 쓰시오.

1 Nick decided to test Mrs. Granger's idea. ☐

2 Mrs. Granger didn't like the idea that students called a pen a *frindle*. ☐

Mrs. Granger said to Nick after class, "This is getting out of hand. Can you tell your friends to stop saying *frindle*?"

"I'm sorry, but I can't stop it. It started as my word, but now it's the students' word."

"Very well. Then I have no choice." Mrs. Granger took out an envelope and asked Nick to sign and date the back. She said, "I'll give this letter to you when all this is over."

Nick thought, "She really hates me."

Next week, Mrs. Granger began a war with *frindle*. She said that she would punish any student for using it. But this only made things worse. The students wanted to use the word more and more. *Frindle* quickly spread to nearby middle and high schools. Shortly after, a local newspaper reporter wrote an article on the situation and everyone in town knew about it. A month later, a national television station covered the news and everyone found out about *frindle*. By the time Nick graduated from elementary school, most students in the country used the word.

Time flew by and Nick turned 21. One day, he received a package. Inside it, he found a pen, an envelope and a dictionary. The envelope had his signature from fifth grade. The dictionary had a yellow note. It said, "Check page 541."

---

more and more: 더욱 더

out of hand: 손을 쓸 수 없는

envelope: 봉투

date: 날짜를 적다

punish: 처벌하다

spread: 퍼지다

nearby: 인근의, 가까이의

local: 지역의, 지방의

article: (신문의) 기사

situation: 상황

cover: 보도하다

graduate: 졸업하다

receive: 받다

signature: 서명

확인문제

● 다음 문장이 본문의 내용과 일치하면 T, 일치하지 않으면 F를 쓰시오.

1 Mrs. Granger wanted students to stop saying *frindle*. ☐

2 Nick thought Mrs. Granger hated him. ☐

3 Students gave up using the word *frindle*. ☐

4 When Nick graduated from elementary school, the word *frindle* was used by most students in the country. ☐

5 There was no signature on the envelope. ☐

● 우리말을 참고하여 빈칸에 알맞은 말을 쓰시오.

1 Nick Allen _____ _____ _____ starting fifth grade, but he _____ _____ one thing — Mrs. Granger's English class.

2 Mrs. Granger _____ _____ _____ her difficult vocabulary lessons.

3 In the first class, Mrs. Granger said, "Everyone _____ _____ _____ _____ _____. You _____ _____ _____ the meanings of new words in it."

4 "Mrs. Granger? Who decides _____ _____ of words? I mean, who decided that 'dog' _____ an animal that barks?" Nick asked.

5 "You did, Nick. You, me, and the _____ _____ and country. We all _____. That gives the word _____ _____."

6 Nick wasn't _____. "When _____ _____ _____?" he said to _____.

7 _____ the way home, he _____ to test Mrs. Granger's idea.

8 He _____ _____ a pen and said, "_____ today, this is a *frindle*."

9 The next day, he _____ five friends _____ _____ the word *frindle*.

10 _____ class, Nick said, "Mrs. Granger, I forgot my *frindle* today."

11 His friend, John, _____ _____ a pen and said, "I have an _____ *frindle*. Do you want _____ _____ my *frindle*?"

12 Mrs. Granger was not _____.

13 She said, "Your new word is cute, _____ it _____ _____ a perfectly good name — a pen."

14 Nick's classmates _____ this _____ and began _____ the word more and more.

15 _____ just three days, it _____ the _____ _____ at school.

1 Nick Allen은 5학년이 시작되는 것이 신났지만, 한 가지가 걱정되었다. 그것은 Granger 선생님의 영어 수업이었다.

2 Granger 선생님은 어려운 어휘 수업으로 유명했다.

3 첫 번째 시간에 Granger 선생님은 말했다. "모두 좋은 사전을 가지고 있어야 해요. 여러분은 사전에서 새 단어의 뜻을 찾을 수 있어요."

4 "Granger 선생님? 단어의 뜻은 누가 정하나요? 그러니까, '개'는 짖는 동물을 뜻한다고 누가 정했나요?" Nick이 물었다.

5 "네가 그랬지, Nick. 너와 나, 그리고 온 마을과 나라가 말이야. 우리 모두가 동의했단다. 그게 그 단어에게 의미를 부여하는 거야."

6 Nick은 마음에 들지 않았다. "내가 언제 동의했지?" 그는 혼잣말을 했다.

7 집에 가는 길에 Nick은 Granger 선생님의 생각을 시험하기로 결심했다.

8 그는 펜을 하나 꺼내서 말했다. "오늘부터 이것은 'frindle'이야."

9 그 다음날 Nick은 다섯 명의 친구들에게 단어 'frindle'을 사용해 달라고 부탁했다.

10 수업 중에 Nick이 말했다. "Granger 선생님, 오늘 'frindle'을 빠뜨리고 왔어요."

11 Nick의 친구인 John이 펜을 하나 들고서는 말했다. "나한테 여분의 'frindle'이 있어. 내 'frindle'을 빌리고 싶니?"

12 Granger 선생님은 즐거워하지 않았다.

13 선생님이 말했다. "너희들의 새 단어는 귀엽지만, 그건 이미 'pen'이라는 완벽하게 좋은 이름이 있단다."

14 Nick의 학급 친구들은 이것을 재미있어 했고 더욱 더 그 단어를 사용하기 시작했다.

15 단지 3일 만에 학교에서 그것은 멋진 단어가 되었다.

16 Mrs. Granger _____ _____ Nick after class, "This is _____ _____ _____ _____. Can you tell your friends _____ _____ _____ *frindle*?"

17 "I'm sorry, but I can't _____ _____. It started _____ my word, but now it's the students' word."

18 "Very well. Then I have _____ _____."

19 Mrs. Granger _____ _____ an envelope and _____ Nick _____ _____ and _____ the back.

20 She said, "_____ _____ this letter _____ _____ when all this _____ _____."

21 Nick thought, "She really _____ me."

22 Next week, Mrs. Granger _____ a war _____ *frindle*.

23 She said that she would _____ any student _____ it.

24 But this only made _____ _____.

25 The students wanted _____ _____ the word _____ _____ _____.

26 *Frindle* quickly _____ _____ _____ middle and high schools.

27 _____ _____, a local newspaper reporter _____ an article _____ the situation and everyone in town _____ _____ _____.

28 A month later, a national television station _____ the news and everyone _____ _____ _____ *frindle*.

29 _____ _____ _____ Nick _____ _____ elementary school, most students in the country _____ the word.

30 Time _____ _____ and Nick turned 21. One day, he _____ a package.

31 _____ _____, he _____ a pen, an envelope and a dictionary.

32 The envelope had his _____ _____ fifth grade.

33 The dictionary had a _____ _____. _____ _____, "Check page 541."

16 Granger 선생님은 수업 후에 Nick에게 말했다. "점점 손을 쓸 수 없게 되어 가는구나. 네 친구들에게 'frindle'을 말하는 것을 멈춰달라고 말해 줄래?"

17 "죄송하지만, 멈추게 할 수가 없어요. 그건 제 단어로 시작됐지만, 이제 그건 학생들의 단어예요."

18 "좋아. 그러면 선택의 여지가 없구나."

19 Granger 선생님은 봉투를 하나 꺼내더니 Nick에게 뒷면에 서명을 하고 날짜를 적게 했다.

20 선생님은 말했다. "이 모든 것이 끝나면 내가 이 편지를 너에게 줄게."

21 Nick은 생각했다. "선생님은 내가 정말 싫은가봐."

22 다음 주에 Granger 선생님은 'frindle'과의 전쟁을 시작했다.

23 선생님은 그 단어를 사용한다면 어떤 학생이든 벌을 줄 것이라고 말했다.

24 하지만 이것은 상황을 더 나쁘게 만들 뿐이었다.

25 학생들은 그 단어를 더욱 더 사용하고 싶어했다.

26 'frindle'은 근처의 중학교와 고등학교로 빠르게 퍼져 나갔다.

27 곧 지역 신문 기자가 그 상황에 관한 기사를 썼고, 마을의 모든 사람들이 그것에 관해 알게 되었다.

28 한 달 후에 한 전국 텔레비전 방송사에 서 그 소식을 다루었고, 모든 사람들이 'frindle'에 관해 알게 되었다.

29 Nick이 초등학교를 졸업할 때쯤에는 이 나라의 대부분의 학생들이 그 단어를 사용했다.

30 시간은 흘러 Nick은 21살이 되었다. 어느 날 Nick은 소포를 하나 받았다.

31 소포 안에는 펜 한 자루, 봉투 한 장, 그리고 사전 한 권이 있었다.

32 봉투에는 5학년 때의 그의 서명이 있었다.

33 사전에는 노란색 쪽지가 있었다. "541쪽을 확인해 봐."라고 적혀 있었다.

● 우리말을 참고하여 본문을 영작하시오.

1 Nick Allen은 5학년이 시작되는 것이 신났지만, 한 가지가 걱정되었다. 그것은 Granger 선생님의 영어 수업이었다.

➡ _____

_____

2 Granger 선생님은 어려운 어휘 수업으로 유명했다.

➡ _____

3 첫 번째 시간에 Granger 선생님은 말했다. "모두 좋은 사전을 가지고 있어야 해요. 여러분은 사전에서 새 단어의 뜻을 찾을 수 있어요."

➡ _____

_____

4 "Granger 선생님? 단어의 뜻은 누가 정하나요? 그러니까, '개'는 짖는 동물을 뜻한다고 누가 정했나요?" Nick이 물었다.

➡ _____

5 "네가 그랬지, Nick. 너와 나, 그리고 온 마을과 나라가 말이야. 우리 모두가 동의했단다. 그게 그 단어에게 의미를 부여하는 거야."

➡ _____

6 Nick은 마음에 들지 않았다. "내가 언제 동의했지?" 그는 혼잣말을 했다.

➡ _____

7 집에 가는 길에 Nick은 Granger 선생님의 생각을 시험하기로 결심했다.

➡ _____

8 그는 펜을 하나 꺼내서 말했다. "오늘부터 이것은 'frindle'이야."

➡ _____

9 그 다음날 Nick은 다섯 명의 친구들에게 단어 'frindle'을 사용해 달라고 부탁했다.

➡ _____

10 수업 중에 Nick이 말했다. "Granger 선생님, 오늘 'frindle'을 빠뜨리고 왔어요."

➡ _____

11 Nick의 친구인 John이 펜을 하나 들고서는 말했다. "나한테 여분의 'frindle'이 있어. 내 'frindle'을 빌리고 싶니?"

➡ _____

12 Granger 선생님은 즐거워하지 않았다.

➡ _____

13 선생님이 말했다. "너희들의 새 단어는 귀엽지만, 그건 이미 'pen'이라는 완벽하게 좋은 이름이 있단다."

➡ _____

14 Nick의 학급 친구들은 이것을 재미있어 했고 더욱 더 그 단어를 사용하기 시작했다.

➡ _____

15 단지 3일 만에 학교에서 그것은 멋진 단어가 되었다.

➡ _____

16 Granger 선생님은 수업 후에 Nick에게 말했다. "점점 손을 쓸 수 없게 되어 가는구나. 네 친구들에게 'frindle'을 말하는 것을 멈춰달라고 말해 줄래?"

➡ _____

_____

17 "죄송하지만, 멈추게 할 수가 없어요. 그건 제 단어로 시작됐지만, 이제 그건 학생들의 단어예요."

➡ _____

18 "좋아. 그러면 선택의 여지가 없구나."

➡ _____

19 Granger 선생님은 봉투를 하나 꺼내더니 Nick에게 뒷면에 서명을 하고 날짜를 적게 했다.

➡ _____

20 선생님은 말했다. "이 모든 것이 끝나면 내가 이 편지를 너에게 줄게."

➡ _____

21 Nick은 생각했다. "선생님은 내가 정말 싫은가봐."

➡ _____

22 다음 주에 Granger 선생님은 'frindle'과의 전쟁을 시작했다.

➡ _____

23 선생님은 그 단어를 사용한다면 어떤 학생이든 벌을 줄 것이라고 말했다.

➡ _____

24 하지만 이것은 상황을 더 나쁘게 만들 뿐이었다.

➡ _____

25 학생들은 그 단어를 더욱 더 사용하고 싶어했다.

➡ _____

26 'frindle'은 근처의 중학교와 고등학교로 빠르게 퍼져 나갔다.

➡ _____

27 곧 지역 신문 기자가 그 상황에 관한 기사를 썼고, 마을의 모든 사람들이 그것에 관해 알게 되었다.

➡ _____

28 한 달 후에 한 전국 텔레비전 방송사에 서 그 소식을 다루었고, 모든 사람들이 'frindle'에 관해 알게 되었다.

➡ _____

29 Nick이 초등학교를 졸업할 때쯤에는 이 나라의 대부분의 학생들이 그 단어를 사용했다.

➡ _____

30 시간은 흘러 Nick은 21살이 되었다. 어느 날 Nick은 소포를 하나 받았다.

➡ _____

31 소포 안에는 펜 한 자루, 봉투 한 장, 그리고 사전 한 권이 있었다.

➡ _____

32 봉투에는 5학년 때의 그의 서명이 있었다.

➡ _____

33 사전에는 노란색 쪽지가 있었다. "541쪽을 확인해 봐."라고 적혀 있었다.

➡ _____

01 다음 짝지어진 단어의 관계가 같도록 빈칸에 알맞은 말을 쓰시오.

> increase : decrease = _____ : disagree

02 다음 문장의 빈칸에 들어갈 말을 〈보기〉에서 골라 쓰시오.

> ┌─ 보기 ─┐
> signature / package / envelope / bark

(1) Why did your dogs _____ last night?

(2) I put my _____ to the document.

(3) Look at the back of the _____, please.

(4) I was so happy when I received my _____ from my sister.

03 다음 우리말을 주어진 단어를 사용하여 영작하시오.

(1) 나는 제주도로 가는 수학여행에 매우 신났었다. (school trip, about)

➡ _____

(2) 나는 수학 시험이 끝난 후 안도감을 느꼈다. (over, test, relaxed)

➡ _____

04 주어진 문장과 같은 의미의 문장을 쓰시오.

(1) David was too tired to meet us last night.

➡ _____

(2) They are tall enough to touch the ceiling.

➡ _____

05 주어진 단어를 이용하여 우리말을 영어로 옮기시오.

(1) 나는 네가 야채를 먹길 원해. (want / vegetables)

➡ _____

(2) 그 의사는 나의 아버지에게 규칙적으로 운동하라고 조언했다. (advise)

➡ _____

06 주어진 단어를 어법에 맞게 빈칸에 쓰시오.

(1) Mr. Park encourages us _____ our best all the time. (do)

(2) I don't want you _____ my books. (borrow)

(3) We found the situation _____. (interest)

[07~12] 다음 글을 읽고 물음에 답하시오.

Nick Allen was excited about starting fifth grade, but he was worried about one thing — Mrs. Granger's English class. Mrs. Granger was famous for her difficult vocabulary lessons. In the first class, Mrs. Granger said, "Everyone should have a good dictionary. You can look up the meanings of new words in it."

"Mrs. Granger? Who decides the meanings of words? I mean, who decided that 'dog' means an animal that barks?" Nick asked.

"You did, Nick. You, me, and the entire town and country. We all agreed. That gives the word its meaning."

Nick wasn't satisfied. "When did I agree?" he said to himself.

On the way home, he decided to test Mrs. Granger's idea. He took out a pen and said, "From today, this is a *frindle*." The next day, he asked five friends to use the word *frindle*. During class, Nick said, "Mrs. Granger, I forgot my *frindle* today." His friend, John, held up a pen and said, "I have an extra *frindle*. Do you want to borrow my *frindle*?" Mrs. Granger was not pleased. She said, "ⓐ Your new word is cute, but it already has a perfectly good name — a pen."

07 What was Nick Allen excited about? Answer in English with a full sentence.

➡ _____

08 What did Mrs. Granger want her students to have? Answer in English with nine words.

➡ _____

09 According to Mrs. Granger, what can students do with a dictionary?

➡ _____

10 밑줄 친 ⓐ가 의미하는 것을 위 글에서 찾아 쓰시오.

➡ _____

11 What did Nick do to test Mrs. Granger's idea? Answer in English with six words.

➡ _____

12 Who was Nick's English teacher?

➡ _____

[13~15] 다음 글을 읽고 물음에 답하시오.

Nick's classmates found this funny and began to use the word more and more. In just three days, it became the cool word at school.

Mrs. Granger said to Nick after class, "This is getting out of hand. Can you tell your friends to stop saying *frindle*?"

"I'm sorry, but I can't stop ⓐit. It started as my word, but now it's the students' word."

"Very well. Then I have no choice." Mrs. Granger took out an envelope and asked Nick to sign and date the back. She said, "I'll give this letter to you when all this is over."

Nick thought, "She really hates me."

(A) She said that she would punish any student for using it.

(B) The students wanted to use the word more and more.

(C) But this only made things worse.

(D) Next week, Mrs. Granger began a war with *frindle*.

Frindle quickly spread to nearby middle and high schools.

13 밑줄 친 ⓐ가 의미하는 것을 우리말로 쓰시오.

➡ _____

14 자연스러운 글이 되도록 (A)~(D)를 바르게 나열하시오.

➡ _____

15 What did Mrs. Granger ask Nick to do after she took out the envelope?

➡ _____

01 출제율 95%

다음 영영풀이가 나타내는 말을 고르시오.

> to make somebody suffer because they have broken the law or done something wrong

① borrow　　　② punish
③ bark　　　　④ cover
⑤ spread

02 출제율 100%

다음 문장의 빈칸에 들어갈 말을 〈보기〉에서 골라 적절한 형태로 쓰시오.

> ┌─ 보기 ─┐
> take out / out of hand / hold up /
> look up / have no choice

(1) He _____ a candy from his pocket and gave it to me.
(2) Did you _____ the meanings of new words in the dictionary?
(3) I _____ but to do this work.
(4) The problem is getting _____.
(5) Would you _____ this board for a while?

03 출제율 90%

다음 문장의 빈칸에 공통으로 들어갈 말로 적절한 것은?

> • The officer gave the letter and asked me to _____ at the bottom.
> • Have you checked the _____ and time of the invitation?
> • Did you fix on a _____ for your journey?

① date　　　　② cover
③ receive　　　④ spread
⑤ chioce

04 출제율 90%

다음 주어진 문장의 밑줄 친 covered와 같은 의미로 쓰인 것은?

> The TV reporter covered the car accident in the morning.

① She covered her eyes with her hands.
② The CNN will cover all the major competition.
③ Be careful. Snow covered the road.
④ Would you cover the seeds with soil?
⑤ Let's cover the label before taking a picture.

05 출제율 95%

다음 밑줄 친 단어의 뜻이 바르지 않은 것은?

① The entire system was broken down. 전체의
② Do you know who planted the tree nearby the red house? 가까이에, 인근의
③ I was pleased with your present. 불쾌한
④ Parents should punish their children in a proper way. 처벌하다
⑤ What do you want to do after you graduate from high school? 졸업하다

06 출제율 85%

다음 우리말을 주어진 단어를 사용하여 영작하시오.

(1) James는 점점 더 많은 시간을 컴퓨터 게임하는 데 쓴다. (and, more)

➡ _____
_____

(2) 나의 영어 선생님은 재미있는 수업으로 유명하다. (funny, for)

➡ _____
_____

07 다음 중 어법상 바르지 <u>않은</u> 것은?

① They forced me to help them.

② Carry was pleased with my gift.

③ Colin is not as handsome as Paul.

④ Although he was busy, he visited us.

⑤ The accident caused us being more careful.

08 다음 중 우리말을 영어로 바르게 옮긴 것은?

나는 네가 나를 초대하면 좋겠어.

① I like to invite you.

② I would like to invite you.

③ I would like you to invite me.

④ I want you to invite yourself.

⑤ I would like you invite me.

09 다음 문장과 같은 의미의 문장은?

Jamie was so interested in the book that he couldn't put it down.

① Jamie was interested in the book enough to put it down.

② Jamie was so interested in the book to put it down.

③ Jamie was too interested in the book to put it down.

④ Jamie was very interested in the book so he put it down.

⑤ Jamie was so interested in the book that he could put it down.

10 다음 중 빈칸에 들어갈 수 <u>없는</u> 말은?

David _____ us to find his wallet.

① forced   ② allowed

③ wanted   ④ encouraged

⑤ made

11 다음 빈칸에 들어갈 말로 가장 적절한 것은?

I want to know. Did she arrive home safely?
= I want to know _____ she arrived home safely.

① how   ② whether   ③ why

④ when   ⑤ that

12 다음 우리말에 맞게 빈칸에 알맞은 말을 쓰시오.

누가 이 편지를 너에게 줬는지 말해 줄래?
Can you tell me _____?

➡ _____

13 다음 중 어법상 <u>어색한</u> 것은?

① We hope to find your son soon.

② Did you decide to get more interesting job?

③ She didn't let me to make the cookies.

④ He taught us to think reasonably.

⑤ They advised me to do the right thing.

14 주어진 단어를 활용하여 다음 우리말을 영어로 쓰시오.

그 선생님은 나를 초조하게 만들어. (make)

➡ _____

[15~20] 다음 글을 읽고 물음에 답하시오.

Nick Allen was excited about starting fifth grade, but he was worried about one thing — Mrs. Granger's English class. Mrs. Granger was famous for her difficult vocabulary lessons.

In the first class, Mrs. Granger said, "Everyone should have a good dictionary. You can look up the meanings of new words in it."

"Mrs. Granger? Who decides the meanings of words? I mean, who decided that 'dog' means an animal that barks?" Nick asked.

"You (A)did, Nick. You, me, and the entire town and country. We all agreed. (B)That gives the word its meaning."

Nick wasn't satisfied. "When did I agree?" he said to himself.

출제율 90%

15 밑줄 친 (A)가 의미하는 것을 위 글에서 찾아 쓰시오.

➡ _____

출제율 95%

16 다음 중 밑줄 친 (B)가 의미하는 것으로 가장 적절한 것은?

① 반 친구들의 설명
② 선생님의 어휘 수업
③ 사회 구성원의 동의
④ 국가의 엄격한 법
⑤ 가족의 따뜻한 사랑

출제율 85%

17 What was Mrs. Granger famous for? Answer in English with a full sentence.

➡ _____

출제율 100%

18 다음 중 위 글의 내용과 일치하지 <u>않는</u> 것은?

① Nick Allen was a fifth grader.
② Mrs. Granger taught English to students.
③ Mrs. Granger wanted students to have a good dictionary.
④ Mrs. Granger wondered who decided the meanings of words.
⑤ Nick didn't feel satisfied with what Mrs. Granger said.

출제율 90%

19 What was Nick worried about?

➡ _____

출제율 95%

20 다음 중 위 글에서 반의어를 찾을 수 <u>없는</u> 것은?

① disagree　　② easy　　③ old
④ whole　　⑤ unknown

[21~26] 다음 글을 읽고 물음에 답하시오.

On the way home, Nick decided to ⓐtest Mrs. Granger's idea. He took out a pen and said, "From today, this is a ①*frindle*."

[A] Mrs. Granger was not pleased. She said, "②Your new word is cute, but it ⓑalready has ③a perfectly good name — a pen."

[B] His friend, John, held up a pen and said, "I have an extra *frindle*. Do you want to ⓒlend my *frindle*?"

[C] The next day, he asked five friends to use the word *frindle*. During class, Nick said, "Mrs. Granger, I forgot my *frindle* today."

Nick's classmates found (A)this ⓓfunny and began to use ④the word more and more. In just three days, ⑤it became the ⓔcool word at school.

21 📝 출제율 95%

자연스러운 글이 되도록 [A]~[C]를 바르게 나열하시오.

➡ _____

22 📝 출제율 95%

밑줄 친 (A)this가 의미하는 것을 우리말로 쓰시오.

➡ _____

23 📝 출제율 90%

①~⑤ 중 의미하는 것이 <u>다른</u> 것을 고르시오.

①   ②   ③   ④   ⑤

24 📝 출제율 85%

How did Mrs. Granger feel about the new word? Answer in English with a full sentence.

➡ _____

25 📝 출제율 100%

ⓐ~ⓔ 중 글의 흐름상 <u>어색한</u> 것은?

① ⓐ   ② ⓑ   ③ ⓒ   ④ ⓓ   ⑤ ⓔ

26 📝 출제율 95%

다음 중 위 글을 읽고 답할 수 <u>없는</u> 것은?

① What did Nick decide to do on the way home?
② What did Nick ask his friends to do?
③ When did Nick tell Mrs. Granger that he forgot his *frindle*?
④ How many classmates were there in Nick's class?
⑤ How long did it take for the word *frindle* to become the cool word at school?

[27~32] 다음 글을 읽고 물음에 답하시오.

Mrs. Granger said to Nick after class, "This is ⓐgetting out of hand. Can you tell your friends to stop (A)[saying / to say] *frindle*?"

"I'm sorry, but I can't stop it. It started as my word, but now it's the students' word."

"Very well. Then I have no choice." Mrs. Granger took out an envelope and asked Nick (B)[signing / to sign] and date the back. She said, "I'll give this letter to you when all this is over."

Nick thought, "She really hates me."

Next week, Mrs. Granger began a war with *frindle*. She said that she would punish any student for using it. But this only made things worse. The students wanted (C)[using / to use] the word more and more.

27 📝 출제율 95%

다음 중 밑줄 친 ⓐ의 의미로 가장 적절한 것은?

① possible to deal with
② beyond my control
③ easy to solve
④ difficult to ask
⑤ hard to get along with

28 📝 출제율 100%

(A)~(C)에서 어법상 옳은 것끼리 바르게 묶은 것은?

① to say – to sign – to use
② to say – signing – using
③ saying – to sign – to use
④ saying – signing – using
⑤ saying – to sign – using

29 출제율 95%

다음 중 위 글의 내용과 일치하는 것은?

① Mrs. Granger told students that they should call a pen a *frindle*.

② The word Nick made became the students' word.

③ Mrs. Granger wrote letters to all of the students.

④ Mrs. Granger thought there were many choices.

⑤ What Mrs. Granger said made things better.

30 출제율 85%

When will Mrs. Granger give the letter to Nick?

➡ _____

31 출제율 90%

What did Mrs. Granger say in order to make her students stop using the word, *frindle*?

➡ _____

_____

32 출제율 95%

What happened after Mrs. Granger began a war with *frindle*?

➡ _____

[33~36] 다음 글을 읽고 물음에 답하시오.

Frindle quickly spread to nearby middle and high schools. Shortly after, a local newspaper reporter wrote an article on the situation and everyone in town knew about it. A month later, a national television station ⓐcovered the news and everyone found out about *frindle*. By the time Nick graduated from elementary school, most students in the country used the word.

Time flew by and Nick turned 21. One day, he received a package. Inside it, he found a pen, an envelope and a dictionary. The envelope had his signature from fifth grade. The dictionary had a yellow note. It said, "Check page 541."

33 출제율 100%

다음 중 위 글을 읽고 대답할 수 없는 것은?

① Who wrote the article on the situation?

② What happened shortly after *frindle* quickly spread to nearby middle and high schools?

③ How old was Nick when he received a package from Mrs. Granger?

④ What was said in the letter?

⑤ How did Nick feel when the word *frindle* became popular?

34 출제율 90%

By the time Nick graduated from elementary school, what happened to the word, *frindle*?

➡ _____

_____

35 출제율 95%

What did Nick find inside the package?

➡ _____

36 출제율 85%

다음 중 밑줄 친 ⓐ와 같은 의미로 쓰인 것은?

① Snow covered the ground.

② Cover the chicken loosely with foil.

③ Much of the country is covered by forest.

④ The front cover of the book is pretty.

⑤ The BBC will cover all the major games.

INSIGHT
on the textbook

교과서 파헤치기

Lesson **7** **Can I Trust It?**

Lesson **8** **Be like Sherlock!**

Lesson **S** **Frindle**

※ 다음 영어를 우리말로 쓰시오.

01	author	22	belief
02	backpack	23	strongly
03	perfect	24	lift
04	connection	25	wisely
05	trip	26	meal
06	award	27	prove
07	difference	28	express
08	mix	29	solve
09	trust	30	navy
10	adventure	31	recommend
11	traditional	32	boring
12	explain	33	touching
13	simple	34	opinion
14	friendship	35	for example
15	especially	36	full of
16	unlike	37	based on
17	truth	38	from now on
18	lie	39	hold on
19	advertisement	40	make a choice
20	worth	41	right now
21	fantasy	42	check out
		43	worth it

※ 다음 우리말을 영어로 쓰시오.

01	믿다, 신뢰하다	22	들어 올리다
02	작가	23	해결하다, 풀다
03	완벽한	24	증명하다
04	감동적인	25	설명하다
05	나타내다, 표현하다	26	전통적인
06	지루한	27	차이점
07	여행	28	섞다
08	남색	29	공상
09	모험	30	추천하다
10	보라색, 자색	31	신념, 생각
11	소설	32	~와 달리
12	의견	33	현명하게
13	광고	34	진실, 사실
14	주머니	35	~을 확인하다
15	간단한, 단순한	36	~을 찾다
16	상	37	지금부터
17	가치가 있는	38	선택하다
18	특히	39	예를 들면
19	식사	40	~로 가득한
20	우정	41	~을 바탕으로
21	강력하게	42	지금
		43	기다려, 멈춰

※ 다음 영영풀이에 알맞은 단어를 <보기>에서 골라 쓴 후, 우리말 뜻을 쓰시오.

1 _____ : to believe that something is true: _____

2 _____ : ideas or feelings about something: _____

3 _____ : to add something to something else: _____

4 _____ : to move something to a higher position: _____

5 _____ : the real facts about something: _____

6 _____ : the foods eaten or prepared at one time: _____

7 _____ : to show what you think or feel: _____

8 _____ : to say or write something that is not true: _____

9 _____ : a small bag that is attached to something: _____

10 _____ : to tell someone that something is good or useful: _____

11 _____ : a notice, picture or short film telling people about something:
_____

12 _____ : the way in which two things are related to each other: _____

13 _____ : to tell somebody about something in a way that is easy to understand:
_____

14 _____ : to use facts, evidence, etc. to show that something is true: _____

15 _____ : a prize such as money, etc. for something that somebody has done:
_____

16 _____ : a large area of land that has very little water and very few plants growing
on it: _____

award	explain	advertisement	lie
mix	opinion	desert	express
prove	connection	pocket	recommend
trust	lift	meal	truth

※ 다음 우리말과 일치하도록 빈칸에 알맞은 말을 쓰시오.

Listen & Speak 1-A

Brian: Can you _____ _____ _____ _____?

Emily: Try *Star Wars*. I _____ _____ it.

Brian: Oh, I _____ _____ it _____.

Emily: It's the _____ _____ movie _____ _____.

Listen & Speak 1-B

W: May I _____ you?

B: Yes. I'm _____ _____ a _____. Can you _____ _____?

W: _____ _____ this red one? Red is _____ _____ _____ _____ _____ _____.

B: _____ _____ _____ was red, so I want a _____ _____.

W: _____ _____ this _____ one? It _____ _____ _____.

B: Oh, that _____ _____. I'll _____ it.

Listen & Speak 2-A

Sue: Tom, you _____ a _____ _____.

Tom: Yes, I did. I'm _____ _____ _____ it.

Sue: _____ do you _____ _____ _____ _____ _____?

Tom: I love the camera. It _____ _____ _____.

Listen & Speak 2-B

Jack: Hi, Suji. _____ _____ you _____ your _____ to Gyeongju?

Suji: I was very _____ _____ it.

Jack: _____ did you _____?

Suji: I _____ Cheomseongdae. It was great.

Jack: _____ _____ _____ you _____?

Suji: Bulguksa. It was a _____ _____.

Jack: _____ _____ the _____ _____.

Suji: Yeah, but _____ _____ to Seokguram _____ _____.

Jack: But _____ _____ it was _____ _____.

Jack: 안녕, 수지야. 경주 여행은 어땠니?
Suji: 매우 즐거웠어.
Jack: 어디를 방문했니?
Suji: 첨성대를 방문했어. 좋았어.
Jack: 또 어디를 방문했니?
Suji: 불국사. 멋진 곳이었어.
Jack: 완벽한 여행이었던 것 같네.
Suji: 응, 하지만 석굴암까지 걸어 올라가는 것은 힘들었어.
Jack: 하지만 그것이 그만한 가치가 있었을 것이라고 확신해.

Real Life Talk – Step 1

Brian: Mina, _____ _____ _____ a good pizza restaurant?

Mina: _____ _____ you try Antonio's? It's _____ _____.

Brian: _____ do you _____ _____ it?

Mina: The food is _____. I _____ the bulgogi pizza.

Brian: _____ are _____ _____?

Mina: I _____ the prices are good, _____.

Brian: _____ _____ a good restaurant. _____ do you _____ _____ _____?

Mina: It's a _____ _____ on the weekends.

Brian: Okay. I'll _____ _____ _____. Thanks.

Mina: No _____. _____ your meal!

Brian: 미나야, 괜찮은 피자 식당을 추천해 줄래?
Mina: Antonio's에 가 보는 게 어때? 내가 가장 좋아하는 곳이야.
Brian: 무엇이 좋은데?
Mina: 음식이 맛있어. 나는 불고기 피자를 추천해.
Brian: 가격은 어때?
Mina: 가격도 괜찮다고 생각해.
Brian: 괜찮은 식당 같네. 서비스는 어때?
Mina: 주말에는 좀 느려.
Brian: 알겠어. 내가 확인해 볼게. 고마워.
Mina: 천만에. 맛있게 먹어!

Real Life Talk – Step 2

Amy: Yujin, can you _____ _____ _____ _____ _____ _____?

Yujin: _____ _____ *The Little Prince*?

Amy: _____ _____ _____ _____ about the book?

Yujin: I like the _____ _____. He is very _____.

Amy: _____ good. I'll _____ it.

Amy: Yujin아, 내게 책을 추천해 줄래?
Yujin: '어린 왕자' 어때?
Amy: 책의 무엇이 마음에 드니?
Yujin: 나는 주인공이 마음에 들어. 그는 매우 특별해.
Amy: 좋은 책 같네. 내가 읽어 볼게.

Step2

※ 다음 우리말에 맞도록 대화를 영어로 쓰시오.

Listen & Speak 1-A

Brian: _____

Emily: _____

Brian: _____

Emily: _____

해석

Brian: 좋은 영화를 추천해 줄래?
Emily: 'Star Wars'를 봐. 정말 좋았어.
Brian: 오, 나는 아직 그 영화를 본 적이 없어.
Emily: 지금 1위 영화야.

Listen & Speak 1-B

W: _____

B: _____

W: _____

B: _____

W: _____

B: _____

W: 도와드릴까요?
B: 네. 배낭을 찾고 있어요. 하나 추천해 주시겠어요?
W: 이 빨간 배낭은 어떤가요? 빨간색은 요즘 가장 인기 있는 색이에요.
B: 제 옛 배낭이 빨간색이어서 다른 색을 원해요.
W: 이 남색 배낭은 어떤가요? 양옆에 주머니가 있어요.
B: 오, 좋아 보여요. 그걸로 살게요.

Listen & Speak 2-A

Sue: _____

Tom: _____

Sue: _____

Tom: _____

Sue: Tom, 새 스마트폰을 샀구나.
Tom: 응, 그래. 나는 정말 만족스러워.
Sue: 무엇이 가장 마음에 드니?
Tom: 카메라가 정말 좋아. 멋진 사진을 찍어.

Listen & Speak 2-B

Jack: _____

Suji: _____

Jack: _____

Suji: _____

Jack: _____

Suji: _____

Jack: _____

Suji: _____

Jack: _____

Jack: 안녕, 수지야. 경주 여행은 어땠니?
Suji: 매우 즐거웠어.
Jack: 어디를 방문했니?
Suji: 첨성대를 방문했어. 좋았어.
Jack: 또 어디를 방문했니?
Suji: 불국사. 멋진 곳이었어.
Jack: 완벽한 여행이었던 것 같네.
Suji: 응, 하지만 석굴암까지 걸어 올라가는 것은 힘들었어.
Jack: 하지만 그것이 그만한 가치가 있었을 것이라고 확신해.

Real Life Talk – Step 1

Brian: _____

Mina: _____

Brian: _____

Mina: _____

Brian: _____

Mina: _____

Brian: _____

Mina: _____

Brian: _____

Mina: _____

Brian: 미나야, 괜찮은 피자 식당을 추천해 줄래?
Mina: Antonio's에 가 보는 게 어때? 내가 가장 좋아하는 곳이야.
Brian: 무엇이 좋은데?
Mina: 음식이 맛있어. 나는 불고기 피자를 추천해.
Brian: 가격은 어때?
Mina: 가격도 괜찮다고 생각해.
Brian: 괜찮은 식당 같네. 서비스는 어때?
Mina: 주말에는 좀 느려.
Brian: 알겠어. 내가 확인해 볼게. 고마워.
Mina: 천만에. 맛있게 먹어!

Real Life Talk – Step 2

Amy: _____

Yujin: _____

Amy: _____

Yujin: _____

Amy: _____

Amy: Yujin아, 내게 책을 추천해 줄래?
Yujin: '어린 왕자' 어때?
Amy: 책의 무엇이 마음에 드니?
Yujin: 나는 주인공이 마음에 들어. 그는 매우 특별해.
Amy: 좋은 책 같네. 내가 읽어 볼게.

※ 다음 우리말과 일치하도록 빈칸에 알맞은 것을 골라 쓰시오.

1 Emma: What _____ you _____, Kyle?

A. doing   B. are

2 Kyle: Oh, Emma. I'm _____ the movie, *Y-Men 7* _____ my
_____.

A. on   B. watching   C. computer

3 Emma: _____ is _____?

A. it   B. how

4 Kyle: _____ ask. It's _____ _____ _____ I want to cry.

A. so   B. don't   C. that   D. boring

5 Emma: I'm _____ _____ _____ that.

A. to   B. sorry   C. hear

6 Kyle: I'm so _____. The movie _____ _____ it was
"The Most Exciting Movie of the Year."

A. advertisement   B. mad   C. said

7 Emma: Well, you can't _____ _____ _____ you _____.

A. that   B. believe   C. everything   D. read

8 Kyle: They _____ _____ the advertisement. I'm going to ask
_____ my money _____.

A. for   B. on   C. back   D. lied

9 Emma: _____ on, Kyle! They didn't really _____ _____
they used _____, not facts.

A. hold   B. because   C. lie   D. opinions

10 Kyle: Huh? I'm _____ _____.

A. you   B. following   C. not

11 Emma: Opinions _____ people's _____ _____, "The
desert is beautiful."

A. like   B. express   C. feelings

12 You can't say _____ it's true or _____. But, _____ can
be _____.

A. not   B. that   C. proven   D. facts

13 _____ _____, "The Atacama Desert is in Chile,"
is a fact. You can _____ that _____ the map.

A. on   B. check   C. example   D. for

14 Kyle: Okay…. But what's _____ _____ _____ movies?

A. with   B. connection   C. the

15 Emma: _____ me _____. What's your _____ movie?

A. explain   B. favorite   C. let

1 Emma: Kyle, 뭐 하고 있니?

2 Kyle: Emma. 나는 컴퓨터로 영화 "Y-Men 7"을 보고 있어.

3 Emma: 어때?

4 Kyle: 묻지 마. 너무 지루해서 울고 싶어.

5 Emma: 유감이야.

6 Klye: 난 정말 화가 나. 영화 광고에는 이것이 "올해의 가장 흥미진진한 영화"라고 쓰여 있었어.

7 Emma: 음, 넌 네가 읽는 것을 모두 믿을 수는 없어.

8 Kyle: 그들은 광고에 거짓말을 한 거야. 돈을 환불해 달라고 해야겠어.

9 Emma: 기다려, Kyle! 그들은 사실이 아닌 의견을 사용했기 때문에 꼭 거짓말을 한 것은 아니야.

10 Kyle: 뭐라고? 네 말을 이해하지 못하겠어.

11 Emma: 의견은 "사막은 아름다워."와 같이 사람들의 감정을 표현하는 것이야.

12 그것이 사실인지 아닌지 말할 수는 없어. 하지만 사실은 증명할 수 있어.

13 예를 들면, "아타카마 사막은 칠레에 있다."는 사실이야. 넌 그것을 지도에서 확인할 수 있어.

14 Kyle: 알겠어… 하지만 그게 영화와 무슨 관련이 있니?

15 Emma: 설명해 줄게. 네가 가장 좋아하는 영화가 뭐니?

16 Kyle: _____ _Forrest_ _____.
    A. _Gump_   B. it's

17 Emma: Okay. _____ look for _____ _____. What does it _____?
    A. say   B. its   C. let's   D. advertisement

18 Kyle: It _____, "Winner of 6 Academy _____ _____ Best Picture."
    A. says   B. including   C. Awards

19 Emma: See? It _____ _____ _____ the _Y-Men 7_ advertisement.
    A. unlike   B. uses   C. facts

20 _____ you _____ the _____?
    A. see   B. difference   C. do

21 Kyle: Not _____. The _Y-Men 7_ ad _____ "Most Exciting Movie" and the _Forrest Gump_ _____ says "Best Picture."
    A. says   B. ad   C. exactly

22 _____ they _____ _____?
    A. opinions   B. aren't   C. both

23 Emma: That's a great _____, Kyle. When people use words _____ "best" or "most," they are usually _____ _____.
    A. like   B. expressing   C. question   D. opinions

24 But in the _Forrest Gump_ _____, "Best Picture" is the _____ which the _____ _____.
    A. award   B. movie   C. ad   D. won

25 We can _____ that _____ the Internet. That's a _____.
    A. fact   B. on   C. check

26 Kyle: Aha! _____ now _____ I'm only going to _____ ads _____ facts.
    A. with   B. from   C. trust   D. on

27 Emma: It's not _____ _____. Most ads _____ facts _____ opinions.
    A. with   B. mix   C. simple   D. that

28 So you _____ to _____ a smart _____ based on _____ of them.
    A. both   B. choice   C. make   D. have

29 Kyle: _____ it! Emma, do you want to _____ the _____ of _Y-Men 7_ _____ me?
    A. rest   B. watch   C. with   D. got

30 Emma: Thanks, but _____ _____. Enjoy the _____ of the movie!
    A. rest   B. thanks   C. no

16 Kyle: "Forest Gump"야.

17 Emma: 좋아. 그 영화의 광고를 찾아보자. 뭐라고 쓰여 있니?

18 Kyle: "Best Picture를 포함하여 아카데미 6개 부문 수상작"이라고 쓰여 있어.

19 Emma: 알겠니? "Y-Men 7" 광고와는 달리 사실을 사용하고 있어.

20 차이를 알겠니?

21 Kyle: 잘 모르겠어. "Y-Men 7" 광고는 "Most Exciting Movie"라고 쓰여 있고 "Forest Gump" 광고는 "Best Picture"라고 쓰여 있잖아.

22 둘 다 의견 아니니?

23 Emma: 좋은 질문이야, Kyle. 사람들이 'best'나 'most'와 같은 말을 사용할 때, 그들은 대개 의견을 표현하는 거야.

24 하지만 "Forest Gump" 광고에서 "Best Picture"는 영화가 받은 상이야.

25 우리는 인터넷에서 그것을 확인할 수 있어. 그건 사실이야.

26 Kyle: 아하! 지금부터 사실로 이루어진 광고만 믿겠어.

27 Emma: 그렇게 간단하지는 않아. 대부분의 광고는 사실과 의견이 섞여 있어.

28 그러니 그 둘을 바탕으로 현명한 선택을 해야 해.

29 Kyle: 알겠어! Emma, "Y-Men 7"의 남은 부분을 나와 함께 볼래?

30 Emma: 고맙지만 사양할게. 영화의 남은 부분 잘 봐!

※ 다음 우리말과 일치하도록 빈칸에 알맞은 말을 쓰시오.

1 Emma: _____ _____ you _____, Kyle?

2 Kyle: Oh, Emma. I'm _____ _____ _____, *Y-Men 7* _____ my computer.

3 Emma: _____ is _____?

4 Kyle: _____ ask. It's _____ _____ _____ I want _____ _____.

5 Emma: I'm _____ _____ _____ _____.

6 Kyle: I'm so _____. The movie _____ said _____ was "_____ _____ _____ _____ of the Year."

7 Emma: Well, you _____ _____ _____ _____ _____ _____ _____.

8 Kyle: They _____ _____ the advertisement. I'm going to _____ _____ _____ _____ _____ _____.

9 Emma: _____ _____, Kyle! They didn't really _____ _____ they _____ _____, not _____.

10 Kyle: Huh? I'm _____ _____ _____.

11 Emma: Opinions _____ _____ _____ like, "The desert is beautiful."

12 You can't say _____ it's _____ _____ _____. But, facts _____ _____ _____.

13 _____ _____, "The Atacama Desert is in Chile," is a fact. You can _____ _____ _____ _____ _____ _____.

14 Kyle: Okay…. But what's _____ _____ _____ movies?

15 Emma: _____ _____ _____. What's your favorite movie?

1 Emma: Kyle, 뭐 하고 있니?

2 Kyle: Emma. 나는 컴퓨터로 영화 "Y-Men 7"을 보고 있어.

3 Emma: 어때?

4 Kyle: 묻지 마. 너무 지루해서 울고 싶어.

5 Emma: 유감이야.

6 Klye: 난 정말 화가 나. 영화 광고에는 이것이 "올해의 가장 흥미진진한 영화"라고 쓰여 있었어.

7 Emma: 음, 넌 네가 읽는 것을 모두 믿을 수는 없어.

8 Kyle: 그들은 광고에 거짓말을 한 거야. 돈을 환불해 달라고 해야겠어.

9 Emma: 기다려, Kyle! 그들은 사실이 아닌 의견을 사용했기 때문에 꼭 거짓말을 한 것은 아니야.

10 Kyle: 뭐라고? 네 말을 이해하지 못하겠어.

11 Emma: 의견은 "사막은 아름다워."와 같이 사람들의 감정을 표현하는 것이야.

12 그것이 사실인지 아닌지 말할 수는 없어. 하지만 사실은 증명할 수 있어.

13 예를 들면, "아타카마 사막은 칠레에 있다."는 사실이야. 넌 그것을 지도에서 확인할 수 있어.

14 Kyle: 알겠어… 하지만 그게 영화와 무슨 관련이 있니?

15 Emma: 설명해 줄게. 네가 가장 좋아하는 영화가 뭐니?

16 Kyle: _____ *Forrest Gump*.

17 Emma: Okay. _____ _____ _____ _____ _____.
What does it say?

18 Kyle: _____ _____, "Winner of 6 Academy Awards _____
Best Picture."

19 Emma: See? It _____ _____ _____ the *Y-Men 7*
advertisement.

20 Do you see _____ _____?

21 Kyle: Not _____. The *Y-Men 7* ad _____ "Most Exciting
Movie" and the *Forrest Gump* ad _____ "Best Picture."

22 _____ they _____ _____?

23 Emma: That's a great question, Kyle. When people use _____
_____ "best" or "most," they are _____ _____ _____.

24 But in the *Forrest Gump* ad, "Best Picture" is the _____
_____ _____ _____ _____.

25 We can _____ _____ _____ _____ _____. That's a
fact.

26 Kyle: Aha! _____ _____ _____ I'm only going to _____
ads _____ facts.

27 Emma: It's not _____ _____. Most ads _____ _____
_____.

28 So you have to _____ _____ _____ _____
_____ _____ of them.

29 Kyle: Got it! Emma, do you want _____ _____ _____
_____ of *Y-Men 7* with me?

30 Emma: Thanks, but _____ _____. Enjoy _____ _____
_____ the movie!

---

16 Kyle: "Forest Gump"야.

17 Emma: 좋아. 그 영화의 광고를 찾아보자. 뭐라고 쓰여 있니?

18 Kyle: "Best Picture를 포함하여 아카데미 6개 부문 수상작"이라고 쓰여 있어.

19 Emma: 알겠니? "Y-Men 7" 광고와는 달리 사실을 사용하고 있어.

20 차이를 알겠니?

21 Kyle: 잘 모르겠어. "Y-Men 7" 광고는 "Most Exciting Movie"라고 쓰여 있고 "Forest Gump" 광고는 "Best Picture"라고 쓰여 있잖아.

22 둘 다 의견 아니니?

23 Emma: 좋은 질문이야, Kyle. 사람들이 'best'나 'most'와 같은 말을 사용할 때, 그들은 대개 의견을 표현하는 거야.

24 하지만 "Forest Gump" 광고에서 "Best Picture"는 영화가 받은 상이야.

25 우리는 인터넷에서 그것을 확인할 수 있어. 그건 사실이야.

26 Kyle: 아하! 지금부터 사실로 이루어진 광고만 믿겠어.

27 Emma: 그렇게 간단하지는 않아. 대부분의 광고는 사실과 의견이 섞여 있어.

28 그러니 그 둘을 바탕으로 현명한 선택을 해야 해.

29 Kyle: 알겠어! Emma, "Y-Men 7"의 남은 부분을 나와 함께 볼래?

30 Emma: 고맙지만 사양할게. 영화의 남은 부분 잘 봐!

※ 다음 문장을 우리말로 쓰시오.

1 Emma: What are you doing, Kyle?

➡ _____

2 Kyle: Oh, Emma. I'm watching the movie, *Y-Men 7* on my computer.

➡ _____

3 Emma: How is it?

➡ _____

4 Kyle: Don't ask. It's so boring that I want to cry.

➡ _____

5 Emma: I'm sorry to hear that.

➡ _____

6 Kyle: I'm so mad. The movie advertisement said it was "The Most Exciting Movie of the Year."

➡ _____

7 Emma: Well, you can't believe everything that you read.

➡ _____

8 Kyle: They lied on the advertisement. I'm going to ask for my money back.

➡ _____

9 Emma: Hold on, Kyle! They didn't really lie because they used opinions, not facts.

➡ _____

10 Kyle: Huh? I'm not following you.

➡ _____

11 Emma: Opinions express people's feelings like, "The desert is beautiful."

➡ _____

12 You can't say that it's true or not. But, facts can be proven.

➡ _____

13 For example, "The Atacama Desert is in Chile," is a fact. You can check that on the map.

➡ _____

14 Kyle: Okay.... But what's the connection with movies?

➡ _____

15 Emma: Let me explain. What's your favorite movie?

➡ _____

16 Kyle: It's *Forrest Gump*.

➡ _____

17 Emma: Okay. Let's look for its advertisement. What does it say?

➡ _____

18 Kyle: It says, "Winner of 6 Academy Awards including Best Picture."

➡ _____

19 Emma: See? It uses facts unlike the *Y-Men 7* advertisement.

➡ _____

20 Do you see the difference?

➡ _____

21 Kyle: Not exactly. The *Y-Men 7* ad says "Most Exciting Movie" and the *Forrest Gump* ad says "Best Picture."

➡ _____

22 Aren't they both opinions?

➡ _____

23 Emma: That's a great question, Kyle. When people use words like "best" or "most," they are usually expressing opinions.

➡ _____

24 But in the *Forrest Gump* ad, "Best Picture" is the award which the movie won.

➡ _____

25 We can check that on the Internet. That's a fact.

➡ _____

26 Kyle: Aha! From now on I'm only going to trust ads with facts.

➡ _____

27 Emma: It's not that simple. Most ads mix facts with opinions.

➡ _____

28 So you have to make a smart choice based on both of them.

➡ _____

29 Kyle: Got it! Emma, do you want to watch the rest of *Y-Men 7* with me?

➡ _____

30 Emma: Thanks, but no thanks. Enjoy the rest of the movie!

➡ _____

※ 다음 괄호 안의 단어들을 우리말에 맞도록 바르게 배열하시오.

1 (Emma: / are / what / doing, / you / Kyle?)
➡ _____

2 (Kyle: / Emma. / oh, // watching / I'm / movie, / the / on / 7 / *Y-Men* / computer. / my)
➡ _____

3 (Emma: / is / it? / how)
➡ _____

4 (Kyle: / ask. / don't // so / it's / that / boring / cry. / to / want / I)
➡ _____

5 (Emma: / sorry / I'm / that. / hear / to)
➡ _____

6 (Klye: / so / mad. / I'm // movie / the / advertisement / it / said / was / Most / "The / Movie / Exciting / of / Year." / the)
➡ _____

7 (Emma: / well, / can't / you / everything / believe / that / read. / you)
➡ _____

8 (Kyle: / lied / they / the / on / advertisement. // going / I'm / ask / to / my / for / back. / money)
➡ _____

9 (Emma: / on, / hold / Kyle! // didn't / they / lie / really / they / because / used / opinions, / facts. / not)
➡ _____

10 (Kyle: / huh? // not / I'm / you. / following)
➡ _____

11 (Emma: / express / opinions / feelings / people's / like, / desert / "the / beautiful." / is)
➡ _____

12 (can't / you / say / it's / that / or / true / not. // but, / can / proven. / be / facts)
➡ _____

13 (example, / for / "The / Desert / Atacama / in / is / Chile," / fact. / a / is // can / you / that / check / map. / the / on)
➡ _____

14 (Kyle: / okay / ..... / what's / but / connection / the / movies? / with)
➡ _____

15 (Emma: / me / let / explain. // your / what's / movie? / favorite)
➡ _____

1 Emma: Kyle, 뭐 하고 있니?

2 Kyle: Emma. 나는 컴퓨터로 영화 "Y-Men 7"을 보고 있어.

3 Emma: 어때?

4 Kyle: 묻지 마. 너무 지루해서 울고 싶어.

5 Emma: 유감이야.

6 Klye: 난 정말 화가 나. 영화 광고에는 이것이 "올해의 가장 흥미진진한 영화"라고 쓰여 있었어.

7 Emma: 음, 넌 네가 읽는 것을 모두 믿을 수는 없어.

8 Kyle: 그들은 광고에 거짓말을 한 거야. 돈을 환불해 달라고 해야겠어.

9 Emma: 기다려, Kyle! 그들은 사실이 아닌 의견을 사용했기 때문에 꼭 거짓말을 한 것은 아니야.

10 Kyle: 뭐라고? 네 말을 이해하지 못하겠어.

11 Emma: 의견은 "사막은 아름다워."와 같이 사람들의 감정을 표현하는 것이야.

12 그것이 사실인지 아닌지 말할 수는 없어. 하지만 사실은 증명할 수 있어.

13 예를 들면, "아타카마 사막은 칠레에 있다."는 사실이야. 넌 그것을 지도에서 확인할 수 있어.

14 Kyle: 알겠어… 하지만 그게 영화와 무슨 관련이 있니?

15 Emma: 설명해 줄게. 네가 가장 좋아하는 영화가 뭐니?

16 (Kyle: / *Forrest* / it's / *Gump*.)
➡ _____

17 (Emma: / okay. / look / let's / for / advertisement. / its // say? / what / it / does)
➡ _____

18 (Kyle: / says, / it / "winner / 6 / of / Awards / Academy / Best / Picture." / including)
➡ _____

19 (Emma: / see? // uses / it / unlike / facts / the / advertisement. / 7 / *Y-Men*)
➡ _____

20 (you / do / see / difference? / the)
➡ _____

21 (Kyle: / exactly. / not // *Y-Men 7* / the / says / ad / "Most Exciting Movie" / and / says / the / "Best Picture." / *Forrest Gump* / ad)
➡ _____

22 (they / aren't / opinions? / both)
➡ _____

23 (Emma: / a / questions, / that's / Kyle. // people / when / words / use / "most," / or / "best" / like / are / they / usually / opinions. / expressing)
➡ _____

24 (in / but / *Forrest Gump* / the / ad, / "Best Picture" / the / is / which / award / won. / movie / the)
➡ _____

25 (can / we / that / check / the / on / Internet. // fact. / a / that's)
➡ _____

26 (Kyle: / aha! // now / from / on / only / I'm / to / going / trust / facts. / with / ads)
➡ _____

27 (Emma: / not / it's / simple. / that // ads / most / facts / mix / opinions. / with)
➡ _____

28 (you / so / to / have / make / smart / a / based / choice / both / on / them. / of)
➡ _____

29 (Kyle: / it! / got / Emma, / you / do / want / watch / to / rest / the / *Y-Men 7* / of / me? / with)
➡ _____

30 (Emma: / but / thanks, / thanks. / no // the / enjoy / rest / movie! / of / the)
➡ _____

16 Kyle: "Forest Gump"야.

17 Emma: 좋아. 그 영화의 광고를 찾아보자. 뭐라고 쓰여 있니?

18 Kyle: "Best Picture를 포함하여 아카데미 6개 부문 수상작"이라고 쓰여 있어.

19 Emma: 알겠니? "Y-Men 7" 광고와는 달리 사실을 사용하고 있어.

20 차이를 알겠니?

21 Kyle: 잘 모르겠어. "Y-Men 7" 광고는 "Most Exciting Movie"라고 쓰여 있고 "Forest Gump" 광고는 "Best Picture"라고 쓰여 있잖아.

22 둘 다 의견 아니니?

23 Emma: 좋은 질문이야, Kyle. 사람들이 'best'나 'most'와 같은 말을 사용할 때, 그들은 대개 의견을 표현하는 거야.

24 하지만 "Forest Gump" 광고에서 "Best Picture"는 영화가 받은 상이야.

25 우리는 인터넷에서 그것을 확인할 수 있어. 그건 사실이야.

26 Kyle: 아하! 지금부터 사실로 이루어진 광고만 믿겠어.

27 Emma: 그렇게 간단하지는 않아. 대부분의 광고는 사실과 의견이 섞여 있어.

28 그러니 그 둘을 바탕으로 현명한 선택을 해야 해.

29 Kyle: 알겠어! Emma, "Y-Men 7"의 남은 부분을 나와 함께 볼래?

30 Emma: 고맙지만 사양할게. 영화의 남은 부분 잘 봐!

※ 다음 우리말을 영어로 쓰시오.

1 Emma: Kyle, 뭐 하고 있니?

➡ _____

2 Kyle: Emma. 나는 컴퓨터로 영화 "Y-Men 7"을 보고 있어.

➡ _____

3 Emma: 어때?

➡ _____

4 Kyle: 묻지 마. 너무 지루해서 울고 싶어.

➡ _____

5 Emma: 유감이야.

➡ _____

6 Klye: 난 정말 화가 나. 영화 광고에는 이것이 "올해의 가장 흥미진진한 영화"라고 쓰여 있었어.

➡ _____

7 Emma: 음, 넌 네가 읽는 것을 모두 믿을 수는 없어.

➡ _____

8 Kyle: 그들은 광고에 거짓말을 한 거야. 돈을 환불해 달라고 해야겠어.

➡ _____

9 Emma: 기다려, Kyle! 그들은 사실이 아닌 의견을 사용했기 때문에 꼭 거짓말을 한 것은 아니야.

➡ _____

10 Kyle: 뭐라고? 네 말을 이해하지 못하겠어.

➡ _____

11 Emma: 의견은 "사막은 아름다워."와 같이 사람들의 감정을 표현하는 것이야.

➡ _____

12 그것이 사실인지 아닌지 말할 수는 없어. 하지만 사실은 증명할 수 있어.

➡ _____

13 예를 들면, "아타카마 사막은 칠레에 있다."는 사실이야. 넌 그것을 지도에서 확인할 수 있어.

➡ _____

14 Kyle: 알겠어…. 하지만 그게 영화와 무슨 관련이 있니?

➡ _____

15 Emma: 설명해 줄게. 네가 가장 좋아하는 영화가 뭐니?

➡ _____

16 Kyle: "Forest Gump"야.

➡ _____

17 Emma: 좋아. 그 영화의 광고를 찾아보자. 뭐라고 쓰여 있니?

➡ _____

18 Kyle: "Best Picture를 포함하여 아카데미 6개 부문 수상작"이라고 쓰여 있어.

➡ _____

19 Emma: 알겠니? "Y-Men 7" 광고와는 달리 사실을 사용하고 있어.

➡ _____

20 차이를 알겠니?

➡ _____

21 Kyle: 잘 모르겠어. "Y-Men 7" 광고는 "Most Exciting Movie"라고 쓰여 있고 "Forest Gump" 광고는 "Best Picture"라고 쓰여 있잖아.

➡ _____

22 둘 다 의견 아니니?

➡ _____

23 Emma: 좋은 질문이야, Kyle. 사람들이 'best'나 'most'와 같은 말을 사용할 때, 그들은 대개 의견을 표현하는 거야.

➡ _____

24 하지만 "Forest Gump" 광고에서 "Best Picture"는 영화가 받은 상이야.

➡ _____

25 우리는 인터넷에서 그것을 확인할 수 있어. 그건 사실이야.

➡ _____

26 Kyle: 아하! 지금부터 사실로 이루어진 광고만 믿겠어.

➡ _____

27 Emma: 그렇게 간단하지는 않아. 대부분의 광고는 사실과 의견이 섞여 있어.

➡ _____

28 그러니 그 둘을 바탕으로 현명한 선택을 해야 해.

➡ _____

29 Kyle: 알겠어! Emma, "Y-Men 7"의 남은 부분을 나와 함께 볼래?

➡ _____

30 Emma: 고맙지만 사양할게. 영화의 남은 부분 잘 봐!

➡ _____

※ 다음 우리말과 일치하도록 빈칸에 알맞은 말을 쓰시오.

Listen and Speak 2 - C

1. A: _____ _____ _____ _____ your bicycle?

2. B: I'm _____ _____ _____ it.

3. A: Why _____?

4. B: It's _____ _____.

1. A: 자전거가 마음에 드니?
2. B: 마음에 들지 않아.
3. A: 왜?
4. B: 너무 무거워.

Think and Write

1. *Harry Potter* is a _____ _____.

2. It _____ _____ _____ J. K. Rowling.

3. Harry Potter is _____ _____ _____ of the book.

4. When Harry goes to _____ _____, his _____ begin.

5. I _____ _____ the _____ of Harry and his friends.

6. The book was _____ _____ _____ I couldn't _____ it _____.

7. I _____ _____ it to everyone.

1. "해리포터"는 공상 소설이다.
2. 이 책은 J. K. Rowling에 의해 쓰였다.
3. Harry Potter는 이 책의 주인공이다.
4. Harry가 마법 학교에 가면서 그의 모험은 시작된다.
5. 나는 특히 Harry와 그의 친구들의 우정을 좋아한다.
6. 이 책은 너무 재미있어서 나는 책을 놓을 수가 없었다.
7. 나는 모두에게 이 책을 강력히 추천한다.

Project

1. Korean _____ _____

2. Facts: It _____ _____ _____ Yongin.

3. There are _____ _____ _____.

4. Visitors _____ _____ nongak and juldagi.

5. Opinions: It's _____ _____ _____ in Yongin.

6. Korean _____ _____ are beautiful.

7. Nongak and juldagi _____ _____ _____.

1. 한국 민속촌
2. 사실: 그것은 용인에 있습니다.
3. 한국 전통 가옥이 있습니다.
4. 방문객들은 농악과 줄타기를 볼 수 있습니다.
5. 의견: 그곳은 용인에 있는 재미있는 장소입니다.
6. 한국 전통 가옥들은 아름답습니다.
7. 농악과 줄타기는 신이 날 겁니다.

※ 다음 우리말을 영어로 쓰시오.

Listen and Speak 2 - C

1. A: 자전거가 마음에 드니?
➡ _____

2. B: 마음에 들지 않아.
➡ _____

3. A: 왜?
➡ _____

4. B: 너무 무거워.
➡ _____

Think and Write

1. "해리포터"는 공상 소설이다.
➡ _____

2. 이 책은 J. K. Rowling에 의해 쓰였다.
➡ _____

3. Harry Potter는 이 책의 주인공이다.
➡ _____

4. Harry가 마법 학교에 가면서 그의 모험은 시작된다.
➡ _____

5. 나는 특히 Harry와 그의 친구들의 우정을 좋아한다.
➡ _____

6. 이 책은 너무 재미있어서 나는 책을 놓을 수가 없었다.
➡ _____

7. 나는 모두에게 이 책을 강력히 추천한다.
➡ _____

Project

1. 한국 민속촌
➡ _____

2. 사실: 그것은 용인에 있습니다.
➡ _____

3. 한국 전통 가옥이 있습니다.
➡ _____

4. 방문객들은 농악과 줄타기를 볼 수 있습니다.
➡ _____

5. 의견: 그곳은 용인에 있는 재미있는 장소입니다.
➡ _____

6. 한국 전통 가옥들은 아름답습니다.
➡ _____

7. 농악과 줄타기는 신이 날 겁니다.
➡ _____

※ 다음 영어를 우리말로 쓰시오.

01 horror	_____	
02 post	_____	
03 broken	_____	
04 thirsty	_____	
05 bronze	_____	
06 feather	_____	
07 rush	_____	
08 flash	_____	
09 poem	_____	
10 strange	_____	
11 thunder	_____	
12 clue	_____	
13 afraid	_____	
14 refrigerator	_____	
15 text	_____	
16 handprint	_____	
17 inside	_____	
18 treasure	_____	
19 crime	_____	
20 dangerous	_____	
21 steal	_____	

22 stranger _____

23 detective _____

24 wonder _____

25 favor _____

26 call _____

27 suddenly _____

28 footprint _____

29 thief _____

30 lightning _____

31 carry _____

32 mop _____

33 principal _____

34 talent _____

35 take care of _____

36 a few _____

37 right now _____

38 win first place _____

39 not ~ anymore _____

40 on the way home _____

41 rush over _____

42 get into trouble _____

43 at the moment _____

※ 다음 우리말을 영어로 쓰시오.

01 발자국 _____

02 은 _____

03 청동 _____

04 번개 _____

05 낯선 사람, 모르는 사람 _____

06 나르다, 옮기다 _____

07 냉장고 _____

08 위험한 _____

09 갑자기 _____

10 궁금해 하다 _____

11 깃털 _____

12 깨진, 부서진 _____

13 재능 _____

14 범죄 _____

15 (급히) 움직이다, 서두르다 _____

16 시 _____

17 섬광, 번쩍임 _____

18 단서, 실마리 _____

19 도둑 _____

20 잃어버리다 _____

21 손자국 _____

22 교장 _____

23 호의, 친절, 부탁 _____

24 목마른 _____

25 공포 _____

26 훔치다 _____

27 이상한 _____

28 탐정 _____

29 ~ 안에 _____

30 물을 주다 _____

31 대걸레로 닦다 _____

32 보물 _____

33 게시하다, 공고하다 _____

34 천둥 _____

35 몇몇의, 조금의 _____

36 집에 가는(오는) 길에 _____

37 더 이상 ~ 않다 _____

38 지금, 곧, 당장 _____

39 ~을 돌보다 _____

40 그 순간에, 그때에 _____

41 ~을 돌려주다 _____

42 곤경에 빠지다 _____

43 달려가다 _____

※ 다음 영영풀이에 알맞은 단어를 <보기>에서 골라 쓴 후, 우리말 뜻을 쓰시오.

1 _____ : in any case: _____

2 _____ : a mark left by a foot or shoe: _____

3 _____ : a strong feeling of shock and fear: _____

4 _____ : the person in charge of a school: _____

5 _____ : activities that involve breaking the law: _____

6 _____ : someone who steals things from another person: _____

7 _____ : in addition to something already mentioned: _____

8 _____ : a bright light that shines for a short time: _____

9 _____ : to clean the floor with a mop: _____

10 _____ : to move or do something very quickly: _____

11 _____ : a natural and special ability to do something well: _____

12 _____ : something that helps a person find something: _____

13 _____ : a yellowish-brown metal containing copper and tin: _____

14 _____ : a person whose job is to find information about something or someone: _____

15 _____ : to take something that does not belong to you in a wrong way: _____

16 _____ : a powerful flash of light in the sky and usually followed by thunder: _____

보기

crime	lightning	footprint	principal
bronze	thief	talent	clue
anyway	detective	flash	rush
steal	else	horror	mop

※ 다음 우리말과 일치하도록 빈칸에 알맞은 말을 쓰시오.

Listen and Speak 1-A

Emily: Jinsu, can I _____ you a _____?

Jinsu: _____. What is it?

Emily: Can you help me _____ _____ _____?

Jinsu: No _____.

Emily: 진수야, 부탁 하나 해도 될까?
Jinsu: 물론이지. 뭔데?
Emily: 설거지하는 것 좀 도와줄래?
Jinsu: 좋아.

Listen and Speak 1-B

Narae: Tony, can you _____ _____ a _____?

Tony: Sure. What is it, Narae?

Narae: Can you _____ _____ _____ my dog this weekend? My family is _____ _____ _____ my grandmother in Busan.

Tony: Oh, _____ _____ _____ _____ _____. My mom doesn't like dogs.

Narae: Oh, _____ _____ _____ _____?

Tony: _____ _____ _____ ask Sumin? Her family _____ dogs.

Narae: Okay. I'll _____ her _____ _____.

Narae: Tony야, 부탁 하나 해도 될까?
Tony: 물론이지. 뭔데, 나래야?
Narae: 이번 주말에 내 개를 돌봐 줄 수 있니? 우리 가족은 부산에 계신 할머니를 방문할 예정이야.
Tony: 오, 미안하지만 안 돼. 엄마께서 개를 좋아하지 않으셔.
Narae: 오, 어떻게 해야 하지?
Tony: 수민이에게 물어보는 게 어때? 그녀의 가족은 개를 정말 좋아해.
Narae: 알겠어. 지금 당장 그녀에게 전화해야겠다.

Listen and Speak 1-C

A: Can you _____ _____ _____ _____?

B: Sure. What is it?

A: Can you _____ _____ _____ the floor?

B: No _____. / _____, I _____.

A: 부탁 하나 해도 될까?
B: 물론이지. 뭔데?
A: 바닥 닦는 것을 도와줄래?
B: 좋아. / 미안하지만 못해.

Listen and Speak 2-A

Brian: Did you see my _____ _____?

Jane: Yes, I saw it _____ _____ _____.

Brian: Really? It's _____ there _____.

Jane: Then I _____ Spot _____ it.

Brian: Oh, there _____ _____. You bad dog, Spot!

Brian: 내 야구 글러브 보았니?
Jane: 그래, 탁자 아래에서 봤어.
Brian: 정말? 더 이상 그곳에 없어.
Jane: 그럼 Spot이 가져간 것 같구나.
Brian: 오, 저기 있네. 이런 나쁜 개, Spot!

Listen and Speak 2-B

G: Good morning, classmates! Nine months _____ _____ so fast, and we are almost _____ _____ _____ _____ this school year. We all had a _____ _____. I guess only _____ _____ of us will _____ _____ _____ _____ next year. Don't be a _____. Say hello when we see _____ _____, okay? Thank you.

Listen and Speak 2-C

A: Guess _____ _____ _____.

B: _____ _____ you're _____ the piano.

A: You're _____. _____ again.

B: I _____ you're _____ _____ the computer.

A: That's _____.

Real Life Talk - Step 1

Brian: Mom, I _____ _____ my smartphone. _____ _____ _____ _____ find it?

Mom: _____ _____ _____ you lost it _____ the house?

Brian: Yes. I just _____ my friend _____ _____ _____ ago.

Mom: _____ _____ you _____ _____ _____?

Brian: In the kitchen. I _____ _____ a sandwich.

Mom: Then I guess you left it _____ in the kitchen.

Brian: I _____ _____ the kitchen, Mom.

Mom: Well, _____ _____ _____ _____ _____. Oh, here _____ _____. Inside the _____.

Brian: Thanks, Mom. You are the _____!

Mom: You're _____, honey.

Real Life Talk - Step 2

A: Can you _____ _____ _____ my baseball glove?

B: Okay. Where _____ you _____ it _____?

A: _____ the bench.

B: I _____ a dog _____ your baseball glove. I can _____ _____ _____ on the bench.

G: 좋은 아침이야, 학급 친구들아! 9개월은 아주 빨리 지나갔고, 우리는 이번 학년의 거의 막바지에 있어. 우리 모두는 멋진 한 해를 보냈어. 우리 중 극소수가 내년에 같은 반이 될 거라고 생각해. 모르는 사람처럼 지내지 말자. 서로 만나면 인사말을 건네자. 알겠지? 고마워.

A: 내가 무엇을 하고 있는지 맞혀 봐.
B: 너는 피아노를 치고 있는 것 같아.
A: 틀렸어. 다시 맞혀 봐.
B: 너는 컴퓨터로 일하고 있는 것 같아.
A: 맞아.

Brian: 엄마, 제 스마트폰을 찾을 수가 없어요. 제가 그것을 찾는 걸 도와주시겠어요?
Mom: 집 안에서 잃어버린 것이 확실하니?
Brian: 네. 불과 몇 분 전에 친구에게 문자 메시지를 보냈어요.
Mom: 너는 그때 어디에 있었니?
Brian: 부엌에요. 샌드위치를 만들고 있었어요.
Mom: 그럼 네가 부엌 어딘가에 놓은 것 같구나.
Brian: 이미 부엌은 확인했어요, 엄마.
Mom: 음, 다시 확인해 보자. 오, 여기 있구나. 냉장고 안에 있어.
Brian: 고마워요, 엄마. 엄마는 최고예요!
Mom: 천만에, 애야.

A: 내 야구 글러브를 찾는 것을 도와줄래?
B: 응. 그것을 어디에서 마지막으로 봤니?
A: 벤치 위에서.
B: 개가 네 야구 글러브를 가져간 것 같아. 벤치 위에 발자국을 볼 수 있어.

※ 다음 우리말에 맞도록 대화를 영어로 쓰시오.

Listen and Speak 1-A

Emily: _____

Jinsu: _____

Emily: _____

Jinsu: _____

Emily: 진수야, 부탁 하나 해도 될까?
Jinsu: 물론이지. 뭔데?
Emily: 설거지하는 것 좀 도와줄래?
Jinsu: 좋아.

Listen and Speak 1-B

Narae: _____

Tony: _____

Narae: _____

_____

Tony: _____

Narae: _____

Tony: _____

Narae: _____

Narae: Tony야, 부탁 하나 해도 될까?
Tony: 물론이지. 뭔데, 나래야?
Narae: 이번 주말에 내 개를 돌봐 줄 수 있니? 우리 가족은 부산에 계신 할머니를 방문할 예정이야.
Tony: 오, 미안하지만 안 돼. 엄마께서 개를 좋아하지 않으셔.
Narae: 오, 어떻게 해야 하지?
Tony: 수민이에게 물어보는 게 어때? 그녀의 가족은 개를 정말 좋아해.
Narae: 알겠어. 지금 당장 그녀에게 전화해야겠다.

Listen and Speak 1-C

A: _____

B: _____

A: _____

B: _____

A: 부탁 하나 해도 될까?
B: 물론이지. 뭔데?
A: 바닥 닦는 것을 도와줄래?
B: 좋아. / 미안하지만 못해.

Listen and Speak 2-A

Brian: _____

Jane: _____

Brian: _____

Jane: _____

Brian: _____

Brian: 내 야구 글러브 보았니?
Jane: 그래, 탁자 아래에서 봤어.
Brian: 정말? 더 이상 그곳에 없어.
Jane: 그럼 Spot이 가져간 것 같구나.
Brian: 오, 저기 있네. 이런 나쁜 개, Spot!

Listen and Speak 2-B

G: _____

_____

_____

_____

G: 좋은 아침이야, 학급 친구들아! 9개월은 아주 빨리 지나갔고, 우리는 이번 학년의 거의 막바지에 있어. 우리 모두는 멋진 한 해를 보냈어. 우리 중 극소수가 내년에 같은 반이 될 거라고 생각해. 모르는 사람처럼 지내지 말자. 서로 만나면 인사말을 건네자. 알겠지? 고마워.

Listen and Speak 2-C

A: _____

B: _____

A: _____

B: _____

A: _____

A: 내가 무엇을 하고 있는지 맞혀 봐.
B: 너는 피아노를 치고 있는 것 같아.
A: 틀렸어. 다시 맞혀 봐.
B: 너는 컴퓨터로 일하고 있는 것 같아.
A: 맞아.

Real Life Talk - Step 1

Brian: _____

Mom: _____

Brian: _____

Mom: _____

Brian: _____

Mom: _____

Brian: _____

Mom: _____

Brian: _____

Mom: _____

Brian: 엄마, 제 스마트폰을 찾을 수가 없어요. 제가 그것을 찾는 걸 도와주시겠어요?
Mom: 집 안에서 잃어버린 것이 확실하니?
Brian: 네. 불과 몇 분 전에 친구에게 문자 메시지를 보냈어요.
Mom: 너는 그때 어디에 있었니?
Brian: 부엌요. 샌드위치를 만들고 있었어요.
Mom: 그럼 네가 부엌 어딘가에 놓은 것 같구나.
Brian: 이미 부엌은 확인했어요, 엄마.
Mom: 음, 다시 확인해 보자. 오, 여기 있구나. 냉장고 안에 있어.
Brian: 고마워요, 엄마. 엄마는 최고예요!
Mom: 천만에, 애야.

Real Life Talk - Step 2

A: _____

B: _____

A: _____

B: _____

A: 내 야구 글러브를 찾는 것을 도와줄래?
B: 응. 그것을 어디에서 마지막으로 봤니?
A: 벤치 위에서.
B: 개가 네 야구 글러브를 가져간 것 같아. 벤치 위에 발자국을 볼 수 있어.

※ 다음 우리말과 일치하도록 빈칸에 알맞은 것을 골라 쓰시오.

1 Mr. Reese, the principal, _____ _____ the _____ playground.
A. across   B. ran   C. wet

2 "Shirley! Shirley! I _____ your _____!"
A. help   B. need

3 Shirley was an _____ _____ _____ at Bakersville Middle School.
A. grade   B. eighth   C. student

4 She was also the _____ _____ in the _____ town.
A. detective   B. whole   C. best

5 "Is there _____ _____?" asked Shirley.
A. wrong   B. something

6 "Someone _____ _____ the gold medal _____ the talent show!"
A. for   B. stolen   C. has

7 Mr. Reese _____ Shirley _____ the _____ of the crime.
A. to   B. took   C. scene

8 There was a _____ _____ a _____ window.
A. broken   B. case   C. with

9 The silver and _____ medals were _____ _____.
A. there   B. bronze   C. still

10 But the gold medal was _____. There was a _____ in _____.
A. place   B. missing   C. poem   D. its

11 Tomorrow is the talent show. _____ _____ the gold medal _____?
A. go   B. did   C. where

12 Look high and _____. You can't _____ me. You're _____ slow.
A. too   B. low   C. catch

13 Shirley asked, "Could you tell me _____ _____ _____?"
A. this   B. when   C. happened

14 "A little _____ nine last night. I was making my _____ when I heard a scream. I _____ _____ and found Jocelyn and the case like this."
A. rounds   B. after   C. over   D. rushed

15 "I _____ _____ _____ _____ here last night."
A. else   B. wonder   C. was   D. who

16 "Sylvia and Harry. They were also _____ _____ the talent show. I'll _____ _____ to my office."
A. call   B. practicing   C. them   D. for

17 Jocelyn was a _____ _____ student with short _____ red hair.
A. grade   B. curly   C. ninth

---

1 Reese 교장은 젖은 운동장을 달려왔다.

2 "Shirley! Shirley! 네 도움이 필요하구나!"

3 Shirley는 Bakersville 중학교의 8학년 학생이었다.

4 그녀는 또한 그 마을 최고의 탐정이었다.

5 "무슨 일이 있나요?" Shirley가 물었다.

6 "누군가 장기 자랑 대회 금메달을 훔쳐갔어!"

7 Reese 교장은 Shirley를 범죄 현장으로 데려갔다.

8 유리창이 깨진 진열장이 있었다.

9 은메달과 동메달은 그곳에 그대로 있었다.

10 하지만 금메달은 사라졌다. 그 자리에는 시가 있었다.

11 내일은 장기 자랑 대회다. 금메달은 어디로 갔을까?

12 구석구석 찾아라. 당신은 나를 잡을 수 없어. 당신은 너무 느려.

13 Shirley는 "언제 이 사건이 일어났는지 말씀해 주시겠어요?"라고 물었다.

14 "어젯밤 9시가 조금 넘은 후에. 내가 순찰을 돌고 있었을 때 비명 소리가 들렸어. 나는 달려가서 Jocelyn과 이 상태인 진열장을 발견했지."

15 "어젯밤에 또 다른 누가 여기 있었는지 궁금해요."

16 "Sylvia와 Harry가 있었어. 그 두 사람 또한 장기 자랑을 위해 연습 중이었어. 내가 그들을 내 사무실로 부르마."

17 Jocelyn은 빨간색 짧은 곱슬머리를 가진 9학년 학생이었다.

18 "I was practicing my song and I became _____ . I stepped outside the classroom to get some water. It was _____ dark. Suddenly, there was a loud sound of _____ . I think the thief broke the window at that moment. Lightning followed right after and it became bright for a second or two. Then I saw someone running _____ from the case."

A. thunder　　　　B. away　　　　C. thirsty　　　　D. completely

19 "Did you _____ the _____ _____ ?"

A. face　　　　B. see　　　　C. thief's

20 "No, I _____ saw the _____ _____ . But the thief had _____ hair."

A. short　　　　B. back　　　　C. thief's　　　　D. only

21 Next was an _____ _____ student, Sylvia. She was tall _____ _____ black hair.

A. with　　　　B. grade　　　　C. long　　　　D. eighth

22 She said, "I was reading my poem _____ in the classroom. I heard a scream and went outside. There was a girl next to the case. With the _____ from the lightning, it was _____ a horror movie. I got _____ so I ran straight home."

A. flash　　　　B. aloud　　　　C. scared　　　　D. like

23 "Did you _____ the window _____ ?"

A. break　　　　B. hear

24 "No, the thunder was _____ _____ . Well, I didn't do it. I was _____ to _____ first place anyway."

A. loud　　　　B. win　　　　C. going　　　　D. too

25 Harry, a _____ grader, had _____ _____ hair.

A. short　　　　B. seventh　　　　C. blonde

26 He said, "Hey, you got the _____ guy. I was practicing my dance _____ . I went home a _____ before nine. I didn't take one step _____ the classroom until then."

A. little　　　　B. outside　　　　C. moves　　　　D. wrong

27 "Did you hear _____ _____ ?"

A. strange　　　　B. anything

28 " _____ _____ I? My music was really _____ ."

A. could　　　　B. loud　　　　C. how

29 "Did you see anyone _____ the _____ _____ ?"

A. way　　　　B. on　　　　C. home

30 "No, I _____ someone _____ really _____ , but I didn't see _____ ."

A. singing　　　　B. heard　　　　C. anyone　　　　D. badly

31 Shirley said, "I don't _____ to hear _____ ." Then she _____ the thief.

A. anymore　　　　B. need　　　　C. to　　　　D. turned

32 "Why don't you _____ the medal _____ before you get _____ some real _____ ?"

A. into　　　　B. bring　　　　C. trouble　　　　D. back

18 "저는 제 노래를 연습하고 있었는데 목이 말랐어요. 저는 물을 가지러 교실 밖으로 나갔어요. 완전히 어두웠어요. 갑자기, 커다란 천둥소리가 났어요. 저는 도둑이 그 순간에 유리창을 깼다고 생각해요. 번개가 바로 뒤 따랐고 1~2초 정도 밝아졌어요. 그때 저는 누군가가 진열장에서 도망치는 걸 봤어요."

19 "도둑의 얼굴을 봤나요?"

20 "아니요, 도둑의 뒷모습만 봤어요. 하지만 그 도둑은 짧은 머리였어요."

21 다음은 8학년 학생인 Sylvia였다. 그녀는 긴 검은색 머리에 키가 컸다.

22 그녀는 말했다. "저는 교실에서 큰 소리로 제 시를 낭송하고 있었어요. 비명 소리를 듣고 밖으로 나갔어요. 진열장 옆에 한 소녀가 있었어요. 번개의 번쩍임과 어우러져 그것은 공포 영화 같았어요. 저는 겁이 나서 곧장 집으로 달려갔어요."

23 "창이 깨지는 소리를 들었나요?"

24 "아니요, 천둥소리가 너무 컸어요. 음, 제가 그런 게 아니에요. 저는 어쨌든 1등을 할 거였으니까요."

25 7학년인 Harry는 짧은 금발을 가지고 있었다.

26 그는 말했다. "이봐요, 사람을 잘못 짚었어요. 저는 제 춤 동작을 연습하고 있었어요. 저는 9시 조금 전에 집에 갔어요. 저는 그때까지 교실 밖으로 한 발자국도 나가지 않았어요."

27 "이상한 소리라도 들었나요?"

28 "제가 어떻게 듣겠어요? 제 음악 소리가 정말 컸어요."

29 "집에 가는 길에 누군가를 보았나요?"

30 "아니요, 누군가가 노래를 정말 끔찍하게 부르는 소리는 들었지만 누구도 보진 못했어요."

31 Shirley는 "더 이상 들을 필요는 없겠네요."라고 말했다. 그러고 나서 그녀는 도둑을 향했다.

32 "정말 곤경에 빠지기 전에 금메달을 돌려주는 게 어때요?"

※ 다음 우리말과 일치하도록 빈칸에 알맞은 말을 쓰시오.

1 Mr. Reese, the principal, _____ _____ the _____ playground.

2 "Shirley! Shirley! I _____ _____ _____!"

3 Shirley was _____ _____ _____ _____ at Bakersville Middle School.

4 She was also _____ _____ _____ in the _____ town.

5 "Is there _____ _____?" _____ Shirley.

6 "Someone _____ _____ the gold medal _____ the _____ _____!"

7 Mr. Reese _____ Shirley _____ the _____ of the crime.

8 There _____ _____ _____ with a _____ window.

9 The silver and _____ medals _____ _____ _____.

10 But the gold medal was _____. There was _____ _____ in _____ _____.

11 Tomorrow is the talent show. _____ _____ the gold medal _____?

12 Look _____ _____ _____. You can't catch me. You're _____ _____.

13 Shirley asked, "Could you tell me _____ _____ _____?"

14 "A little _____ nine last night. I was _____ _____ _____ when I heard a scream. I _____ _____ and found Jocelyn and the case _____ this."

15 "I wonder _____ _____ _____ _____ last night."

16 "Sylvia and Harry. They were also _____ _____ the talent show. I'll _____ _____ to my office."

17 Jocelyn was a _____ _____ student _____ _____ red hair.

1 Reese 교장은 젊은 운동장을 달려왔다.

2 "Shirley! Shirley! 네 도움이 필요하구나!"

3 Shirley는 Bakersville 중학교의 8학년 학생이었다.

4 그녀는 또한 그 마을 최고의 탐정이었다.

5 "무슨 일이 있나요?" Shirley가 물었다.

6 "누군가 장기 자랑 대회 금메달을 훔쳐갔어!"

7 Reese 교장은 Shirley를 범죄 현장으로 데려갔다.

8 유리창이 깨진 진열장이 있었다.

9 은메달과 동메달은 그곳에 그대로 있었다.

10 하지만 금메달은 사라졌다. 그 자리에는 시가 있었다.

11 내일은 장기 자랑 대회다. 금메달은 어디로 갔을까?

12 구석구석 찾아라. 당신은 나를 잡을 수 없어. 당신은 너무 느려.

13 Shirley는 "언제 이 사건이 일어났는지 말씀해 주시겠어요?"라고 물었다.

14 "어젯밤 9시가 조금 넘은 후에. 내가 순찰을 돌고 있었을 때 비명 소리가 들렸어. 나는 달려가서 Jocelyn과 이 상태인 진열장을 발견했지."

15 "어젯밤에 또 다른 누가 여기 있었는지 궁금해요."

16 "Sylvia와 Harry가 있었어. 그 두 사람 또한 장기 자랑을 위해 연습 중이었어. 내가 그들을 내 사무실로 부르마."

17 Jocelyn은 빨간색 짧은 곱슬머리를 가진 9학년 학생이었다.

18 "I was _____ my song and I _____ _____. I _____ the classroom _____ _____ some water. _____ was _____ dark. _____, there was a loud sound of _____. I think the thief _____ the window at that moment. _____ _____ right after and it became bright for _____ or _____. Then I _____ someone _____ _____ from the case."

19 "Did you see the _____ _____?"

20 "No, I _____ _____ the thief's _____. But the thief had _____ hair."

21 Next was an _____ _____ student, Sylvia. She was tall _____ _____ _____ hair.

22 She said, "I was _____ my poem _____ in the classroom. I heard a scream and _____ _____. There was a girl _____ _____ the case. With the _____ from the lightning, it was _____ _____ _____ _____. I got _____ so I _____ _____ home."

23 "Did you _____ the window _____?"

24 "No, the thunder was _____ _____. Well, I didn't do it. I _____ _____ _____ _____ first place anyway."

25 Harry, a _____ grader, had _____ _____ hair.

26 He said, "Hey, you got the _____ guy. I was practicing my dance _____. I went home _____ _____ _____ nine. I didn't _____ one step _____ the classroom _____ then."

27 "Did you _____ _____ _____?"

28 "_____ _____ I? My music was really loud."

29 "Did you see anyone _____ _____ _____ _____ _____?"

30 "No, I _____ _____ _____ really badly, but I didn't see anyone."

31 Shirley said, "I don't _____ _____ _____ _____." Then she _____ _____ the thief.

32 "Why don't you _____ _____ before you _____ _____ some real _____?"

18 "저는 제 노래를 연습하고 있었는데 목이 말랐어요. 저는 물을 가지러 교실 밖으로 나갔어요. 완전히 어두웠어요. 갑자기, 커다란 천둥소리가 났어요. 저는 도둑이 그 순간에 유리창을 깼다고 생각해요. 번개가 바로 뒤따랐고 1~2초 정도 밝아졌어요. 그때 저는 누군가가 진열장에서 도망치는 걸 봤어요."

19 "도둑의 얼굴을 봤나요?"

20 "아니요, 도둑의 뒷모습만 봤어요. 하지만 그 도둑은 짧은 머리였어요."

21 다음은 8학년 학생인 Sylvia였다. 그녀는 긴 검은색 머리에 키가 컸다.

22 그녀는 말했다. "저는 교실에서 큰 소리로 제 시를 낭송하고 있었어요. 비명 소리를 듣고 밖으로 나갔어요. 진열장 옆에 한 소녀가 있었어요. 번개의 번쩍임과 어우러져 그것은 공포 영화 같았어요. 저는 겁이 나서 곧장 집으로 달려갔어요."

23 "창이 깨지는 소리를 들었나요?"

24 "아니요, 천둥소리가 너무 컸어요. 음, 제가 그런 게 아니에요. 저는 어쨌든 1등을 할 거였으니까요."

25 7학년인 Harry는 짧은 금발을 가지고 있었다.

26 그는 말했다. "이봐요, 사람을 잘못 짚었어요. 저는 제 춤 동작을 연습하고 있었어요. 저는 9시 조금 전에 집에 갔어요. 저는 그때까지 교실 밖으로 한 발자국도 나가지 않았어요."

27 "이상한 소리라도 들었나요?"

28 "제가 어떻게 듣겠어요? 제 음악 소리가 정말 컸어요."

29 "집에 가는 길에 누군가를 보았나요?"

30 "아니요, 누군가가 노래를 정말 끔찍하게 부르는 소리는 들었지만 누구도 보진 못했어요."

31 Shirley는 "더 이상 들을 필요는 없겠네요."라고 말했다. 그러고 나서 그녀는 도둑을 향했다.

32 "정말 곤경에 빠지기 전에 금메달을 돌려주는 게 어때요?"

※ 다음 문장을 우리말로 쓰시오.

1 Mr. Reese, the principal, ran across the wet playground.
➡ _____

2 "Shirley! Shirley! I need your help!"
➡ _____

3 Shirley was an eighth grade student at Bakersville Middle School.
➡ _____

4 She was also the best detective in the whole town.
➡ _____

5 "Is there something wrong?" asked Shirley.
➡ _____

6 "Someone has stolen the gold medal for the talent show!"
➡ _____

7 Mr. Reese took Shirley to the scene of the crime.
➡ _____

8 There was a case with a broken window.
➡ _____

9 The silver and bronze medals were still there.
➡ _____

10 But the gold medal was missing. There was a poem in its place.
➡ _____

11 Tomorrow is the talent show. Where did the gold medal go?
➡ _____

12 Look high and low. You can't catch me. You're too slow.
➡ _____

13 Shirley asked, "Could you tell me when this happened?"
➡ _____

14 "A little after nine last night. I was making my rounds when I heard a scream. I rushed over and found Jocelyn and the case like this."
➡ _____

15 "I wonder who else was here last night."
➡ _____

16 "Sylvia and Harry. They were also practicing for the talent show. I'll call them to my office."
➡ _____

17 Jocelyn was a ninth grade student with short curly red hair.
➡ _____

18 "I was practicing my song and I became thirsty. I stepped outside the classroom to get some water. It was completely dark. Suddenly, there was a loud sound of thunder. I think the thief broke the window at that moment. Lightning followed right after and it became bright for a second or two. Then I saw someone running away from the case."

➡ _____

_____

_____

19 "Did you see the thief's face?"

➡ _____

20 "No, I only saw the thief's back. But the thief had short hair."

➡ _____

21 Next was an eighth grade student, Sylvia. She was tall with long black hair.

➡ _____

22 She said, "I was reading my poem aloud in the classroom. I heard a scream and went outside. There was a girl next to the case. With the flash from the lightning, it was like a horror movie. I got scared so I ran straight home."

➡ _____

_____

23 "Did you hear the window break?"

➡ _____

24 "No, the thunder was too loud. Well, I didn't do it. I was going to win first place anyway."

➡ _____

25 Harry, a seventh grader, had short blonde hair.

➡ _____

26 He said, "Hey, you got the wrong guy. I was practicing my dance moves. I went home a little before nine. I didn't take one step outside the classroom until then."

➡ _____

_____

27 "Did you hear anything strange?"

➡ _____

28 "How could I? My music was really loud."

➡ _____

29 "Did you see anyone on the way home?"

➡ _____

30 "No, I heard someone singing really badly, but I didn't see anyone."

➡ _____

31 Shirley said, "I don't need to hear anymore." Then she turned to the thief.

➡ _____

32 "Why don't you bring the medal back before you get into some real trouble?"

➡ _____

※ 다음 괄호 안의 단어들을 우리말에 맞도록 바르게 배열하시오.

1 (Reese, / Mr. / principal, / the / across / ran / wet / playground. / the)
➡ _____

2 ("Shirley! / I / Shirley! / help!" / your / need)
➡ _____

3 (was / Shirley / eighth / an / grade / student / Bakersville / at / School. / Middle)
➡ _____

4 (was / she / the / also / best / in / detective / the / town. / whole)
➡ _____

5 (there / "is / wrong?" / something / Shirley. / asked)
➡ _____

6 (has / "someone / the / stolen / medal / gold / for / show!" / talent / the)
➡ _____

7 (Reese / Mr. / took / to / Shirley / the / crime. / of / the / scene)
➡ _____

8 (was / there / case / a / with / window. / broken / a)
➡ _____

9 (silver / the / and / medals / bronze / were / there. / still)
➡ _____

10 (the / but / gold / was / medal / missing. // was / there / poem / a / place. / its / in)
➡ _____

11 (is / tomorrow / the / show. / talent // did / where / gold / go? / medal / the)
➡ _____

12 (high / look / low. / and // you / catch / can't / me. // too / you're / slow.)
➡ _____

13 (asked, / Shirley / "could / tell / you / me / this / happened?" / when)
➡ _____

14 (little / "a / after / last / nine / night. // I / making / was / rounds / my / when / heard / I / scream. / a // I / over / rushed / and / Jocelyn / found / and / case / the / this." / like)
➡ _____

15 (wonder / "I / else / who / was / last / night." / here)
➡ _____

16 (Harry. / and / "Sylvia // were / they / practicing / also / for / talent / the / show. // call / I'll / to / them /. office." / my)
➡ _____

17 (was / Jocelyn / a / grade / ninth / student / with / curly / short / hair. / red)
➡ _____

1 Reese 교장은 젖은 운동장을 달려왔다.

2 "Shirley! Shirley! 네 도움이 필요하구나!"

3 Shirley는 Bakersville 중학교의 8학년 학생이었다.

4 그녀는 또한 그 마을 최고의 탐정이었다.

5 "무슨 일이 있나요?" Shirley가 물었다.

6 "누군가 장기 자랑 대회 금메달을 훔쳐갔어!"

7 Reese 교장은 Shirley를 범죄 현장으로 데려갔다.

8 유리창이 깨진 진열장이 있었다.

9 은메달과 동메달은 그곳에 그대로 있었다.

10 하지만 금메달은 사라졌다. 그 자리에는 시가 있었다.

11 내일은 장기 자랑 대회다. 금메달은 어디로 갔을까?

12 구석구석 찾아라. 당신은 나를 잡을 수 없어. 당신은 너무 느려.

13 Shirley는 "언제 이 사건이 일어났는지 말씀해 주시겠어요?"라고 물었다.

14 "어젯밤 9시가 조금 넘은 후에. 내가 순찰을 돌고 있었을 때 비명 소리가 들렸어. 나는 달려가서 Jocelyn과 이 상태인 진열장을 발견했지."

15 "어젯밤에 또 다른 누가 여기 있었는지 궁금해요."

16 "Sylvia와 Harry가 있었어. 그 두 사람 또한 장기 자랑을 위해 연습 중이었어. 내가 그들을 내 사무실로 부르마."

17 Jocelyn은 빨간색 짧은 곱슬머리를 가진 9학년 학생이었다.

18 ("I / practicing / was / song / and / my / became / thirsty. I // I / outside / stepped / classroom / the / to / some / get / water. // was / it / dark. / completely // suddenly, / was / there / loud / a / sound / of / thunder. // I / the / think / thief / the / broke / window / of / that / at / moment. // lightning / right / followed / after / and / it / bright / became / a / for / second / two. / or // then / saw / I / running / someone / away / the / case." / from)

➡ _____
_____
_____
_____

19 (you / "did / see / thief's / the / face?")

➡ _____

20 ("no, / only / I / saw / thief's / the / back. // but / thief / the / hair." / short / had)

➡ _____

21 (was / next / eighth / an / student, / grade / Sylvia. // was / she / with / tall / black / long / hair.)

22 (said, / she / "I / reading / was / poem / my / in / aloud / classroom. / the // I / heard / scream / a / and / outside. / went // was / there / girl / a / to / next / case. / the // the / with / from / flash / lightning, / the / was / it / like / horror / movie. / a // I / scared / got / I / so / home." / straight / ran)

➡ _____
_____
_____
_____

23 (you / "did / hear / the / break?" / window)

➡ _____

24 (the / "no, / was / thunder / loud. / too // well, / didn't / I / it. / do // was / I / to / going / win / place / first / anyway.")

➡ _____
_____

25 (a / Harry, / grader, / seventh / had / hair. / blonde / short)

26 (said, / he / "hey, / got / you / wrong / the / guy. // was / practicing / I / dance / moves. / my // went / I / home / little / a / nine. / before // didn't / I / one / take / step / outside / the / then." / until / classroom)

➡ _____
_____
_____

27 (you / "did / anything / hear / strange?")

➡ _____

28 (could / "how / I? // music / my / really / was / loud.")

29 (you / "did / anyone / see / the / on / home?" / way)

➡ _____

30 ("no, / heard / I / singing / someone / really / badly, / I / but / see / didn't /. anyone.")

➡ _____

31 (said, / Shirley / "I / need / don't / hear / to / anymore." // she / then / to / turned / thief. / the)

➡ _____

32 ("why / you / don't / bring / medal / the / before / back / get / you / into / real / trouble?" / some)

➡ _____

---

18 "저는 제 노래를 연습하고 있었는데 목이 말랐어요. 저는 물을 가지러 교실 밖으로 나갔어요. 완전히 어두웠어요. 갑자기, 커다란 천둥소리가 났어요. 저는 도둑이 그 순간에 유리창을 깼다고 생각해요. 번개가 바로 뒤 따랐고 1~2초 정도 밝아졌어요. 그때 저는 누군가가 진열장에서 도망치는 걸 봤어요."

19 "도둑의 얼굴을 봤나요?"

20 "아니요. 도둑의 뒷모습만 봤어요. 하지만 그 도둑은 짧은 머리였어요."

21 다음은 8학년 학생인 Sylvia였다. 그녀는 긴 검은색 머리에 키가 컸다.

22 그녀는 말했다. "저는 교실에서 큰 소리로 제 시를 낭송하고 있었어요. 비명 소리를 듣고 밖으로 나갔어요. 진열장 옆에 한 소녀가 있었어요. 번개의 번쩍임과 어우러져 그것은 공포 영화 같았어요. 저는 겁이 나서 곧장 집으로 달려갔어요."

23 "창이 깨지는 소리를 들었나요?"

24 "아니요. 천둥소리가 너무 컸어요. 음, 제가 그런 게 아니에요. 저는 어쨌든 1등을 할 거였으니까요."

25 7학년인 Harry는 짧은 금발을 가지고 있었다.

26 그는 말했다. "이봐요, 사람을 잘못 짚었어요. 저는 제 춤 동작을 연습하고 있었어요. 저는 9시 조금 전에 집에 갔어요. 저는 그때까지 교실 밖으로 한 발자국도 나가지 않았어요."

27 "이상한 소리라도 들었나요?"

28 "제가 어떻게 듣겠어요? 제 음악 소리가 정말 컸어요."

29 "집에 가는 길에 누군가를 보았나요?"

30 "아니요, 누군가가 노래를 정말 끔찍하게 부르는 소리는 들었지만 누구도 보진 못했어요."

31 Shirley는 "더 이상 들을 필요는 없겠네요."라고 말했다. 그러고 나서 그녀는 도둑을 향했다.

32 "정말 곤경에 빠지기 전에 금메달을 돌려주는 게 어때요?"

※ 다음 우리말을 영어로 쓰시오.

1 Reese 교장은 젖은 운동장을 달려왔다.

➡ _____

2 "Shirley! Shirley! 네 도움이 필요하구나!"

➡ _____

3 Shirley는 Bakersville 중학교의 8학년 학생이었다.

➡ _____

4 그녀는 또한 그 마을 최고의 탐정이었다.

➡ _____

5 "무슨 일이 있나요?" Shirley가 물었다.

➡ _____

6 "누군가 장기 자랑 대회 금메달을 훔쳐갔어!"

➡ _____

7 Reese 교장은 Shirley를 범죄 현장으로 데려갔다.

➡ _____

8 유리창이 깨진 진열장이 있었다.

➡ _____

9 은메달과 동메달은 그곳에 그대로 있었다.

➡ _____

10 하지만 금메달은 사라졌다. 그 자리에는 시가 있었다.

➡ _____

11 내일은 장기 자랑 대회다. 금메달은 어디로 갔을까?

➡ _____

12 구석구석 찾아라. 당신은 나를 잡을 수 없어. 당신은 너무 느려.

➡ _____

13 Shirley는 "언제 이 사건이 일어났는지 말씀해 주시겠어요?"라고 물었다.

➡ _____

14 "어젯밤 9시가 조금 넘은 후에. 내가 순찰을 돌고 있었을 때 비명 소리가 들렸어. 나는 달려가서 Jocelyn과 이 상태인 진열장을 발견했지."

➡ _____

15 "어젯밤에 또 다른 누가 여기 있었는지 궁금해요."

➡ _____

16 "Sylvia와 Harry가 있었어. 그 두 사람 또한 장기 자랑을 위해 연습 중이었어. 내가 그들을 내 사무실로 부르마."

➡ _____

17 Jocelyn은 빨간색 짧은 곱슬머리를 가진 9학년 학생이었다.

➡ _____

18 "저는 제 노래를 연습하고 있었는데 목이 말랐어요. 저는 물을 가지러 교실 밖으로 나갔어요. 완전히 어두웠어요. 갑자기, 커다란 천둥소리가 났어요. 저는 도둑이 그 순간에 유리창을 깼다고 생각해요. 번개가 바로 뒤따랐고 1~2초 정도 밝아졌어요. 그때 저는 누군가가 진열장에서 도망치는 걸 봤어요."

➡ _____

_____

19 "도둑의 얼굴을 봤나요?"

➡ _____

20 "아니요, 도둑의 뒷모습만 봤어요. 하지만 그 도둑은 짧은 머리였어요."

➡ _____

21 다음은 8학년 학생인 Sylvia였다. 그녀는 긴 검은색 머리에 키가 컸다.

➡ _____

22 그녀는 말했다. "저는 교실에서 큰 소리로 제 시를 낭송하고 있었어요. 비명 소리를 듣고 밖으로 나갔어요. 진열장 옆에 한 소녀가 있었어요. 번개의 번쩍임과 어우러져 그것은 공포 영화 같았어요. 저는 겁이 나서 곧장 집으로 달려갔어요."

➡ _____

_____

23 "창이 깨지는 소리를 들었나요?"

➡ _____

24 "아니요, 천둥소리가 너무 컸어요. 음, 제가 그런 게 아니에요. 저는 어쨌든 1등을 할 거였으니까요."

➡ _____

25 7학년인 Harry는 짧은 금발을 가지고 있었다.

➡ _____

26 그는 말했다. "이봐요, 사람을 잘못 짚었어요. 저는 제 춤 동작을 연습하고 있었어요. 저는 9시 조금 전에 집에 갔어요. 저는 그때까지 교실 밖으로 한 발자국도 나가지 않았어요."

➡ _____

27 "이상한 소리라도 들었나요?"

➡ _____

28 "제가 어떻게 듣겠어요? 제 음악 소리가 정말 컸어요."

➡ _____

29 "집에 가는 길에 누군가를 보았나요?"

➡ _____

30 "아니요, 누군가가 노래를 정말 끔찍하게 부르는 소리는 들었지만 누구도 보진 못했어요."

➡ _____

31 Shirley는 "더 이상 들을 필요는 없겠네요."라고 말했다. 그러고 나서 그녀는 도둑을 향했다.

➡ _____

32 "정말 곤경에 빠지기 전에 금메달을 돌려주는 게 어때요?"

➡ _____

구석구석 지문 Test

※ 다음 우리말과 일치하도록 빈칸에 알맞은 말을 쓰시오.

Project

1. To the _____ _____,

2. Hello. We _____ _____ our treasure in the classroom. It is _____ _____.

3. Do you want to know _____ it is? Then _____ _____ _____.

4. First, _____ _____ a plant _____ the window. Look _____ the plant. You'll find a key.

5. Second, _____ _____ the key and _____ _____ _____ _____ of the classroom. You'll see the lockers.

6. The treasure is in the _____ _____ _____ _____ _____.

7. It _____ _____, so use the key _____ _____ it. Got it? Help _____.

1. 보물 사냥꾼들에게,
2. 안녕. 우리는 교실에 우리 보물을 숨겼어. 그것은 맛있는 것이야.
3. 그것이 어디에 있는지 알고 싶니? 그러면 다음 단계를 따라 봐.
4. 우선, 창문 옆에 있는 식물을 찾아. 그 식물 아래를 봐. 너는 열쇠 하나를 찾을 거야.
5. 두 번째, 그 열쇠를 들고 교실 뒤쪽으로 걸어가. 너는 사물함을 볼 거야.
6. 보물은 왼쪽에서 세 번째 사물함 안에 있어.
7. 그것은 잠겼으니 그것을 열기 위해 열쇠를 사용해. 알겠지? 많이 먹으렴.

Think and Write

1. When Rapunzel was a baby, a witch _____ _____ _____ a tall tower.

2. Rapunzel _____ _____ in the tower. She had _____ _____.

3. The witch used it _____ _____ _____ the tower.

4. The witch always said, "The _____ _____ is very dangerous."

5. One day, a prince _____ _____ _____ _____.

6. He said, "_____ _____. The world outside is wonderful."

7. Rapunzel said, "I don't know _____ _____ _____ _____." Rapunzel _____ _____.

8. Finally, she _____ _____ her mind. She _____ her hair and _____ _____ from the tower.

9. When she _____ the world _____ _____ _____ _____ _____, she couldn't believe her eyes. "_____ _____ _____ _____ _____!"

1. Rapunzel이 아기였을 때, 한 마녀가 그녀를 높은 탑에 가뒀다.
2. Rapunzel은 그 탑에서 자랐다. 그녀는 긴 머리카락을 가지고 있었다.
3. 마녀는 탑을 올라가기 위해 그 머리카락을 사용했다.
4. 마녀는 항상 "바깥세상은 매우 위험해."라고 말했다.
5. 어느 날, 한 왕자가 Rapunzel이 노래를 아름답게 부르고 있는 것을 들었다.
6. 그는 "내려와요. 바깥세상은 멋져요."라고 말했다.
7. Rapunzel은 "누가 사실을 말하고 있는지 모르겠어."라고 말했다. Rapunzel은 혼란스러웠다.
8. 마침내, 그녀는 결심했다. 그녀는 머리카락을 자르고 탑에서 내려왔다.
9. 그녀가 처음으로 세상과 마주했을 때, 그녀는 자신의 눈을 믿을 수 없었다. "정말 아름다운 세상이야!"

Check Up

1. A: Can _____ do _____ _____ _____?

2. B: _____. What is it?

3. A: Can you _____ _____ _____ _____ these balloons?

4. B: No _____.

1. A: 부탁 하나 해도 될까?
2. B: 물론이지. 뭔데?
3. A: 이 풍선들을 부는 것 좀 도와줄 수 있니?
4. B: 좋아.

※ 다음 우리말을 영어로 쓰시오.

Project

1. 보물 사냥꾼들에게.
   ➡ _____

2. 안녕. 우리는 교실에 우리 보물을 숨겼어. 그것은 맛있는 것이야.
   ➡ _____

3. 그것이 어디에 있는지 알고 싶니? 그러면 다음 단계를 따라 봐.
   ➡ _____

4. 우선, 창문 옆에 있는 식물을 찾아. 그 식물 아래를 봐. 너는 열쇠 하나를 찾을 거야.
   ➡ _____

5. 두 번째, 그 열쇠를 들고 교실 뒤쪽으로 걸어가. 너는 사물함을 볼 거야.
   ➡ _____

6. 보물은 왼쪽에서 세 번째 사물함 안에 있어.
   ➡ _____

7. 그것은 잠겼으니 그것을 열기 위해 열쇠를 사용해. 알겠지? 많이 먹으렴.
   ➡ _____

Think and Write

1. Rapunzel이 아기였을 때, 한 마녀가 그녀를 높은 탑에 가뒀다.
   ➡ _____

2. Rapunzel은 그 탑에서 자랐다. 그녀는 긴 머리카락을 가지고 있었다.
   ➡ _____

3. 마녀는 탑을 올라가기 위해 그 머리카락을 사용했다.
   ➡ _____

4. 마녀는 항상 "바깥세상은 매우 위험해."라고 말했다.
   ➡ _____

5. 어느 날, 한 왕자가 Rapunzel이 노래를 아름답게 부르고 있는 것을 들었다.
   ➡ _____

6. 그는 "내려와요. 바깥세상은 멋져요."라고 말했다.
   ➡ _____

7. Rapunzel은 "누가 사실을 말하고 있는지 모르겠어."라고 말했다. Rapunzel은 혼란스러웠다.
   ➡ _____

8. 마침내, 그녀는 결심했다. 그녀는 머리카락을 자르고 탑에서 내려왔다.
   ➡ _____

9. 그녀가 처음으로 세상과 마주했을 때, 그녀는 자신의 눈을 믿을 수 없었다. "정말 아름다운 세상이야!"
   ➡ _____

Check Up

1. A: 부탁 하나 해도 될까?
   ➡ _____

2. B: 물론이지. 뭔데?
   ➡ _____

3. A: 이 풍선들을 부는 것 좀 도와줄 수 있니?
   ➡ _____

4. B: 좋아.
   ➡ _____

※ 다음 영어를 우리말로 쓰시오.

01 bark

02 spread

03 package

04 cover

05 date

06 agree

07 signature

08 borrow

09 cool

10 meaning

11 entire

12 perfectly

13 envelope

14 situation

15 graduate

16 punish

17 inside

18 local

19 mean

20 receive

21 article

22 funny

23 grade

24 classmate

25 nearby

26 reporter

27 extra

28 decide

29 pleased

30 excited

31 satisfied

32 vocabulary

33 war

34 dictionary

35 have no choice

36 be over

37 by the time

38 take out

39 hold up

40 be worried about

41 on the way home

42 be famous for

43 be excited about

※ 다음 우리말을 영어로 쓰시오.

01 (개가) 짖다

02 의미하다

03 봉투

04 빌리다

05 서명

06 학년

07 받다

08 멋진

09 날짜를 적다; 날짜

10 기쁜, 기뻐하는

11 의미

12 처벌하다, 벌주다

13 (신문의) 기사

14 여분의, 추가의

15 만족하는

16 신이 난

17 재미있는

18 상황

19 퍼지다, 확산되다

20 졸업하다

21 소포

22 안에

23 지역의, 지방의

24 결정하다

25 완벽하게

26 기자

27 사전

28 보도하다, 덮다

29 인근의, 가까이의

30 재빨리, 빠르게

31 전체의, 온

32 어휘

33 전쟁

34 동의하다

35 더욱 더, 갈수록 더

36 ～로 유명하다

37 선택의 여지가 없다

38 쥐다, 잡다

39 (사전 등에서) 찾아보다

40 손을 쓸 수 없는

41 그때까지, ～할 때까지

42 집으로 가는 길에

43 ～에 대해 걱정하다

※ 다음 영영풀이에 알맞은 단어를 <보기>에서 골라 쓴 후, 우리말 뜻을 쓰시오.

1 _____ : to complete a course in education: _____

2 _____ : a flat paper container used for sending letters in: _____

3 _____ : to have the same opinion as somebody: _____

4 _____ : including everything, everyone or every part: _____

5 _____ : the idea that is represented by a word, phrase, etc.: _____

6 _____ : all the words that a person knows or uses: _____

7 _____ : more than is usual, expected, or than exists already: _____

8 _____ : a piece of writing about a particular subject in a newspaper: _____

9 _____ : a person who is or was in the same class as you at school or college: _____

10 _____ : a box, bag, etc. in which things are wrapped or packed: _____

11 _____ : a person who collects and reports news for newspapers, radio or television: _____

12 _____ : your name as you usually write it, for example at the end of a letter: _____

13 _____ : to take and use something that belongs to somebody else, and return it to them at a later time: _____

14 _____ : all the circumstances and things that are happening at a particular time and in a particular place: _____

15 _____ : to make somebody suffer because they have broken the law or done something wrong: _____

16 _____ : a book that gives a list of the words of a language in alphabetical order and explains what they mean, or gives a word for them in a foreign language: _____

보기			
vocabulary	dictionary	article	envelope
punish	entire	package	signature
reporter	borrow	situation	agree
extra	graduate	meaning	classmate

※ 다음 우리말과 일치하도록 빈칸에 알맞은 것을 골라 쓰시오.

1 Nick Allen was _____ about starting _____ _____, but he was _____ about one thing — Mrs. Granger's English class.

　　A. worried　　　B. grade　　　C. fifth　　　D. excited

2 Mrs. Granger was _____ _____ her _____ vocabulary _____.

　　A. lessons　　　B. famous　　　C. difficult　　　D. for

3 In the first _____, Mrs. Granger said, "Everyone should have a good _____. You can look _____ the _____ of new words in it."

　　A. meanings　　　B. class　　　C. dictionary　　　D. up

4 "Mrs. Granger? Who decides the _____ of words? I mean, who _____ that 'dog' _____ an animal that _____?" Nick asked.

　　A. means　　　B. meanings　　　C. barks　　　D. decided

5 "You did, Nick. You, me, and the _____ town and country. We all _____. That gives the word _____ _____."

　　A. agreed　　　B. meaning　　　C. entire　　　D. its

6 Nick wasn't _____. "When did I _____?" he said to _____.

　　A. agree　　　B. satisfied　　　C. himself

7 _____ the way home, he _____ to _____ Mrs. Granger's idea.

　　A. decided　　　B. on　　　C. test

8 He _____ _____ a pen and said, "_____ today, this is a *frindle*."

　　A. from　　　B. out　　　C. took

9 The next day, he _____ five friends to _____ the _____ *frindle*.

　　A. use　　　B. asked　　　C. word

10 _____ _____, Nick said, "Mrs. Granger, I _____ my *frindle* today."

　　A. forgot　　　B. class　　　C. during

11 His friend, John, _____ _____ a pen and said, "I have an _____ *frindle*. Do you want to _____ my *frindle*?"

　　A. up　　　B. extra　　　C. help　　　D. borrow

12 Mrs. Granger was _____ _____.

　　A. pleased　　　B. not

13 She said, "Your new word is cute, _____ it _____ has a _____ good name — a pen."

　　A. perfectly　　　B. already　　　C. but

14 Nick's classmates _____ this _____ and began to _____ the word _____ and more.

　　A. more　　　B. funny　　　C. use　　　D. found

15 _____ just three days, it _____ the _____ at school.

　　A. word　　　B. in　　　C. cool　　　D. became

1 Nick Allen은 5학년이 시작되는 것이 신났지만, 한 가지가 걱정되었다. 그것은 Granger 선생님의 영어 수업이었다.

2 Granger 선생님은 어려운 어휘 수업으로 유명했다.

3 첫 번째 시간에 Granger 선생님은 말했다. "모두 좋은 사전을 가지고 있어야 해요. 여러분은 사전에서 새 단어의 뜻을 찾을 수 있어요."

4 "Granger 선생님? 단어의 뜻은 누가 정하나요? 그러니까, '개'는 짖는 동물을 뜻한다고 누가 정했나요?" Nick이 물었다.

5 "네가 그랬지, Nick. 너와 나, 그리고 온 마을과 나라가 말이야. 우리 모두가 동의했단다. 그게 그 단어에게 의미를 부여하는 거야."

6 Nick은 마음에 들지 않았다. "내가 언제 동의했지?" 그는 혼잣말을 했다.

7 집에 가는 길에 Nick은 Granger 선생님의 생각을 시험하기로 결심했다.

8 그는 펜을 하나 꺼내서 말했다. "오늘부터 이것은 'frindle'이야."

9 그 다음날 Nick은 다섯 명의 친구들에게 단어 'frindle'을 사용해 달라고 부탁했다.

10 수업 중에 Nick이 말했다. "Granger 선생님, 오늘 'frindle'을 빠뜨리고 왔어요."

11 Nick의 친구인 John이 펜을 하나 들고서는 말했다. "나한테 여러분의 'frindle'이 있어. 내 'frindle'을 빌리고 싶니?"

12 Granger 선생님은 즐거워하지 않았다.

13 선생님이 말했다. "너희들의 새 단어는 귀엽지만, 그건 이미 'pen'이라는 완벽하게 좋은 이름이 있단다."

14 Nick의 학급 친구들은 이것을 재미있어 했고 더욱 더 그 단어를 사용하기 시작했다.

15 단지 3일 만에 학교에서 그것은 멋진 단어가 되었다.

16 Mrs. Granger said to Nick after class, "This is _____ out of _____. Can you tell your friends to _____ _____ *frindle*?"

    A. hand   B. getting   C. saying   D. stop

17 "I'm sorry, but I can't _____ it. It started _____ my word, but now it's the students' _____."

    A. as   B. stop   C. word

18 "Very well. Then I _____ _____ _____."

    A. choice   B. no   C. have

19 Mrs. Granger _____ _____ an envelope and asked Nick to _____ and _____ the back.

    A. date   B. out   C. sign   D. took

20 She said, "I'll _____ this letter to you _____ all this is _____."

    A. over   B. give   C. when

21 Nick _____, "She really _____ me."

    A. hates   B. thought

22 _____ week, Mrs. Granger _____ a war _____ *frindle*.

    A. began   B. next   C. with

23 She said that she would _____ any student _____ _____ it.

    A. using   B. punish   C. for

24 But this _____ made _____ _____.

    A. only   B. worse   C. things

25 The students wanted _____ _____ the word _____ and more.

    A. use   B. more   C. to

26 *Frindle* quickly _____ _____ middle and high schools.

    A. nearby   B. spread   C. to

27 _____ _____, a local newspaper reporter _____ an article on the situation and everyone in town _____ about it.

    A. wrote   B. after   C. knew   D. shortly

28 A month _____, a national television station _____ the news and everyone _____ _____ about *frindle*.

    A. out   B. covered   C. found   D. later

29 _____ the time Nick _____ _____ elementary school, most students in the country _____ the word.

    A. used   B. from   C. graduated   D. by

30 Time _____ _____ and Nick turned 21. _____ day, he _____ a package.

    A. received   B. by   C. flew   D. one

31 _____ it, he _____ a pen, an _____ and a dictionary.

    A. found   B. inside   C. envelope

32 The envelope had his _____ _____ fifth _____.

    A. grade   B. from   C. signature

33 The dictionary had a yellow _____. It _____, "_____ page 541."

    A. said   B. note   C. check

---

16 Granger 선생님은 수업 후에 Nick에게 말했다. "점점 손을 쓸 수 없게 되어 가는구나. 네 친구들에게 'frindle'을 말하는 것을 멈춰달라고 말해 줄래?"

17 "죄송하지만, 멈추게 할 수가 없어요. 그건 제 단어로 시작됐지만, 이제 그건 학생들의 단어예요."

18 "좋아. 그러면 선택의 여지가 없구나."

19 Granger 선생님은 봉투를 하나 꺼내더니 Nick에게 뒷면에 서명을 하고 날짜를 적게 했다.

20 선생님은 말했다. "이 모든 것이 끝나면 내가 이 편지를 너에게 줄게."

21 Nick은 생각했다. "선생님은 내가 정말 싫은가봐."

22 다음 주에 Granger 선생님은 'frindle'과의 전쟁을 시작했다.

23 선생님은 그 단어를 사용한다면 어떤 학생이든 벌을 줄 것이라고 말했다.

24 하지만 이것은 상황을 더 나쁘게 만들 뿐이었다.

25 학생들은 그 단어를 더욱 더 사용하고 싶어했다.

26 'frindle'은 근처의 중학교와 고등학교로 빠르게 퍼져 나갔다.

27 곧 지역 신문 기자가 그 상황에 관한 기사를 썼고, 마을의 모든 사람들이 그것에 관해 알게 되었다.

28 한 달 후에 한 전국 텔레비전 방송사에서 그 소식을 다루었고, 모든 사람들이 'frindle'에 관해 알게 되었다.

29 Nick이 초등학교를 졸업할 때쯤에는 이 나라의 대부분의 학생들이 그 단어를 사용했다.

30 시간은 흘러 Nick은 21살이 되었다. 어느 날 Nick은 소포를 하나 받았다.

31 소포 안에는 펜 한 자루, 봉투 한 장, 그리고 사전 한 권이 있었다.

32 봉투에는 5학년 때의 그의 서명이 있었다.

33 사전에는 노란색 쪽지가 있었다. "541쪽을 확인해 봐."라고 적혀 있었다.

※ 다음 우리말과 일치하도록 빈칸에 알맞은 말을 쓰시오.

1 Nick Allen _____ _____ _____ starting _____ _____, but he _____ _____ _____ one thing — Mrs. Granger's English class.

2 Mrs. Granger _____ _____ _____ her difficult _____ _____.

3 In the first class, Mrs. Granger said, "Everyone _____ _____ _____ _____ _____. You _____ _____ _____ the _____ of _____ _____ in it."

4 "Mrs. Granger? Who decides _____ _____ of words? I mean, who decided that 'dog' _____ an animal that _____?" Nick asked.

5 "You did, Nick. You, me, and the _____ _____ and country. We all _____. That gives the word _____ _____."

6 Nick wasn't _____. "When _____ _____ _____ _____?" he _____ _____ _____.

7 _____ the way home, he _____ to test Mrs. Granger's idea.

8 He _____ _____ a pen and said, "_____ today, this is a *frindle*."

9 The next day, he _____ five friends _____ _____ the word *frindle*.

10 _____ _____, Nick said, "Mrs. Granger, I _____ my *frindle* today."

11 His friend, John, _____ _____ a pen and said, "I have an _____ *frindle*. Do you want _____ _____ my *frindle*?"

12 Mrs. Granger _____ _____ _____.

13 She said, "Your new word is cute, _____ it _____ _____ a _____ good name — a pen."

14 Nick's classmates _____ this _____ and began _____ the word _____ _____ _____.

15 _____ just three days, it _____ the _____ _____ at school.

1 Nick Allen은 5학년이 시작되는 것이 신났지만, 한 가지가 걱정되었다. 그것은 Granger 선생님의 영어 수업이었다.

2 Granger 선생님은 어려운 어휘 수업으로 유명했다.

3 첫 번째 시간에 Granger 선생님은 말했다. "모두 좋은 사전을 가지고 있어야 해요. 여러분은 사전에서 새 단어의 뜻을 찾을 수 있어요."

4 "Granger 선생님? 단어의 뜻은 누가 정하나요? 그러니까, '개'는 짖는 동물을 뜻한다고 누가 정했나요?" Nick이 물었다.

5 "네가 그랬지, Nick. 너와 나, 그리고 온 마을과 나라가 말이야. 우리 모두가 동의했단다. 그게 그 단어에게 의미를 부여하는 거야."

6 Nick은 마음에 들지 않았다. "내가 언제 동의했지?" 그는 혼잣말을 했다.

7 집에 가는 길에 Nick은 Granger 선생님의 생각을 시험하기로 결심했다.

8 그는 펜을 하나 꺼내서 말했다. "오늘부터 이것은 'frindle'이야."

9 그 다음날 Nick은 다섯 명의 친구들에게 단어 'frindle'을 사용해 달라고 부탁했다.

10 수업 중에 Nick이 말했다. "Granger 선생님, 오늘 'frindle'을 빠뜨리고 왔어요."

11 Nick의 친구인 John이 펜을 하나 들고서는 말했다. "나한테 여분의 'frindle'이 있어. 내 'frindle'을 빌리고 싶니?"

12 Granger 선생님은 즐거워하지 않았다.

13 선생님이 말했다. "너희들의 새 단어는 귀엽지만, 그건 이미 'pen'이라는 완벽하게 좋은 이름이 있단다."

14 Nick의 학급 친구들은 이것을 재미있어 했고 더욱 더 그 단어를 사용하기 시작했다.

15 단지 3일 만에 학교에서 그것은 멋진 단어가 되었다.

16 Mrs. Granger _____ _____ Nick _____ _____, "This is _____ _____ _____ _____. Can you tell your friends _____ _____ _____ *frindle*?"

17 "I'm sorry, but I can't _____ _____. It started _____ my word, but now it's the _____ _____."

18 "Very well. Then I have _____ _____."

19 Mrs. Granger _____ _____ an envelope and _____ Nick _____ _____ and _____ the back.

20 She said, "_____ _____ this letter _____ _____ when all this _____ _____."

21 Nick _____, "She really _____ me."

22 Next week, Mrs. Granger _____ a war _____ *frindle*.

23 She said that she would _____ any student _____ _____ it.

24 But this only _____ _____ _____.

25 The students wanted _____ _____ the word _____ _____ _____.

26 *Frindle* quickly _____ _____ _____ middle and high schools.

27 _____ _____, a local newspaper reporter _____ an article _____ the situation and everyone in town _____ _____ _____.

28 _____ _____ _____, a national television station _____ the news and everyone _____ _____ _____ *frindle*.

29 _____ _____ _____ Nick _____ _____ elementary school, _____ _____ in the country _____ the word.

30 Time _____ _____ and Nick turned 21. _____ _____, he _____ a package.

31 _____ _____, he _____ a pen, an _____ and a _____.

32 The envelope had his _____ _____ _____ _____.

33 The dictionary had a _____ _____. _____ _____, "Check page 541."

---

16 Granger 선생님은 수업 후에 Nick에게 말했다. "점점 손을 쓸 수 없게 되어 가는구나. 네 친구들에게 'frindle'을 말하는 것을 멈춰달라고 말해 줄래?"

17 "죄송하지만, 멈추게 할 수가 없어요. 그건 제 단어로 시작됐지만, 이제 그건 학생들의 단어예요."

18 "좋아. 그러면 선택의 여지가 없구나."

19 Granger 선생님은 봉투를 하나 꺼내더니 Nick에게 뒷면에 서명을 하고 날짜를 적게 했다.

20 선생님은 말했다. "이 모든 것이 끝나면 내가 이 편지를 너에게 줄게."

21 Nick은 생각했다. "선생님은 내가 정말 싫은가봐."

22 다음 주에 Granger 선생님은 'frindle'과의 전쟁을 시작했다.

23 선생님은 그 단어를 사용한다면 어떤 학생이든 벌을 줄 것이라고 말했다.

24 하지만 이것은 상황을 더 나쁘게 만들 뿐이었다.

25 학생들은 그 단어를 더욱 더 사용하고 싶어했다.

26 'frindle'은 근처의 중학교와 고등학교로 빠르게 퍼져 나갔다.

27 곧 지역 신문 기자가 그 상황에 관한 기사를 썼고, 마을의 모든 사람들이 그것에 관해 알게 되었다.

28 한 달 후에 한 전국 텔레비전 방송사에서 그 소식을 다루었고, 모든 사람들이 'frindle'에 관해 알게 되었다.

29 Nick이 초등학교를 졸업할 때쯤에는 이 나라의 대부분의 학생들이 그 단어를 사용했다.

30 시간은 흘러 Nick은 21살이 되었다. 어느 날 Nick은 소포를 하나 받았다.

31 소포 안에는 펜 한 자루, 봉투 한 장, 그리고 사전 한 권이 있었다.

32 봉투에는 5학년 때의 그의 서명이 있었다.

33 사전에는 노란색 쪽지가 있었다. "541쪽을 확인해 봐."라고 적혀 있었다.

※ 다음 문장을 우리말로 쓰시오.

1 ▶ Nick Allen was excited about starting fifth grade, but he was worried about one thing
— Mrs. Granger's English class.

➡ _____

2 ▶ Mrs. Granger was famous for her difficult vocabulary lessons.

➡ _____

3 ▶ In the first class, Mrs. Granger said, "Everyone should have a good dictionary.
You can look up the meanings of new words in it."

➡ _____

_____

4 ▶ "Mrs. Granger? Who decides the meanings of words? I mean, who decided that 'dog' means
an animal that barks?" Nick asked.

➡ _____

5 ▶ "You did, Nick. You, me, and the entire town and country. We all agreed.
That gives the word its meaning."

➡ _____

_____

6 ▶ Nick wasn't satisfied. "When did I agree?" he said to himself.

➡ _____

7 ▶ On the way home, he decided to test Mrs. Granger's idea.

➡ _____

8 ▶ He took out a pen and said, "From today, this is a *frindle* ."

➡ _____

9 ▶ The next day, he asked five friends to use the word *frindle*.

➡ _____

10 ▶ During class, Nick said, "Mrs. Granger, I forgot my frindle today."

➡ _____

11 ▶ His friend, John, held up a pen and said, "I have an extra *frindle* . Do you want to borrow my *frindle*?"

➡ _____

12 ▶ Mrs. Granger was not pleased.

➡ _____

13 ▶ She said, "Your new word is cute, but it already has a perfectly good name — a pen."

➡ _____

14 ▶ Nick's classmates found this funny and began to use the word more and more.

➡ _____

15 ▶ In just three days, it became the cool word at school.

➡ _____

16 Mrs. Granger said to Nick after class, "This is getting out of hand. Can you tell your friends to stop saying *frindle*?"
➡ _____
_____

17 "I'm sorry, but I can't stop it. It started as my word, but now it's the students' word."
➡ _____

18 "Very well. Then I have no choice."
➡ _____

19 Mrs. Granger took out an envelope and asked Nick to sign and date the back.
➡ _____

20 She said, "I'll give this letter to you when all this is over."
➡ _____

21 Nick thought, "She really hates me."
➡ _____

22 Next week, Mrs. Granger began a war with *frindle*.
➡ _____

23 She said that she would punish any student for using it.
➡ _____

24 But this only made things worse.
➡ _____

25 The students wanted to use the word more and more.
➡ _____

26 *Frindle* quickly spread to nearby middle and high schools.
➡ _____

27 Shortly after, a local newspaper reporter wrote an article on the situation and everyone in town knew about it.
➡ _____

28 A month later, a national television station covered the news and everyone found out about *frindle*.
➡ _____

29 By the time Nick graduated from elementary school, most students in the country used the word.
➡ _____

30 Time flew by and Nick turned 21. One day, he received a package.
➡ _____

31 Inside it, he found a pen, an envelope and a dictionary.
➡ _____

32 The envelope had his signature from fifth grade.
➡ _____

33 The dictionary had a yellow note. It said, "Check page 541."
➡ _____

※ 다음 괄호 안의 단어들을 우리말에 맞도록 바르게 배열하시오.

1 (Allen / Nick / excited / was / starting / about / grade, / fifth / but / was / he / about / worried / thing / one / — / Granger's / Mrs. / class. / English)
➡ _____

2 (Granger / Mrs. / famous / was / her / for / vocabulary / lessons. / difficult)
➡ _____

3 (the / in / class, / first / Granger / Mrs. / said, / "everyone / have / should / a / dictionary. / good // can / you / look / the / up / meanings / new / of / it." / in / words)
➡ _____

4 (Granger? / "Mrs. // decides / who / meanings / words? / of / the // mean, / I / decided / who / 'dog' / that / an / means / barks?" / that / animal // asked. / Nick)
➡ _____

5 (did, / "you / Nick. // me, / you, / and / entire / the / country. / and / town // all / we / agreed. // gives / that / word / the / meaning." / its)
➡ _____

6 (wasn't / Nick / satisfied. // "when / I / did / agree?" / said / he / himself. / to)
➡ _____

7 (the / on / home, / way / decided / he / test / to / Granger's / Mrs. / idea.)
➡ _____

8 (took / he / a / out / and / pen / said, / "from / today, / is / this / *frindle*." / a)
➡ _____

9 (next / the / day, / asked / he / friends / five / use / to / *frindle*. / word / the)
➡ _____

10 (class, / during / said, / Nick / Granger, / "Mrs. / forgot / I / today." / *frindle* / my)
➡ _____

11 (friend, / his / John, / up / held / pen / a / and / said, / "I / an / extra / have / *frindle*. // you / do / want / borrow / to / *frindle*?" / my)
➡ _____

12 (Granger / Mrs. / was / pleased. / not)
➡ _____

13 (said, / she / "your / word / new / cute, / is / it / but / already / has / perfectly / a / name / good / — / pen." / a)
➡ _____

14 (classmates / Nick's / this / found / funny / began / and / use / to / word / the / more / and / more.)
➡ _____

15 (just / in / days, / three / became / it / cool / the / school. / at / word)
➡ _____

1 Nick Allen은 5학년이 시작되는 것이 신났지만, 한 가지가 걱정되었다. 그것은 Granger 선생님의 영어 수업이었다.

2 Granger 선생님은 어려운 어휘 수업으로 유명했다.

3 첫 번째 시간에 Granger 선생님은 말했다. "모두 좋은 사전을 가지고 있어야 해요. 여러분은 사전에서 새 단어의 뜻을 찾을 수 있어요."

4 "Granger 선생님? 단어의 뜻은 누가 정하나요? 그러니까, '개'는 짖는 동물을 뜻한다고 누가 정했나요?" Nick이 물었다.

5 "네가 그랬지, Nick. 너와 나, 그리고 온 마을과 나라가 말이야. 우리 모두가 동의했단다. 그게 그 단어에게 의미를 부여하는 거야."

6 Nick은 마음에 들지 않았다. "내가 언제 동의했지?" 그는 혼잣말을 했다.

7 집에 가는 길에 Nick은 Granger 선생님의 생각을 시험하기로 결심했다.

8 그는 펜을 하나 꺼내서 말했다. "오늘부터 이것은 'frindle'이야."

9 그 다음날 Nick은 다섯 명의 친구들에게 단어 'frindle'을 사용해 달라고 부탁했다.

10 수업 중에 Nick이 말했다. "Granger 선생님, 오늘 'frindle'을 빠뜨리고 왔어요."

11 Nick의 친구인 John이 펜을 하나 들고서는 말했다. "나한테 여분의 'frindle'이 있어. 내 'frindle'을 빌리고 싶니?"

12 Granger 선생님은 즐거워하지 않았다.

13 선생님이 말했다. "너희들의 새 단어는 귀엽지만, 그건 이미 'pen'이라는 완벽하게 좋은 이름이 있단다."

14 Nick의 학급 친구들은 이것을 재미있어 했고 더욱 더 그 단어를 사용하기 시작했다.

15 단지 3일 만에 학교에서 그것은 멋진 단어가 되었다.

16 (Granger / Mrs. / to / said / after / Nick / class, / "this / getting / is / of / out / hand. // you / can / your / tell / to / friends / saying / stop / *frindle?*")
➡ _____

17 (sorry, / "I'm / but / can't / I / it. / stop // started / it / my / as / word, / now / but / it's / word." / students' / the)
➡ _____

18 (well. / "very // I / then / choice." / no / have)
➡ _____

19 (Granger / Mrs. / out / took / envelope / an / and / Nick / asked / to / date / and / sign / back. / the)
➡ _____

20 (said, / she / "I'll / this / give / letter / you / to / when / this / all / over." / is)
➡ _____

21 (thought, / Nick / "she / hates / really / me.")
➡ _____

22 (week, / next / Granger / Mrs. / a / began / war / *frindle.* / with)
➡ _____

23 (said / she / that / would / she / punish / student / any / it. / using / for)
➡ _____

24 (this / but / made / only / worse. / things)
➡ _____

25 (students / the / to / wanted / use / word / the / and / more / more.)
➡ _____

26 (quickly / *frindle* / to / spread / middle / nearby / and / schools. / high)
➡ _____

27 (after, / shortly / local / a / reporter / newspaper / an / wrote / article / the / on / situation / and / in / everyone / knew / town / it. / about)
➡ _____

28 (month / a / later, / national / a / station / television / covered / news / the / and / found / everyone / about / out / *frindle.*)
➡ _____

29 (the / by / time / graduated / Nick / from / school, / elementary / students / most / the / in / country / word. / the / used)
➡ _____

30 (flew / time / and / by / Nick / 21. / turned // day, / one / received / package. / a / he)
➡ _____

31 (it, / inside / found / he / pen, / a / envelope / an / and / dictionary. / a)
➡ _____

32 (envelope / the / his / had / from / signature / grade. / fifth)
➡ _____

33 (dictionary / the / a / had / yellow / note. // said, / it / page / "check / 541.")
➡ _____

16 Granger 선생님은 수업 후에 Nick에게 말했다. "점점 손을 쓸 수 없게 되어 가는구나. 네 친구들에게 'frindle'을 말하는 것을 멈춰달라고 말해 줄래?"

17 "죄송하지만, 멈추게 할 수가 없어요. 그건 제 단어로 시작됐지만, 이제 그건 학생들의 단어예요."

18 "좋아. 그러면 선택의 여지가 없구나."

19 Granger 선생님은 봉투를 하나 꺼내더니 Nick에게 뒷면에 서명을 하고 날짜를 적게 했다.

20 선생님은 말했다. "이 모든 것이 끝나면 내가 이 편지를 너에게 줄게."

21 Nick은 생각했다. "선생님은 내가 정말 싫은가봐."

22 다음 주에 Granger 선생님은 'frindle'과의 전쟁을 시작했다.

23 선생님은 그 단어를 사용한다면 어떤 학생이든 벌을 줄 것이라고 말했다.

24 하지만 이것은 상황을 더 나쁘게 만들 뿐이었다.

25 학생들은 그 단어를 더욱 더 사용하고 싶어했다.

26 'frindle'은 근처의 중학교와 고등학교로 빠르게 퍼져 나갔다.

27 곧 지역 신문 기자가 그 상황에 관한 기사를 썼고, 마을의 모든 사람들이 그것에 관해 알게 되었다.

28 한 달 후에 한 전국 텔레비전 방송사에 서 그 소식을 다루었고, 모든 사람들이 'frindle'에 관해 알게 되었다.

29 Nick이 초등학교를 졸업할 때쯤에는 이 나라의 대부분의 학생들이 그 단어를 사용했다.

30 시간은 흘러 Nick은 21살이 되었다. 어느 날 Nick은 소포를 하나 받았다.

31 소포 안에는 펜 한 자루, 봉투 한 장, 그리고 사전 한 권이 있었다.

32 봉투에는 5학년 때의 그의 서명이 있었다.

33 사전에는 노란색 쪽지가 있었다. "541쪽을 확인해 봐."라고 적혀 있었다.

※ 다음 우리말을 영어로 쓰시오.

1 Nick Allen은 5학년이 시작되는 것이 신났지만, 한 가지가 걱정되었다. 그것은 Granger 선생님의 영어 수업이었다.

➡ _____

_____

2 Granger 선생님은 어려운 어휘 수업으로 유명했다.

➡ _____

3 첫 번째 시간에 Granger 선생님은 말했다. "모두 좋은 사전을 가지고 있어야 해요. 여러분은 사전에서 새 단어의 뜻을 찾을 수 있어요."

➡ _____

_____

4 "Granger 선생님? 단어의 뜻은 누가 정하나요? 그러니까, '개'는 짖는 동물을 뜻한다고 누가 정했나요?" Nick이 물었다.

➡ _____

5 "네가 그랬지, Nick. 너와 나, 그리고 온 마을과 나라가 말이야. 우리 모두가 동의했단다. 그게 그 단어에게 의미를 부여하는 거야."

➡ _____

6 Nick은 마음에 들지 않았다. "내가 언제 동의했지?" 그는 혼잣말을 했다.

➡ _____

7 집에 가는 길에 Nick은 Granger 선생님의 생각을 시험하기로 결심했다.

➡ _____

8 그는 펜을 하나 꺼내서 말했다. "오늘부터 이것은 'frindle'이야."

➡ _____

9 그 다음날 Nick은 다섯 명의 친구들에게 단어 'frindle'을 사용해 달라고 부탁했다.

➡ _____

10 수업 중에 Nick이 말했다. "Granger 선생님, 오늘 'frindle'을 빠뜨리고 왔어요."

➡ _____

11 Nick의 친구인 John이 펜을 하나 들고서는 말했다. "나한테 여분의 'frindle'이 있어. 내 'frindle'을 빌리고 싶니?"

➡ _____

12 Granger 선생님은 즐거워하지 않았다.

➡ _____

13 선생님이 말했다. "너희들의 새 단어는 귀엽지만, 그건 이미 'pen'이라는 완벽하게 좋은 이름이 있단다."

➡ _____

14 Nick의 학급 친구들은 이것을 재미있어 했고 더욱 더 그 단어를 사용하기 시작했다.

➡ _____

15 단지 3일 만에 학교에서 그것은 멋진 단어가 되었다.

➡ _____

16 Granger 선생님은 수업 후에 Nick에게 말했다. "점점 손을 쓸 수 없게 되어 가는구나. 네 친구들에게 'frindle'을 말하는 것을 멈춰달라고 말해 줄래?"

➡ _____

_____

17 "죄송하지만, 멈추게 할 수가 없어요. 그건 제 단어로 시작됐지만, 이제 그건 학생들의 단어예요."

➡ _____

18 "좋아. 그러면 선택의 여지가 없구나."

➡ _____

19 Granger 선생님은 봉투를 하나 꺼내더니 Nick에게 뒷면에 서명을 하고 날짜를 적게 했다.

➡ _____

20 선생님은 말했다. "이 모든 것이 끝나면 내가 이 편지를 너에게 줄게."

➡ _____

21 Nick은 생각했다. "선생님은 내가 정말 싫은가봐."

➡ _____

22 다음 주에 Granger 선생님은 'frindle'과의 전쟁을 시작했다.

➡ _____

23 선생님은 그 단어를 사용한다면 어떤 학생이든 벌을 줄 것이라고 말했다.

➡ _____

24 하지만 이것은 상황을 더 나쁘게 만들 뿐이었다.

➡ _____

25 학생들은 그 단어를 더욱 더 사용하고 싶어했다.

➡ _____

26 'frindle'은 근처의 중학교와 고등학교로 빠르게 퍼져 나갔다.

➡ _____

27 곧 지역 신문 기자가 그 상황에 관한 기사를 썼고, 마을의 모든 사람들이 그것에 관해 알게 되었다.

➡ _____

28 한 달 후에 한 전국 텔레비전 방송사에 서 그 소식을 다루었고, 모든 사람들이 'frindle'에 관해 알게 되었다.

➡ _____

29 Nick이 초등학교를 졸업할 때쯤에는 이 나라의 대부분의 학생들이 그 단어를 사용했다.

➡ _____

30 시간은 흘러 Nick은 21살이 되었다. 어느 날 Nick은 소포를 하나 받았다.

➡ _____

31 소포 안에는 펜 한 자루, 봉투 한 장, 그리고 사전 한 권이 있었다.

➡ _____

32 봉투에는 5학년 때의 그의 서명이 있었다.

➡ _____

33 사전에는 노란색 쪽지가 있었다. "541쪽을 확인해 봐."라고 적혀 있었다.

➡ _____

영어 기출 문제집

적중100

2학기

정답 및 해설

동아 | 이병민

중 2

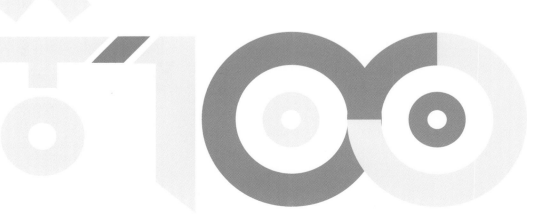

Lesson
7

Can I Trust It?

시험대비 실력평가   p.08

01 simple   02 ②   03 ④
04 (1) express (2) advertisement (3) belief
05 ③   06 ①
07 (1) purple (2) beliefs (3) genre (4) friendship

01 주어진 단어의 관계는 반의어 관계를 나타낸다. simple: 간단
　 한, complex: 복잡한
02 누군가가 한 무언가에 대한 돈 등과 같은 상을 가리키는 말은
　 award(상)이다. penalty: 벌금 fare: 운임 fee: 요금
03 prove: 증명하다
05 주어진 문장에서 touching은 '감동적인'을 뜻하며 이와 같은 의
　 미로 쓰인 것은 ③번이다. 나머지는 모두 '만지다'를 의미한다.
06 navy: 해군, 남색
07 belief: 신념, purple: 보라색, genre: 장르, friendship: 우
　 정

서술형 시험대비   p.09

01 difference 02 (1) lie (2) pocket (3) based
03 (1) traditional (2) desert (3) author
　 (4) connection (5) award (6) fantasy
04 (1) From now on, let's start playing the soccer
　 game.
　 (2) Before you go out, check out the light again.
　 (3) Who is the main character in this movie?
05 (1) Can you explain the rules of the game?
　 (2) If you mix red with blue, you can get purple.
　 (3) I can prove that he didn't break the window.
　 (4) Did you see the advertisement on the
　 newspaper?

01 주어진 빈칸에 different의 명사형 difference가 와야 한다.
02 lie: 거짓말하다, pocket: 주머니, be based on: ~을 바탕으로
　 하다
03 fantasy: 공상, traditional: 전통적인, connection: 연관성,
　 author: 작가, desert: 사막, award: 상 primarily: 주로

교과서 Conversation

핵심 Check   p.10~11

1 (1) recommend / How about (2) Can you suggest
　 / Why (3) What do you think would be
2 (1) How do you like (2) I'm not satisfied with it
　 (3) What do you like

교과서 대화문 익히기

Check(√) True or False   p.12

1 T 2 T 3 T 4 F

교과서 확인학습   p.14~15

Listen & Speak 1-A
recommend / yet / number one

Listen & Speak 1-B
help / backpack, recommend one / How about, these
days / different / navy, pockets / take

Listen & Speak 2-A
got / like most about it / takes

Listen & Talk 2-B
like, trip / happy / Where else / wonderful place /
perfect trip / walking up / worth it

Real Life Talk – Step 1
can you recommend / Why don't / about / delicious,
recommend / the prices / think, too / Sounds like,
How, the service / slow / check it out / problem, Enjoy

Real Life Talk – Step 2
recommend a book for me / about / What, like / main
character, special / Sounds

시험대비 기본평가   p.16

01 Can you recommend a good movie?
02 ⑤   03 What do you like most about it?
04 (B) the new smartphone (C) the camera

01 ④ → was   02 ②   03 ④

04 can you recommend a book for me?

05 She likes the main character.

06 ①   07 ⓐ Antonio's   ⓑ the service

08 ⑤   09 ②   10 ⑤   11 ③

12 ⑤

01 동명사가 주어로 쓰였으므로 동사는 단수 형태인 was가 적절하다.

02 문맥상 상반의 접속사 but이 알맞다.

03 ④ Jack은 석굴암까지 걸어 올라가는 것이 가치가 있었을 것이라고 믿었다.

06 주어진 문장은 식당을 추천하고 있는 표현이므로 (A)가 적절하다.

09 이어지는 대화에서 빨간색을 추천한 이유를 설명하고 있으므로 (B)가 적절하다.

10 소년의 오래된 배낭이 얼마나 많은 주머니를 갖고 있었는지는 알 수 없다.

11 (A)의 빈칸에 들어갈 말로 만족을 나타내는 표현이 알맞다. ③은 실망을 나타내고 있다.

12 ⑤ 위 대화를 통해 Tom이 언제 멋진 사진을 찍었는지 알 수 없다.

01 I haven't seen it yet.

02 She recommended *Star Wars*.

03 It's *Star Wars*.   04 It is red.

05 It has side pockets.

06 Because his old backpack was red.

07 (A) How   (B) Where   (C) Where

08 (A) Gyeongju   (B) Bulguksa   (C) Seokguram

02 Emily는 Brian에게 *Star Wars*를 추천하였다.

03 지금 1위 영화는 *Star Wars*이다.

04 요즘 가장 인기 있는 색은 빨간색이다.

05 남색 가방은 양옆에 주머니가 있다.

06 소년이 빨간색 배낭을 원하지 않은 이유는 그의 옛 배낭이 빨간색이기 때문이다.

08 나는 경주 여행을 갔다. 이곳은 정말로 멋지고 아름다운 도시였다. 나는 첨성대뿐만 아니라 불국사도 방문했다. 그들은 모두 훌륭한 곳이었다. 나는 석굴암까지 올라갔을 때 피곤했다. 그러나 그것은 가치있는 일이었다. 나는 경주로 간 완벽한 여행이 정말 마음에 들었다.

1 (1) so bright that   (2) so small that   (3) so lazy that

2 (1) that(또는 which) Elizabeth made

(2) that(또는 which) he lost

(3) that(또는 which) Molly really liked

(4) who(m)(또는 that) she saw

01 (1) who → which(또는 that)

(2) which → who(m)(또는 that)   (3) very → so

(4) so → too

02 (1) who(m) Tom likes   (2) so easy that

(3) so rich that, that   (4) that I sit on[in]

03 (1) She didn't touch the food that she didn't like.

(2) Those babies whom the woman is looking after look very cute.

(3) The shoes are so tight that my feet hurt.

(4) Her commute was so far that she bought a car.

01 (1), (2) 목적격 관계대명사가 쓰이고 있으므로 생략해도 무방하다. (3) 'so ~ that'은 원인과 결과를 나타내는 어구이며 that은 완전한 절을 이끈다. 'too ~ to V'는 '너무 ~해서 …할 수 없는'의 의미이다.

02 (1), (4) 'Tom이 많이 좋아하는 그 소녀', '내가 앉아 있는 이 의자'이므로 관계사절로 명사를 수식할 수 있다. (2), (3) 'so ~ that'은 원인과 결과를 나타내는 어구이다.

03 (1), (2) '좋아하지 않는 음식', '그 여자가 돌보고 있는 저 아기들'이므로 the food that she didn't like, the babies whom she is looking after로 쓰는 것이 옳다.

01 ④   02 ④   03 ②, ④

04 The book which[that] you borrowed from the library was written by my mother.

05 ③   06 ②   07 ⑤

08 The computer is so small that I can carry it around.

09 ③   10 ③

11 Julia studied so hard that she could pass the important exam.

12 The traffic was so heavy that I couldn't be here on time.

p.26~27

13 ③   14 ⑤   15 which[that] we watched last week   16 ②   17 ②

18 that they sang together was beautiful   19 ⑤

20 ④   21 I am so shy that I can't talk in front of many people.

22 (1) which[that] I am interested

   (2) which I am interested

01 피곤한 것이 원인이고 일찍 잔 것은 결과이므로 ④번이 옳다.

02 어제 만난 여자가 너무 상냥해서 친구가 되고 싶었다는 의미이다. 원인과 결과를 나타내는 어구인 'so ~ that' 구문을 쓰는 것이 옳다.

03 목적격 관계대명사가 적절하다. 사물이 선행사이므로 which나 that이 옳다.

04 목적격 관계대명사를 이용하면 '네가 도서관에서 빌린 그 책은 우리 엄마에 의해 쓰였다.'는 의미의 문장을 만들 수 있다.

05 'too ~ to V'는 '너무 ~해서 V할 수 없는'이라는 의미이다. 'so ~ that ... can't'와 같다.

06 ② 핵심 주어인 자전거는 단수이므로 is라고 쓰는 것이 옳다.

07 hard는 부사로 '세게'라는 의미를 갖는다. hardly 역시 부사이지만 '거의 ~하지 않는'이라는 의미이다. 두 번째 빈칸에는 목적격 관계대명사가 쓰이므로 that 혹은 which가 온다.

08 컴퓨터가 너무 작은 것이 원인이 되어 내가 가지고 다닐 수 있게 되었다. 따라서 'so ~ that' 구문을 이용하여 문장을 만들 수 있다. carry around: 휴대하다, 가지고 다니다

09 ③번은 주격 관계대명사이다. 목적격 관계대명사 혹은 '주격 관계대명사+be동사'는 생략 가능하다. run across: 우연히 마주치다

10 모두 완전한 명사절을 이끄는 접속사 that이지만, ③번은 불완전한 절을 이끄는 관계대명사 that이다.

11 Julia가 공부를 열심히 해서 그 결과 시험에 합격할 수 있었다는 하나의 문장을 쓸 수 있다.

12 원인과 결과를 나타내는 어구를 이용하여 늦은 이유를 설명하면 된다. 주어진 단어를 이용한다면 '교통 체증이 너무 심해서 제때에 올 수 없었다.'라고 쓸 수 있다.

13 결과를 나타내는 절을 이끌거나 목적격 관계대명사 역할을 할 수 있는 것은 that이다.

14 ⑤ 'Where is the dog which follows you all the time?'이라고 쓰는 것이 옳다.

15 목적격 관계대명사이므로 that을 써도 무방하다.

16 'so ~ that'은 원인과 결과를 나타내는 어구이다. 같은 의미가 되기 위해서는 빈칸에 because를 쓰는 것이 옳다.

17 나를 슬프게 하는 것이 원인이고 라디오를 끈 것이 결과이므로 ②번이 가장 적절하다.

18 목적격 관계대명사 that을 대신하여 which를 쓰거나 생략해도 무방하다.

19 'too ~ to V'는 '너무 ~해서 V할 수 없는'이란 의미이다. 따라서 ⑤번이 옳다.

20 ① looks ② couldn't ③ whom(또는 that) ⑤ diligent

21 너무 수줍어서 많은 사람들 앞에서 말할 수 없다는 문장을 쓸 수 있다.

22 관계대명사 that은 전치사의 목적어로 쓰일 수 없는 것에 유의하여 답을 쓴다.

🦉 서술형 시험대비 p.26~27

01 The girl whom you introduced to me is very popular.

02 was so heavy that Sandra couldn't carry it. 또는 was too heavy for Sandra to carry

03 which Ross wrote was so amazing that I was moved to tears

04 (1) which(또는 that)   (2) who(또는 that)

   (3) whom(또는 that)

05 (1) Penny couldn't eat anything because she was very sick.

   (2) Penny was so sick that she couldn't eat anything.

06 (1) which Tom is driving is not his

   (2) picked some roses which Catherine planted

   (3) know the person who(m) you took a trip with

07 so warm that he doesn't need to buy another coat

08 (1) Sally speaks English so well that you would think it is her native language.

   (2) The music was so loud that you could hear it from miles away.

   (3) Gabriel is so beautiful that any man would love to be with her.

09 The soup was so hot that it burned my tongue.

10 Jody is the student who(m) Ms. Galler is looking for.

11 (1) The boy who(m) you saw yesterday is my brother.

   (2) The dress which she is wearing was designed by a famous person.

12 The people whom I call most often are my mother and my sisters.

13 so happy that

14 The party was so enjoyable that no one wanted to leave.

15 She woke up so early that she was tired.

01 '네가 나에게 소개해 준 그 소녀'이므로 관계사절이 the girl을 수식하도록 문장을 만든다.

02 상자가 너무 무거워서 Sandra는 그것을 나르지 않았다고 쓸 수
있다.

03 which 대신 that을 쓰거나 또는 생략할 수 있다.

04 (1), (3)번에 쓰인 관계대명사는 목적격이므로 생략해도 무방하
다.

05 Penny는 너무 아파서 아무것도 먹을 수 없었다는 의미이다.

06 목적격 관계대명사를 이용하여 하나의 문장으로 이어주었으므로
모두 that으로 쓰거나 생략해도 무방하다.

07 Avian의 외투가 너무 따뜻해서 다른 것을 살 필요가 없다는 문
장을 쓸 수 있다.

08 원인과 결과를 나타내는 'so ~ that' 구문을 이용하여 문장을 하
나로 만든다.

09 수프가 너무 뜨거워서 혀를 데였다는 문장으로 쓸 수 있다.

10 목적격 관계대명사이므로 that을 쓰거나 생략해도 무방하다.

11 모두 목적격 관계대명사이므로 that으로 쓰거나 생략해도 무방
하다.

12 '내가 가장 자주 전화하는'이 '사람들'을 수식하고 있으므로 관계
사절 The people whom I call most often이라고 쓰는 것이
옳다.

13 Jason에 따르면 Lisa는 너무 행복해서 방에서 춤을 추고 있다
고 말할 수 있다.

14 파티가 너무 즐거워서 누구도 파티를 떠나고 싶어 하지 않았다
는 문장을 쓸 수 있다.

15 원인과 결과를 나타내는 'so ~ that' 구문을 이용하여 문장을 만
든다.

[교과서]
Reading

확인문제	p.28

1 T 2 F 3 T

확인문제	p.29

1 F 2 F 3 T 4 T

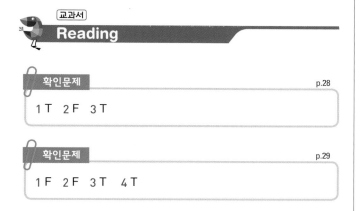

교과서 확인학습 A	p.30~31

01 are, doing
02 watching, on
03 How
04 so boring that
05 to hear that
06 advertisement, it, The Most Exciting Movie
07 everything that you read
08 ask for my money back

09 Hold on, lie because
10 not following you
11 express people's feelings
12 that, can be proven
13 For example, check that on the map
14 the connection with
15 Let me explain
16 It's
17 look for its advertisement
18 It says
19 uses facts unlike
20 the difference
21 exactly, says, says
22 Aren't, both opinions
23 words like, usually expressing opinions
24 which the movie won
25 that on the Internet
26 From now on, trust, with
27 that simple, mix, with
28 make a smart choice, both
29 to watch
30 the rest of

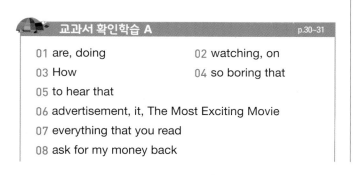

교과서 확인학습 B	p.32~33

1 Emma: What are you doing, Kyle?

2 Kyle: Oh, Emma. I'm watching the movie, *Y-Men 7*
on my computer.

3 Emma: How is it?

4 Kyle: Don't ask. It's so boring that I want to cry.

5 Emma: I'm sorry to hear that.

6 Kyle: I'm so mad. The movie advertisement said it
was "The Most Exciting Movie of the Year."

7 Emma: Well, you can't believe everything that you
read.

8 Kyle: They lied on the advertisement. I'm going to
ask for my money back.

9 Emma: Hold on, Kyle! They didn't really lie
because they used opinions, not facts.

10 Kyle: Huh? I'm not following you.

11 Emma: Opinions express people's feelings like,
"The desert is beautiful."

12 You can't say that it's true or not. But, facts can be
proven.

13 For example, "The Atacama Desert is in Chile," is
a fact. You can check that on the map.

14 Kyle: Okay.... But what's the connection with
movies?

15 Emma: Let me explain. What's your favorite
movie?

16 Kyle: It's *Forrest Gump*.

17 Emma: Okay. Let's look for its advertisement.
What does it say?

18 Kyle: It says, "Winner of 6 Academy Awards
including Best Picture."

19 Emma: See? It uses facts unlike the *Y-Men 7* advertisement.

20 Do you see the difference?

21 Kyle: Not exactly. The *Y-Men 7* ad says "Most Exciting Movie" and the *Forrest Gump* ad says "Best Picture."

22 Aren't they both opinions?

23 Emma: That's a great question, Kyle. When people use words like "best" or "most," they are usually expressing opinions.

24 But in the *Forrest Gump* ad, "Best Picture" is the award which the movie won.

25 We can check that on the Internet. That's a fact.

26 Kyle: Aha! From now on I'm only going to trust ads with facts.

27 Emma: It's not that simple. Most ads mix facts with opinions.

28 So you have to make a smart choice based on both of them.

29 Kyle: Got it! Emma, do you want to watch the rest of *Y-Men 7* with me?

30 Emma: Thanks, but no thanks. Enjoy the rest of the movie!

시험대비 실력평가
p.34~37

01 ①, ②　　　02 ③　　　03 opinions
04 It's because the movie is so boring.
05 ②　　　06 ④　　　07 아타카마 사막이 칠레에 있는 것
08 ③　　　09 ⑤　　　10 a fact
11 ③　　　12 facts and opinions　　　13 ①
14 People usually express their opinions with words like "best" or "most."
15 ④　　　16 ⑤　　　17 ④
18 He is watching the movie, Y-Men 7 on his computer.　　　19 ④
20 The movie advertisement said it was "The Most Exciting Movie of the Year."
21 ④　　　22 ②　　　23 an opinion, a fact
24 ④　　　25 ⑤
26 (D) → (A) → (C) → (B)　　　27 ③
28 영화 "Forest Gump"가 "Best Picture" 상을 받은 것
29 facts and opinions

---

01 사물을 선행사로 취하는 목적격 관계대명사가 들어가는 것이 옳다.

02 ③ Kyle은 영화에 만족하지 않는다. be fooled by: ~에 의해 속다

03 어떤 것에 대한 감정이나 생각은 '의견'이다.

04 Kyle이 울고 싶은 이유는 영화가 너무 지루하기 때문이다.

05 기다리라는 의미이다. 따라서 wait이 옳다. way to go: 잘 했어

06 앞 문장의 내용을 예를 들어 설명하고 있다.

07 "Atacama Desert is in Chile."를 가리키는 말이다.

08 Emma가 가장 좋아하는 영화는 글을 읽고 알 수 없다.

09 증명될 수 있는 것이 사실이다. 따라서 ⑤번이 사실이다.

10 의견과 사실의 차이점을 설명하는 글이다. 의견이 어떤 것인지를 설명한 후 사실에 관하여 설명하고 있다.

11 ① 오랫동안 ② 당분간 ③ 지금부터 ④, ⑤ 가끔

12 사실과 의견 둘 다 가리키는 말이다.

13 both 뒤에는 복수명사가 쓰인다.

14 사람들은 "best" 또는 "most"와 같은 말을 사용하여 그들의 의견을 표현한다.

15 ④ 대부분의 광고는 사실과 의견이 섞여 있다고 하였다.

16 ⓐ는 감정의 원인을 나타내는 to부정사이다. 따라서 ⑤번이 옳다.

17 그들이 거짓말을 한 것이 아니라는 이유를 설명하고 있으므로 because가 옳다.

18 Kyle은 컴퓨터로 영화 "Y-Men 7"을 보고 있다.

19 (A) 답변으로 미루어 보아 영화가 어떤지를 물었다고 볼 수 있으므로 how, (B) 지루함을 유발할 때에는 boring, (C) be going to V: V할 예정이다.

20 영화 광고에는 그 영화가 "올해의 가장 흥미진진한 영화"라고 쓰여 있었다.

21 that은 아타카마 사막이 칠레에 있다는 것을 받는다.

22 (A) 사실은 증명이 되는 것이므로 수동태, (B) 사역동사+목적어+원형부정사: 목적어가 V하게 하다 (C) '~을 포함하여'라는 의미의 전치사가 쓰여야 하므로 including

23 글의 내용에 따르면, 그 아기가 가장 예쁘다는 것은 의견이고, 에베레스트 산이 세계에서 가장 높은 산이라는 것은 사실이라고 할 수 있다.

24 모두 확인 가능한 사실이지만 '혼자 해변 가에 가는 것은 안전하지 않다'는 것은 의견이다.

25 "Forest Gump"는 "Best Picture'를 포함하여 여섯 개의 아카데미상을 받았다고 하였다.

26 (D) 둘 다 의견이 아니냐는 질문 → (A) 의견과 사실의 차이를 설명 → (C) 이해한 후 사실만 있는 광고를 믿겠다고 말함 → (B) 보통 광고에는 사실과 의견이 섞여 있다고 말해 줌.

27 mix A with B: A와 B를 섞다. with: ~을 가진, ~을 포함한

28 영화가 상을 받은 사실을 인터넷을 통해 확인할 수 있다는 것이다.

29 대부분의 광고에는 사실과 의견 모두 있다고 하였다.

01 I am going to ask for my money back.

02 It's so boring that I want to cry.

03 They used not facts but opinions, so they didn't really lie.

04 It is *Y–Men 7*.　　05 excited

06 be proven　　07 We can check that on the map.

08 doesn't use facts

09 Did you see the movie that won 6 Academy Awards?

10 Kyle's favorite movie is *Forrest Gump*.

11 Aren't they both opinions?

12 "Best Picture" is the award. The movie won the award.

13 People who use words like 'best' or 'most' are usually expressing opinions.

14 base, facts and opinions

01 ask for ~ back: ~을 돌려달라고 청하다

02 원인과 결과를 나타내는 'so ~ that' 구문을 이용하여 문장을 만들 수 있다.

03 그들은 사실이 아니라 의견을 사용했으므로 꼭 거짓말을 한 것은 아니다. so는 결과를 이끄는 접속사이다. not A but B: A가 아니라 B(= B, not A)

04 Kyle이 보고 있는 영화의 제목은 "Y–Men 7"이다.

05 가장 흥미진진한 영화라는 광고와는 달리 Kyle은 흥미진진함을 느끼지 못했다고 말하는 것이 옳다.

06 사실은 '증명이 되는 것'이므로 수동태를 쓰는 것이 옳다. 조동사 뒤에 동사원형을 쓰는 것에 유의한다.

07 밑줄 친 문장이 사실이라는 것은 지도를 확인하여 알 수 있다.

08 "Y-Men 7" 광고와는 달리 사실을 사용하고 있다고 하였으므로 "Y-Men 7" 광고는 사실을 사용하지 않는다는 것을 알 수 있다.

09 관계대명사 that을 대신하여 which를 써도 무방하다.

10 Kyle이 가장 좋아하는 영화는 "Forest Gump"라고 하였다.

11 답변으로 미루어 보아 '둘 다 의견이 아니니?'라고 질문했음을 알 수 있다.

12 관계대명사를 이용하여 두 문장을 하나의 문장으로 쓴 것이다. 선행사를 이용하여 두 개의 문장으로 쓸 수 있다.

13 'best'나 'most'와 같은 말을 사용하는 사람이라고 하였으므로 관계사절이 people을 수식하도록 문장을 만든다.

14 대부분의 광고에는 사실과 의견이 섞여 있기 때문에 결정을 내릴 때 사실과 의견을 바탕으로 선택해야 한다.

01 full　　02 ④　　03 ④

04 (1) How do you like the present?

　　(2) There is no evidence to prove his claim.

05 (1) make a choice　(2) check out　(3) full of

06 ③　　07 ①　　08 ②　　09 ③

10 ②　　11 ②　　12 ⑤

13 How did you like your trip to Gyeongju?

14 worth　　15 ⑤　　16 ⑤　　17 ⑤

18 ②　　19 ①, ②, ⑤

20 It was so hot that we went swimming yesterday.

21 ②　　22 ⑤

23 The drug that[which] the man stole was for his son.　　24 ③

25 We eat the carrots which my grandfather grew on the farm.

26 There are so many leaves on a single tree that it is impossible to count them.

27 Tell me about the museum that you visited last week.

28 The movie that[which] Kyle chose used opinions in the advertisement.

29 ③, ⑤　　30 ⑤　　31 ①　　32 ⑤

33 It's because most ads mix facts with opinions.

01 주어진 단어의 관계는 반의어 관계를 나타낸다. empty: 텅 빈, full: 가득 찬

02 사실이 아닌 무언가를 말하거나 쓰는 것을 가리키는 말은 lie(거짓말하다)이다.

03 worth: 가치가 있는

04 How do you like ~?: ~가 마음에 드니?, claim: 주장

05 make a choice: 선택하다, check out: 확인하다, be full of: ~로 가득 차다

06 주어진 문장에서 lie는 '거짓말하다'를 뜻하며 이와 같은 의미로 쓰인 것은 ③번이다. 나머지는 모두 '눕다'를 뜻한다.

07 worth: 가치가 있는, be worth ~ing: ~할 가치가 있다

10 여자와 소년은 점원과 손님의 관계임을 알 수 있다.

11 these days: 요즘에 = nowadays

14 무언가에 대해 충분히 중요하거나 좋거나 즐길 만한 것을 나타내는 말은 worth(가치가 있는)이다.

16 ⑤ 배낭의 무엇이 가장 마음에 드는지에 대한 구체적인 답변이 이어져야 한다.

17 관계대명사 that과 접속사 that을 구별하는 문제이다. 관계대명사는 불완전한 절을 이끌고 접속사는 완전한 절을 이끈다는 사실에 유의하자.

18 날씨가 나빴기 때문에 우리 여행을 미루었다는 의미이다. 따라서 '날씨가 너무 나빠서 여행을 미루었다'는 ②번이 가장 적절하다.

19 목적격 관계대명사가 들어가야 한다. 사람이 선행사이므로 who, whom, that이 쓰일 수 있으며 생략도 가능하다.

20 너무 더워서 수영하러 갔다는 문장으로 쓸 수 있다. go Ving: V하러 가다

21 원인과 결과를 나타내는 문장이므로 because가 옳다.

22 모두 Maya가 비행을 너무 무서워해서 비행기로 여행할 수 없다는 의미이지만, ⑤번은 비행이 무섭다 할지라도 비행기로 여행한다는 의미이다.

23 that[which]은 생략할 수 있다.

24 목적격 관계대명사나 '주격 관계대명사+be동사'는 생략 가능하다.

25 which 대신 that을 쓰거나 생략해도 좋다.

26 한 그루의 나무에 잎이 너무 많아서 그것을 세는 것이 불가능하다는 문장으로 쓸 수 있다.

27 that을 대신하여 which를 쓰거나 목적격 관계대명사이므로 생략해도 무방하다.

28 'Kyle이 선택한 영화'라고 하였으므로 관계사절이 the movie를 수식하도록 문장을 만든다.

29 (A)는 인칭대명사로 the movie를 가리키는 말이다. it은 가주어, 비인칭 주어, 인칭대명사로 쓰일 수 있다.

30 Emma가 Kyle에 관해 어떻게 생각하는지는 알 수 없다.

31 모두 관계대명사 that이 들어갈 수 있으니 ①번에는 의문대명사 who나 what이 들어간다.

32 사실과 의견을 바탕으로 현명한 선택을 해야 한다고 하였으므로 ⑤번이 가장 적절하다.

33 대부분의 광고들은 사실과 의견을 섞기 때문에 사실로 이루어진 광고만 믿는다는 것은 간단한 일이 될 수 없다

단원별 예상문제　　　　　　　　　p.46~49

01 ⑤　　02 (1) wisely　(2) recommend
(3) strongly　　03 (1) number one　(2) look for
(3) right now　(4) Hold on　(5) worth it
04 (E) → (A) → (C) → (D) → (B)　　05 ⑤
06 I was very happy with it.　　07 ④
08 Cheomseongdae, Bulguksa
09 ⑤　　10 ⑤　　11 ③　　12 ④
13 Can you give me back the pen that you borrowed from me?
14 ②　　15 ⑤
16 The barbell was so light that I could lift it up.
17 ②　　18 ④　　19 facts, opinions
20 They are mainly talking about the difference between facts and opinions.　　21 ③
22 The book was so touching that I read it many times.　　23 ⑤
24 Charlotte's Web is a children's novel which E. B. White wrote.

01 무언가를 다른 무언가에 더하는 것을 가리키는 말은 mix(섞다)이다.

03 (4) hold on: 기다리다 (5) worth it: 그만한 가치가 있는

04 (E) 도움 요청 → (A) 가방 추천 → (C) 거절 및 이유 설명 → (D) 다른 가방 추천 → (B) 반응 및 구매

05 이어지는 대화에서 자전거가 마음에 들지 않는 이유를 설명하고 있으므로 ⑤번처럼 무엇이 마음에 드는지 묻는 표현은 어색하다.

07 (A) How do you like ~?:~가 마음에 드니? (B)에는 주어 That이 생략되어 있으므로 sounds, (C)에는 동명사 주어 walking이 적절하다.

09 주어진 빈칸에 들어갈 말로 추천하는 이유를 설명하는 표현이 적절하다.

10 Brian이 Antonio's에 가격이 좋은지 아닌지 확인하려고 갈 것이라는 설명은 대화의 내용과 일치하지 않는다.

11 관계대명사와 의문대명사를 구별하는 문제이다. 관계대명사는 해석되지 않으나 의문대명사는 '누구'라고 해석된다.

12 일을 열심히 한 것이 원인이고 그 결과로 그가 아프게 된 것이므로 ④번이 옳다.

13 '네가 나에게 빌려간 펜'이므로 the pen that you borrowed from me라고 쓰는 것이 옳다.

14 '의자에 앉다'는 표현은 sit on이다. 따라서 on which라고 쓰는 것이 적절하며 관계대명사 that은 전치사의 목적어로 쓰이지 않는 것에 유의하자.

15 전치사의 목적어로 관계대명사 that은 쓰일 수 없다. 따라서 to whom으로 쓰는 것이 적절하다.

16 가벼운 것이 원인이고 내가 들어 올릴 수 있었다는 것이 결과이므로 'so light that ~'을 쓴다.

17 Emma가 하는 말을 이해할 수 없다는 의미이다.

18 (B)는 명사절을 이끄는 접속사로 완전한 절을 이끈다. ④번은 불완전한 절을 이끄는 관계대명사 that이다.

19 사실은 증명될 수 있는 것이라고 하였다. 따라서 '사실과는 다르게 의견은 증명될 수 없다'라고 쓰는 것이 옳다.

20 사실과 의견의 차이에 관하여 주로 이야기하고 있다.

21 모두 확인할 수 있는 사실이지만 ③번은 의견이다.

22 '이 책은 너무 감동적이어서 나는 이 책을 여러 번 읽었다'는 의미이다.

23 Wilbur가 몇 명의 친구를 가지고 있는지는 알 수 없다.

24 which를 대신하여 that을 써도 무방하다.

서술형 실전문제　　　　　　　　　p.50~51

01 Her favorite restaurant is Antonio's.
02 She recommends the bulgogi pizza.
03 She thinks it is a little slow on the weekends.
04 (C) → (B) → (A) → (D)

05 I can't find the cup which my husband likes to use.

06 (1) The wind blew my hat off my head because it was strong.

(2) The wind was so strong that it blew my hat off my head.

07 who[whom] Peter fell in love with left him / with whom Peter fell in love left him

08 that you baked / so delicious that

09 The jewel is so precious that it is priceless.

10 It says, "Winner of 6 Academy Awards including Best Picture."

11 She is using the advertisement of Forrest Gump.

12 의견은 진짜인지 아닌지 말할 수 없지만 사실은 확인할 수 있다.

13 opinions, facts

14 The book was so interesting that I couldn't put it down.

15 The genre of the book is fantasy.

01 미나가 가장 좋아하는 식당은 Antonio's이다.

02 미나는 불고기 피자를 추천하였다.

03 미나는 주말에는 서비스가 좀 느리다고 생각했다.

04 (C) 새 스마트폰을 갖게 된 것을 언급 → (B) 대답 및 만족 표현 → (A) 가장 마음에 드는 점 질문 → (D) 가장 마음에 드는 특징 설명

05 목적격 관계대명사이므로 생략해도 무방하며 that으로 써도 좋다.

06 원인은 바람이 강한 것이고, 그 결과로 내 머리에서 모자가 벗겨진 것이다.

07 'Peter가 사랑에 빠졌던 그 여자는 몇 주 전 그를 떠났다'는 문장을 쓸 수 있다. who[whom] 대신 that을 쓰거나 생략해도 좋다.

08 관계대명사 that은 생략하거나 which로 바꾸어 써도 좋다.

09 priceless: 값을 매길 수 없는, 대단히 귀중한

10 "Forest Gump" 영화 광고에는 "Winner of 6 Academy Awards including Best Picture."라고 쓰여 있다.

11 Emma는 Kyle이 가장 좋아하는 영화의 광고를 사용하여 사실과 의견의 차이점을 설명하고 있다.

12 의견은 사람의 감정을 나타내어 어떠한 것이 사실인지 아닌지 말할 수 없지만, 사실은 확인할 수 있는 차이가 있다고 하였다.

13 해석: 광고에는 우리가 믿을 수 없는 많은 의견들이 있다. 우리는 많은 사실을 가진 광고가 필요해.

14 원인과 결과를 이끄는 'so ~ that' 구문을 이용하여 문장을 만들 수 있다. 재미있는 것이 원인이고, 책을 놓을 수 없었던 것이 결과임에 유의한다.

15 책의 장르는 공상 소설(a fantasy novel)이라고 하였다.

창의사고력 서술형 문제 p.52

|모범답안|

01 (A) the bulgogi pizza (B) prices (C) a little slow

02 (1) Tom was so busy that he couldn't answer the phone.

(2) The waves were so high that we couldn't swim in the sea.

03 **Facts**

It is located in Yongin.

/ There are Korean traditional houses.

/ Visitors can watch nongak and jultagi.

Opinions

It's a fun place in Yongin.

/ They are beautiful.

/ Nongak and jultagi are very exciting to see.

01 제가 가장 좋아하는 식당, Antonio's를 소개하고자 합니다. 이곳은 괜찮은 피자 식당이에요. 저는 불고기 피자를 추천합니다. 이것은 진짜 맛있어요. 만약 여러분이 주말에 이곳에 방문한다면, 서비스는 조금 느릴 수 있어요. Antonio's를 방문해 보는 게 어떨까요?

단원별 모의고사 p.53~56

01 ⑤   02 ②

03 It was difficult for her. 04 ③   05 ⑤

06 (A) red (B) a different color

(C) the navy backpack (D) side pockets

07 They are talking about Tom's new smartphone.

08 He is really happy with it.

09 He likes the camera most about his smartphone.

10 ⓓ → check it out   11 ⑤

12 (1) Mix the butter with the sugar.

(2) Jack lifted the chair.

(3) Are you telling the truth?

13 ④   14 ②

15 His speech was so famous that everyone knew about it.   16 ⑤

17 It is so cold that my mouth is frozen. 18 ③

19 ④   20 ⑤   21 ④

22 ⓕ → unlike   23 fact, an opinion

24 ④   25 that I read is so touching that / recommend it to you

02 경주 여행에 매우 만족함을 알 수 있다.

03 Suji에게 석굴암까지 올라가는 것은 어려웠다.

04 이어지는 대화에서 추천하는 표현이 이어지므로 빈칸에 추천하는 표현이 적절하다. recommend: 추천하다

9

05 ⑤번을 제외한 나머지는 모두 추천을 하는 표현이다.

06 나는 오늘 새로운 배낭을 사서 기분이 좋았다. 나는 빨간색 배낭을 메곤 했었다. 그래서 나는 다른 색을 사고 싶었다. 점원은 내게 남색 배낭을 추천하였는데 이것은 양쪽에 주머니를 갖고 있었다. 나는 이것이 매우 마음에 들어서 샀다. 나는 내일 새 배낭을 메는 것을 기대하고 있다.

07 Tom과 Sue는 Tom의 새 스마트폰에 대해 이야기하고 있다.

08 Tom은 그의 스마트폰을 정말 만족스러워하고 있다.

09 Tom은 그의 스마트폰에서 카메라를 가장 좋아한다.

10 check out과 같이 '동사+부사'로 이루어진 구동사의 목적어가 인칭대명사일 때는 동사와 부사 사이에 목적어가 위치한다.

11 위 대화에서 Antonio's에서 불고기 피자가 얼마인지는 알 수 없다.

12 mix: 섞다, lift: 들어 올리다. tell the truth: 진실을 말하다

13 모두 날씨가 너무 좋아서 우리가 밖으로 나갔다는 의미이지만 ④번은 날씨가 너무 좋아서 밖으로 나갈 수 없었다는 의미이다.

14 모두 불완전한 절을 이끄는 관계대명사 that이지만 ②번은 접속사 that으로 완전한 절을 이끈다.

15 유명한 것이 원인이고 모두가 아는 것이 결과이다. 따라서 so famous that everyone knew about it이라고 쓰는 것이 옳다.

16 주어가 복수 명사인 The women이므로 are friendly라고 쓰는 것이 옳다.

17 너무 추워서 내 입이 얼었다는 문장으로 쓸 수 있다.

18 무엇을 하고 있는지 묻는 말에 ⓒ 대답 → ⓐ 영화가 어떠냐는 질문에 → ⓓ 너무 지루하다는 대답 → ⓑ 이 대답에 유감이라고 답하는 순서가 자연스럽다.

19 hold on: 기다리다

20 광고에는 사실과 의견이 모두 있다고 하였으므로 ⑤번이 글의 내용과 일치한다.

21 ④ "Forest Gump"의 광고를 가리키는 대명사이다.

22 "Y-Men 7" 광고에는 의견이 사용되었고 "Forest Gump" 광고에는 사실이 사용되었다고 하였으므로 unlike를 쓰는 것이 옳다.

23 어떠한 것이 증명될 수 있으면 사실이지만, 진실인지 아닌지 확인할 수 없는 것은 의견이라고 말할 수 있다.

24 ignore: 무시하다, 못 본 체하다

25 '내가 읽은 책'이라고 하였으므로 관계사절이 the book을 수식하도록 문장을 만든다.

Be like Sherlock!

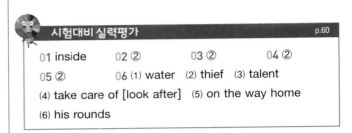

01 inside   02 ②   03 ②   04 ②
05 ②   06 (1) water   (2) thief   (3) talent
(4) take care of [look after]   (5) on the way home
(6) his rounds

01 주어진 단어의 관계는 반의어 관계를 나타낸다. inside: ~안에, outside: ~ 밖에

02 무언가를 잘하는 타고난, 특별한 능력을 가리키는 말은 talent(재능)이다.

03 lightning: 번개

04 주어진 문장에서 post는 '게시하다'를 뜻하며 이와 같은 의미로 쓰인 것은 ②번이다. 나머지는 모두 '우편, 우편물'을 의미한다.

05 문장에 공통으로 들어갈 말은 text이며 명사로 '본문, 문자메시지', 동사로 '문자를 보내다'를 의미한다.

06 water: 물을 주다, thief: 도둑, talent:재능, take care of=look after: ~을 돌보다, on the way home: 집에 오는 길에, make one's round: 순찰을 돌다

01 lose   02 (1) refrigerator   (2) thunder   (3) clue
(4) afraid   (5) poem   (6) carry
03 (1) strange   (2) suddenly   (3) post
04 (1) His life was not happy anymore.
　(2) When we get into a trouble, we should try to overcome.
　(3) He won first place in the talent show.
05 (1) The crime rate is rising.
　(2) He showed a talent for dancing.
　(3) Her dog is afraid of thunder.
　(4) Could you mop the floor?
　(5) She hired a detective to solve the problem.
　(6) Her bag is as light as a feather.

01 주어진 단어의 관계는 반의어 관계를 나타낸다. find: 찾다, lose: 잃어버리다

02 afraid: 두려워하는, refrigerator: 냉장고, carry: 나르다, 옮기다, poem: 시, clue: 단서, thunder: 천둥

03 strange: 이상한, suddenly: 갑자기, post: 게시하다

04 not ~ anymore: 더 이상 ~ 않는, overcome: 극복하다, win first place: 일등을 하다

05 crime rate: 범죄율, be afraid of: ~을 두려워하다, mop: 닦다, detective: 탐정, feather: 깃털

[교과서]
Conversation

핵심 Check
p.62~63

1 (1) favor / Can you help me (2) favor / What is it / post / afraid

2 (1) Guess / I guess (2) wrong (3) Maybe

교과서 대화문 익히기

Check(√) True or False
p.64

1 T 2 F 3 T 4 F

교과서 확인학습
p.66~67

Listen and Speak 1-A
favor / wash the dishes

Listen and Speak 1-B
take care of / I'm sorry but I can't / what should I do / Why don't you / right now

Listen and Speak 1-C
do me a favor / help me mop / problem, can't

Listen and Speak 2-A
under the table / anymore / guess / he is

Listen and Speak 2-B
have passed, at the end of, wonderful year, a few, stranger, each other

Listen and Speak 2-C
what I'm doing / I guess / wrong / working on / right

Real Life Talk - Step 1
Can you help me / inside / texted / Where were / was making / somewhere / checked / let's check it again, it is, refrigerator / welcome

Real Life Talk - Step 2
help me find / did, see, last / guess, took, see its footprints

시험대비 기본평가
p.68

01 can I ask you a favor?   02 ⑤
03 Brian's baseball glove   04 ③

시험대비 실력평가
p.69~70

01 ①   02 ③, ⑤   03 ⑤
04 (E) → (C) → (A) → (D) → (B)
05 I guess a dog took your baseball glove.
06 ④   07 ⓐ → find (또는 to find)   08 ④
09 ③   10 classmates   11 ②
12 ⑤

01 (A)는 도움 요청에 대해 거절하는 표현으로 ①번과 바꾸어 쓸 수 있다.

02 (B)는 제안하는 표현이다.

04 (E) 야구 글러브를 보았는지 질문 → (C) 대답 및 설명 → (A) 그곳에 없음을 설명 → (D) 추측 표현하기 → (B) 야구 글러브 발견

06 ④ Jack이 야구 글러브를 갖고 도망가는 개를 보았다는 설명은 대화의 내용과 일치하지 않는다.

07 help는 준사역동사로서 목적보어로 동사원형 또는 to부정사를 취한다.

08 위 대화를 통해 Brian이 친구에게 왜 문자메시지를 보냈는지는 알 수 없다.

09 irritated: 짜증난, confused: 혼란스러워 하는, pleased: 기쁜, dissatisfied: 불만족한, nervous: 긴장된, upset: 화난

10 학교나 대학에서 당신과 같은 학급에 있는 사람들을 가리키는 말은 classmates(급우들)이다.

11 (A) 현재완료로 have passed, (B) 셀 수 있는 명사를 수식하는 a few, (C) each other: 서로

12 수진과 학급 친구들은 극소수만 같은 반이 될 것이다.

서술형 시험대비
p.71

01 stranger   02 I guess only a few of us will be in the same class next year.
03 Can you help me find it?
04 He used it in the kitchen last.
05 It was in the refrigerator.   06 footprint
07 Because he can see its footprints on the bench.

01 당신이 모르는 사람을 가리키는 말은 stranger(모르는 사람)이다.

04 Brian은 그의 스마트폰을 부엌에서 마지막으로 사용하였다.

11

05 Brian의 스마트폰은 냉장고에 있었다.

06 발 또는 신발에 의해 남겨진 자국을 의미하는 것은 footprint(발자국)이다.

07 Jack이 Amy의 야구 글러브를 개가 가져갔다고 생각하는 이유는 그가 벤치 위에서 개의 발자국들을 볼 수 있기 때문이다.

교과서 Grammar

핵심 Check   p.72~73

1 (1) something noisy   (2) something wrong
   (3) something strange
2 (1) when the movie starts   (2) what he ate
   (3) how much the watch is

시험대비 기본평가   p.74

01 (1) nice anyone → anyone nice
   (2) can I → I can   (3) to see pretty → pretty to see
   (4) that → if[whether]
02 (1) who she is   (2) what made her angry
   (3) something comfortable to sit on
   (4) how old she is   (5) there something cold
03 (1) I want to eat something sweet.
   (2) Do you have anything bigger than this?
   (3) Jason doesn't know how his mom found him.
   (4) We don't know when they will come.

01 (1), (3) -thing, -body, -one으로 끝나는 부정대명사는 형용사가 뒤에서 수식한다. 단, 이러한 대명사를 형용사와 to부정사가 동시에 수식하는 경우 '대명사+형용사+to부정사'의 어순임에 유의한다. (2), (4) 간접의문문의 어순은 '의문사+주어+동사'이며, 의문사가 없는 의문문의 간접의문문은 'if/whether+주어+동사'로 쓴다.

02 (1), (4) 간접의문문의 어순은 '의문사+주어+동사'이다. (2) what이 의문대명사로 주어로 쓰이고 있다. (3) 형용사와 to부정사가 동시에 something을 수식하는 경우 '대명사+형용사+to부정사'의 어순이다. (5) -thing으로 끝나는 부정대명사는 형용사의 수식을 뒤에서 받는다.

03 (1), (2) -thing으로 끝나는 부정대명사는 형용사의 수식을 뒤에서 받는다. (3), (4) 간접의문문의 어순은 '의문사+주어+동사'의 어순이다.

시험대비 실력평가   p.75~77

01 ⑤   02 ②   03 ④
04 She doesn't have anyone kind to talk with.
05 ⑤   06 ④   07 ①, ④
08 when we are going to meet
09 ⑤   10 ④   11 ③
12 There is something important to deal with.
13 ②   14 ④   15 ⑤
16 I wonder who he is talking with now.
17 ③   18 ⑤
19 Could you tell me when this happened?
20 Do you know who brought this T-shirt?
21 ③   22 ③   23 ③
24 someone strong and healthy .

01 주어진 우리말을 영어로 옮기면 'I want to see something colorful and beautiful.'이다.

02 간접의문문의 어순은 '의문사+주어+동사'이며 의문사가 주어 역할을 하는 경우는 '의문사+동사'의 어순이 가능하다.

03 -thing으로 끝나는 대명사는 형용사의 수식을 뒤에서 받으며, '신나는 것을 유발'할 때에는 현재분사를 쓰는 것이 적절하다. 간접의문문의 어순은 '의문사+주어+동사'이다.

04 -thing으로 끝나는 대명사가 형용사와 to부정사의 수식을 동시에 받을 때 '-thing+형용사+to부정사' 어순임에 유의하여 답을 쓴다.

05 빈칸에는 someone을 수식하는 형용사가 들어가는 것이 적절하다. ⑤는 부사이다.

06 ④번을 영어로 바르게 옮기면 Do you know who saw her?이다.

07 의문사가 없는 문장의 간접의문문은 if나 whether를 써서 만들 수 있다.

08 remember의 목적어로 '의문사+주어+동사' 어순의 간접의문문을 쓸 수 있다.

09 형용사와 to부정사가 동시에 something을 수식할 때에는 '형용사+to부정사'의 어순으로 수식하는 것이 일반적이다. 따라서 something fun to talk about이 적절하다.

10 대답으로 미루어 보아 길을 묻는 말이 들어가는 것이 가장 적절하다.

11 공을 찬 주체가 누구인지 궁금하다는 의미이므로 의문대명사 who를 이용하여 간접의문문을 완성할 수 있다.

12 important와 to deal with가 something을 동시에 수식하므로 something important to deal with 어순으로 쓴다.

13 -thing으로 끝나는 대명사를 수식할 때 '형용사+to부정사' 어순이며, remember라는 동사의 목적어로 간접의문문이 쓰이고 있으므로 '의문사+주어+동사' 어순으로 빈칸을 채운다.

14 ④번의 두 문장을 간접의문문으로 옮기면 I don't know who helped you.이다.

15 -one으로 끝나는 대명사 뒤에는 형용사가 수식한다. care는 명사이므로 빈칸에 쓰일 수 없다.

16 '그가 지금 누구와 이야기하고 있는지'가 wonder의 목적어이다. 따라서 간접의문문을 활용하여 who he is talking with now를 wonder의 목적어로 쓰는 것이 적절하다.

17 주어진 문장의 밑줄 친 who는 간접의문문을 만드는 의문대명사로 '누가'라고 해석된다. guess의 목적어로 간접의문문을 이끌고 있는 ③번이 답이다. 나머지는 모두 앞선 명사를 수식하는 관계대명사 who이다.

18 know의 목적어 역할을 하는 간접의문문이므로 who he is라고 쓰는 것이 적절하다.

19 간접의문문을 활용하여 '언제 이게 발생했는지'가 tell의 직접목적어가 되도록 문장을 만들 수 있다. '의문사+주어+동사'의 어순에 유의하여 답을 쓴다.

20 간접의문문의 어순은 '의문사+주어+동사'이지만, 의문사가 주어 역할을 하는 경우 '의문사+동사' 어순이다.

21 의문사가 없는 문장의 간접의문문은 if 혹은 whether를 써서 만든다.

22 ③ anything heavy라고 쓰는 것이 적절하다.

23 주어진 문장을 영어로 옮기면 He tries to do something good for others.이다.

24 답변으로 미루어 보아 의학 실험을 위해서 튼튼하고 건강한 누군가가 필요하다는 말을 했음을 유추할 수 있다. 긍정문이므로 someone을 쓰고 -one으로 끝나는 대명사이므로 형용사가 뒤에서 수식하도록 빈칸을 채운다.

서술형 시험대비
p.78~79

01 I need someone reliable.
02 (1) Do you know how she bakes these cookies?
　(2) I'll ask Jason where he lives.
　(3) Do you remember what Brad's last name is?
　(4) I wonder if[whether] they will go abroad to study English.
　(5) Can you tell me if[whether] she is going to run or walk?
　(6) I don't understand what they wanted to do.
　(7) I want to know who made the decision last night.
03 Let me know how old he is.
04 when[what time] I came
05 A: I met someone interesting at a party yesterday.
　B: Tell me who he was.
06 Mike wanted to meet someone brave to be admired.
07 what the story is about
08 something strange / it is　　09 if
10 I need something colorful to decorate this tree.
11 A: I don't know what he wants
　B: He wants something different.
12 Do you know what this word means?
13 something to drink
14 I don't remember where I put my purse yesterday.
15 A: what they are　B: something surprising

01 someone은 형용사의 수식을 뒤에서 받는 대명사이다.

02 간접의문문은 의문사가 이끄는 문장이 '의문사+주어+동사'의 어순으로 주절에서 명사 역할을 하는 것이다. 단, 의문사가 없는 경우 'if/ whether+주어+동사'의 어순임에 유의한다.

03 know의 목적어로 간접의문문 how old he is를 써서 문장을 완성한다.

04 답변으로 미루어 보아 '언제[몇 시에] 집에 왔는지를 기억할 수 없다'는 말이 들어가는 것이 적절하다.

05 someone을 수식하는 interesting은 뒤에서 someone을 수식한다. '그가 누구였는지'는 Tell의 직접목적어로 쓰여 '의문사+주어+동사' 어순으로 나타낼 수 있다.

06 '존경 받을 만한 용감한 누군가'라고 하였으므로 someone을 brave와 to be admired가 수식하도록 문장을 만든다. 이때 '형용사+to부정사'의 어순으로 대명사 someone을 뒤에서 수식하는 것에 유의한다.

07 그 이야기가 어떤 것에 관한 것인지 알고 싶다는 말에 대한 답변이 이어지고 있으므로 what the story is about이라고 쓰는 것이 적절하다.

08 이상하게 생긴 어떤 것을 발견했다고 하자, 정말로 이상하게 보인다며 무엇인지 아냐고 물어보고, 이에 모르겠다고 답하는 것이 자연스럽다.

09 조건의 부사절과 간접의문문을 이끌 수 있는 것은 접속사 if이다.

10 '이 트리를 장식할 다채로운 무언가'라고 하였으므로 colorful과 to decorate this tree가 something을 수식하도록 문장을 만든다. 이때, 'something+형용사+to부정사'의 어순임에 유의한다.

11 '그가 무엇을 원하는지'가 동사 know의 목적어이므로 I don't know what he wants.라고 쓴다. '다른 무언가'라고 하였으므로 부정대명사 something을 형용사 different가 뒤에서 수식하도록 문장을 만든다.

12 동사 know의 목적어로 간접의문문 what this word means를 써서 문장을 완성할 수 있다.

13 대답으로 미루어 보아 마실 것을 원한다는 말이 들어가는 것이 적절하다.

14 간접의문문의 어순은 '의문사+주어+동사'이다.

15 해석: A: 나는 그들이 무엇을 보고 있는지 궁금해. B: 그들은 극장에서 어떤 놀라운 것을 보고 있어.

Reading

확인문제
p.80

1 T 2 F 3 F 4 T

확인문제
p.81

1 F 2 T 3 T

교과서 확인학습 A
p.82~83

01 ran across
02 need, help
03 eighth grade
04 the best detective
05 something wrong
06 has stolen, for
07 took, to, scene
08 was, broken
09 were still there
10 missing, a poem, its place
11 Where did, go
12 high and low, too
13 when this happened
14 after, making my rounds, rushed over
15 who else was here
16 practicing, call them
17 ninth grade, curly
18 practicing, thirsty, stepped outside, to get, It, completely, Suddenly, thunder, broke, Lightning followed, running away
19 face
20 back, short
21 eighth grade, with long black
22 reading, aloud, next to, flash, like a horror movie, scared
23 hear, break
24 too loud, was going to win
25 short blonde
26 wrong, moves, a little before, take, outside, until
27 anything strange
28 How could
29 on the way home
30 singing
31 to hear anymore, turned to
32 bring the medal back

교과서 확인학습 B
p.84~85

1 Mr. Reese, the principal, ran across the wet playground.
2 "Shirley! Shirley! I need your help!"
3 Shirley was an eighth grade student at Bakersville Middle School.
4 She was also the best detective in the whole town.
5 "Is there something wrong?" asked Shirley.
6 "Someone has stolen the gold medal for the talent show!"
7 Mr. Reese took Shirley to the scene of the crime.
8 There was a case with a broken window.
9 The silver and bronze medals were still there.
10 But the gold medal was missing. There was a poem in its place.
11 Tomorrow is the talent show. Where did the gold medal go?
12 Look high and low. You can't catch me. You're too slow.
13 Shirley asked, "Could you tell me when this happened?"
14 "A little after nine last night. I was making my rounds when I heard a scream. I rushed over and found Jocelyn and the case like this."
15 "I wonder who else was here last night."
16 "Sylvia and Harry. They were also practicing for the talent show. I'll call them to my office."
17 Jocelyn was a ninth grade student with short curly red hair.
18 "I was practicing my song and I became thirsty. I stepped outside the classroom to get some water. It was completely dark. Suddenly, there was a loud sound of thunder. I think the thief broke the window at that moment. Lightning followed right after and it became bright for a second or two. Then I saw someone running away from the case."
19 "Did you see the thief's face?"
20 "No. I only saw the thief's back. But the thief had short hair."
21 Next was an eighth grade student, Sylvia. She was tall with long black hair.
22 She said, "I was reading my poem aloud in the classroom. I heard a scream and went outside. There was a girl next to the case. With the flash from the lightning, it was like a horror movie. I got scared so I ran straight home."
23 "Did you hear the window break?"
24 "No, the thunder was too loud. Well, I didn't do it. I was going to win first place anyway."
25 Harry, a seventh grader, had short blonde hair.
26 He said, "Hey, you got the wrong guy. I was practicing my dance moves. I went home a little before nine. I didn't take one step outside the classroom until then."
27 "Did you hear anything strange?"

28 "How could I? My music was really loud."

29 "Did you see anyone on the way home?"

30 "No. I heard someone singing really badly, but I didn't see anyone."

31 Shirley said, "I don't need to hear anymore." Then she turned to the thief.

32 "Why don't you bring the medal back before you get into some real trouble?"

시험대비 실력평가 　　　　　　　p.86~89

01 ②　　　　02 in the case　　　03 ④
04 Someone stole it.
05 Jocelyn, Sylvia and Harry　　　06 ③
07 ②　　　　08 The thief had short hair.
09 thief　　　10 ⑤
11 if[whether] you saw anyone on the way home
12 the thunder was too loud　　　13 ③
14 when this happened　15 ④, ⑤　16 ②, ④
17 the gold medal　　18 ⑤　　19 ④
20 ③　　　　21 Because she wanted to get some
water.　　　　22 She was tall with long black hair.
23 ②　　　　24 ③
25 He was practicing his dance moves.

01 위 글에서 금메달은 이미 사라지고 난 이후이므로 ②번은 위 글에서 찾아볼 수 없다.

02 진열장을 가리키는 말이다.

03 위 글에서 쓰인 case는 '진열장'을 의미한다.

04 누군가가 장기자랑 대회 금메달을 훔쳐갔다고 하였다.

05 어젯밤에 학교에 있었던 세 사람을 가리키는 말이다.

06 물을 가지러 교실 밖으로 나갔다고 하였으므로 교실 안에서 물을 마셨다는 것은 글의 내용과 일치하지 않는다.

07 ⓑ는 날짜, 날씨, 거리, 명암 등을 나타내는 비인칭 주어 It이다.
①, ④ 가주어 It ② 비인칭 주어 ③, ⑤ 인칭대명사

08 도둑이 짧은 머리인 것을 Jocelyn이 보았다.

09 다른 사람에게서 무언가를 훔치는 사람은 '도둑'이다.

10 음악 소리가 정말 커서 이상한 소리를 들을 수 없었다는 것이 자연스럽다.

11 집에 가는 길에 누군가를 보았느냐는 물음에 대한 답이 이어지고 있다. 의문사가 없는 의문문의 간접의문문은 if나 whether를 써서 만든다.

12 천둥소리가 너무 커서 창이 깨지는 소리를 듣지 못했다고 하였다.

13 Syliva는 공포영화를 본 것이 아니라, 번개의 번쩍임에 본 진열장 옆의 소녀의 모습이 공포 영화 같았다고 하였다.

14 이어지는 대답이 '지난 밤 9시가 조금 넘은 후'라는 것으로 보아

언제 이 사건이 일어났는지 묻는 말이 들어가는 것이 가장 적절하다.

15 도둑이 쓴 시에 장기 자랑 대회가 내일이라고 적혀 있었다.

16 시의 내용으로 보아, 시를 쓴 사람은 도둑이며 학교 장기 자랑 대회는 사건 다음 날 개최될 예정이었다.

17 은메달과 동메달은 그대로 남아 있었다고 하였으므로 범인은 진열장에서 오직 금메달만을 가지고 갔다.

18 번개로 인하여 1~2초 정도 밝아졌을 때 범인이 진열장에서 도망치는 것을 보았다는 것이 자연스럽다.

19 공포영화를 본 것 같았다고 하였으므로 '무서움'을 느꼈다는 것이 적절하다.

20 천둥이 쳤을 때 Syliva는 교실 밖으로 나와 진열장 옆에 있던 소녀를 보고 있었다.

21 Jocelyn은 물을 가지러 교실 밖으로 나갔다고 하였다.

22 Sylvia는 길고 검은 머리를 가진 키가 큰 소녀이다.

23 (A) -thing으로 끝나는 대명사이므로 뒤에서 형용사의 수식을 받는다. (B) 지각동사의 목적격 보어로 원형부정사 혹은 현재분사이다. (C) Why don't you+동사원형 ~?

24 뒤에 이어지는 문장으로 보아 이상한 소리를 들을 수 없었다는 의미이다.

25 Harry는 교실 안에서 춤 동작을 연습하고 있었다고 하였다.

서술형 시험대비 　　　　　　　p.90~91

01 Is there something wrong?
02 principal / eighth, best detective
03 They were in the broken case.
04 calling, Mr. Reese, stole the gold medal, broken, poem, the gold medal .　05 천둥소리가 나던 순간
06 what you were doing
07 Mr. Reese, Jocelyn, Sylvia, and Harry were in the school.
08 It was because his music was really loud.
09 She saw a girl next to the case.
10 Because she got scared.
11 The flash from the lightning did.
12 went home → went outside, heard → didn't hear
13 I found out who stole the gold medal.

01 무슨 일이 있는지를 묻는 표현이 들어가는 것이 적절하다. -thing으로 끝나는 부정대명사이므로 형용사의 수식을 뒤에서 받는 것에 유의한다.

02 Mr. Reese는 Bakersville 중학교의 교장 선생님이다. Shirley는 8학년이고 마을 최고의 탐정이다.

03 은메달과 동메달은 깨진 진열장 안에 있었다.

04 해석: 내가 걷고 있을 때, 누군가가 내 이름을 부르는 소리를 들었다. 그것은 Mr. Reese였다. 그는 누군가가 장기 자랑 대회

금메달을 훔쳤다고 말했다. 나는 그와 함께 범죄의 현장으로 갔다. 나는 진열장의 유리창이 깨져 있는 것을 보았다. 금메달 대신에 시가 있었다.

05 커다란 천둥소리가 났을 때 도둑이 유리창을 깼다고 생각한다는 의미이다.

06 비명소리를 들었을 때 Mr. Reese는 순찰을 돌고 있었다고 하였다.

07 교장 선생님, Jocelyn, Sylvia, Harry가 사건 당시에 학교에 있었다.

08 음악 소리가 너무 커서 이상한 소리를 듣지 못했다는 의미이다.

09 밖으로 나온 Sylvia는 진열장 옆에 있는 한 소녀를 보았다.

10 Sylvia는 무서웠기 때문에 곧장 집으로 달려갔다고 하였다.

11 번개의 번쩍임이 범죄 현장을 공포 영화처럼 보이게 만들었다고 하였다.

12 Sylvia는 비명소리를 듣고 밖으로 나갔다고 하였고, 커다란 천둥소리 때문에 창문이 깨지는 소리를 듣지 못했다고 하였다.

13 '누가 금메달을 훔쳤는지'가 find out의 목적어가 되어야 하므로 간접의문문을 이용하여 쓸 수 있다.

영역별 핵심문제
p.93~97

01 footprint 　　02 ⑤　　　　03 ②
04 (1) thirsty　 (2) detective　 (3) footprint　 (4) broken
05 ②
06 (1) She gave me a silver necklace.
　 (2) I'll carry your luggage to your room.
　 (3) This story is about a witch who flies in the sky.
07 ⑤　　　　　08 Can you help me wash the dishes?
09 ⑤　　　　　10 ②
11 can you give me a hand?　　　　12 ⑤
13 She is making her speech at the end of the
　 school year.
14 She is asking them to say hello when they see
　 each other.　　　　15 ④　　　 16 ④
17 ③　　　 18 ②　　　 19 ④
20 Do you know what color her bag is?　 21 ⑤
22 ④　　　 23 ⑤
24 She bought something special for her mother.
25 ③　　　 26 I need someone trustful to depend
on.　　　 27 ③　　　 28 ④　　　 29 ②
30 She cut her hair.　　　 31 ⑤

01 주어진 단어의 관계는 반의어 관계를 나타낸다. handprint: 손 자국, footprint: 발자국

02 favor: 호의, 부탁

03 주어진 문장에서 principal은 '교장'을 뜻한다. ②번은 '주요한, 주된'을 의미한다.

04 broken: 깨진, 부서진, footprint: 발자국, thirsty: 목마른, detective: 탐정

05 pass는 각각 '통과하다, 합격하다, 건네주다, 지나다'를 의미한다.

06 silver: 은, necklace: 목걸이, luggage: 짐, witch: 마녀

07 위 대화의 밑줄 친 (A)와 나머지는 도움을 요청하는 표현이다. ⑤번은 도움을 제안하는 표현이다.

09 추측해 대한 반응으로 '그것 참 안됐구나.'라는 대답은 어색하다.

10 주어진 문장은 (B)의 앞에 나오는 Tony의 질문에 대한 답으로 적절하다.

12 위 대화를 통해 나래가 그녀의 개를 어떻게 돌보는지는 알 수 없다.

13 이 연설은 학년의 막바지에 하고 있다.

14 수진은 서로 만나면 인사말을 건넬 것을 부탁하고 있다.

15 ⓓ는 부엌을 가리키며 나머지는 모두 스마트폰을 가리킨다.

17 who found your purse라고 쓰는 것이 적절하다.

18 주어진 우리말을 영어로 옮기면 I want to do something exciting for my birthday party.이다.

19 '누가 너를 그 파티에 초대했는지'라고 하였으므로 의문대명사 who를 이용하여 간접의문문을 만든다.

20 의문사가 이끄는 문장을 동사 know의 목적어로 만든다. 이때 어순은 '의문사+주어+동사'의 어순임에 유의한다.

21 -thing으로 끝나는 부정대명사를 형용사와 to부정사가 동시에 수식할 때는 '형용사+to부정사' 어순으로 수식한다.

22 간접의문문의 어순은 '의문사+주어+동사'이고, -thing으로 끝나는 부정대명사는 '형용사+to부정사'의 어순으로 수식받는다. 의문사가 없는 의문문의 간접의문문은 if 혹은 whether를 써서 나타낸다.

23 부정대명사를 수식하는 어순은 '형용사+to부정사'이다. 따라서 nothing precious to keep이라고 써야 한다.

24 부정대명사는 뒤에서 형용사의 수식을 받는다. 따라서 something special이라고 쓰는 것이 적절하다.

25 그녀가 왜 늦었는지를 모르겠다는 말이 적절하다. 이때 간접의문문의 어순인 '의문사+주어+동사'에 맞게 빈칸을 채운다.

26 someone은 부정대명사이므로 '형용사+to부정사' 어순으로 뒤에서 수식받는다.

27 Mr. Reese가 범죄 현장으로 달려갔을 때 Jocelyn을 보았다고 하였으므로 그가 가장 먼저 도착했다고 볼 수 없다.

28 Mr. Reese는 학교에서 순찰을 돌고 있었다고 하였으므로 ④번은 글의 내용과 일치하지 않는다.

29 라푼젤은 긴 머리카락을 가지고 있었는데 (B) 마녀는 그것을 이용해서 탑으로 올라갔고 세상이 위험하다고 말함. 어느 날 지나가던 왕자가 그녀가 노래하는 것을 듣고 (A) 세상이 아름답다고 말하며 라푼젤에게 내려오라고 함 (C) 마침내 결심한 라푼젤은 탑에서 내려옴.

30 탑에서 내려오기 전에 라푼젤은 머리카락을 잘랐다.

31 탑에서 내려오기 위해서 라푼젤이 무엇을 사용했는지는 알 수 없다.

01 ③   02 (C) → (B) → (D) → (A)

03 ④   04 ⑤

05 Can you take care of my dog this weekend?

06 ①, ③   07 ④   08 ⑤

09 She asks him to help her wash the dishes.

10 Can you give me a hand to wash the dishes?

11 ④   12 ③   13 ④   14 ⑤

15 warm to wear

16 Please ask him what time he can pick me up.

17 who built it   18 who is telling the
truth   19 ④   20 ②

21 (C)–(B)–(A)–(D)   22 ⑤   23 ④

24 who stole, practicing her song, reading her poem

25 ⑤

01 구리와 주석을 포함한 황갈색의 금속을 가리키는 말은
   bronze(청동)이다.

02 (C) 도움 요청하기 → (B) 대답 및 질문 → (D) 필요한 도움
   설명 → (A) 승낙

03 주어진 문장은 어디에 있었는지에 대한 대답이므로 (D)가 적절
   하다.

04 Briain의 스마트폰이 냉장고에서 발견되었다는 설명이 대화의
   내용과 일치한다.

07 ④번은 모르는 사람을 친구로 만드는 법을 배워야 한다는 것으
   로 Sujin이 학급 친구들에게 모르는 사람처럼 지내지 말고 내년
   에 서로 인사하며 지내자고 부탁하는 내용에 어색하다.

08 수진이 모르는 사람들을 만날 때마다 무엇을 해야 하는지는 알
   수 없다.

09 Emily는 Jinsu에게 설거지를 도와줄 것을 요청한다.

10 give a hand: 도와주다

11 빈칸에는 간접의문문을 목적어로 받을 수 있는 동사가 쓰이는
   것이 적절하다. know, tell, remember는 모두 목적어를 취할
   수 있는 타동사이지만 happen은 자동사이다.

12 대답으로 보아 누가 깃발을 찾았는지 궁금하다는 말이 들어가는
   것이 적절하다.

13 '형용사+to부정사'의 어순으로 부정대명사 something을 뒤에
   서 수식하는 ④번이 옳다. discuss: ~에 관하여 논의하다

14 ① who kicked the ball ② someone old ③ if she likes
   ④ what he would want라고 쓰는 것이 적절하다.

15 입을 따뜻한 무언가를 원한다는 말이 들어가는 것이 가장 적절
   하다.

16 ask의 직접목적어로 간접의문문을 활용하여 문장을 쓴다. 이때
   '의문사+주어+동사'의 어순임에 유의한다.

17 대답으로 미루어 보아 누가 그것을 지었는지 아는지를 묻는 말
   이 적절하다.

18 간접의문문을 이용하여 문장을 완성할 수 있다. 이때 who는 의

문대명사로 의문사이자 주어 역할을 동시에 한다.

19 혼란스러웠지만 마침내 결정을 내렸다는 것이 가장 자연스럽다.
   따라서 Finally가 가장 적절하다.

20 긴 머리를 가진 사람은 Rapunzel이다.

21 목이 말라서 (C) 물을 가지러 교실 밖으로 나옴 - (B) 갑자기
   커다란 천둥이 치고 - (A) 바로 그 순간에 도둑이 창문을 깼다
   고 생각함. 이후에 번개가 쳤고 1~2초 정도 밝아짐 - (D) 그때
   도둑이 진열장에서 달아나는 것을 봄

22 지각동사의 목적격 보어는 동사원형이나 현재분사이다.

23 Sylvia는 어쨌든 자신이 1등을 할 거였다고 말했으므로 Teo가
   글의 내용을 제대로 이해하였다.

24 Shirley는 누가 금메달을 훔쳤는지 찾기를 원했고. Jocelyn은
   사건 당시 노래를 연습하고 있었고, Sylvia는 시를 낭송하고 있
   었다고 하였다.

25 Sylvia가 비명소리를 몇 시에 들었는지는 알 수 없다.

01 She asks him to take care of her dog this
   weekend.

02 Tony's mother doesn't like dogs.

03 Because Sumin's family loves dogs.

04 if[whether] Donna was satisfied with my[our]
   service.

05 I wonder if[whether] she has something round.

06 I can't remember what it is called in English.

07 something sweet to eat[have] .

08 I really don't understand why she is crying.

09 She used Rapunzel's long hair to climb up the
   tower.

10 Because the world outside was beautiful unlike
   what the witch said.

11 It happened at Bakersville Middle School last
   night.

12 He found Jocelyn and the case with a broken
   window.

13 He took Shirley to the scene of the crime.

14 He is the principal of Bakersville Middle School.

15 the gold medal

01 나래는 Tony에게 이번 주말에 그녀의 개를 돌봐줄 것을 요청하
   였다.

02 Tony의 엄마는 개를 좋아하지 않는다.

03 Sumin의 가족은 개를 좋아하기 때문에 나래에게 추천하였다.

04 Donna가 서비스에 만족을 했는지 묻고 싶다는 말이 들어가는
   것이 적절하다.

05 부정대명사 something은 형용사의 수식을 뒤에서 받는다.

동사 remember의 목적어로 간접의문문을 쓴다. 어순은 '의문사+주어+동사'이므로 'what it is called ~'라고 쓰는 것이 적절하다.

07 대답으로 미루어 보아 먹을 단것을 원한다고 말했음을 알 수 있다. -thing으로 끝나는 부정대명사의 수식은 '형용사+to부정사'의 어순임에 유의한다.

08 understand의 목적어로 간접의문문을 써야 하며, 이때 어순은 '의문사+주어+동사'이다.

09 마녀는 탑으로 올라가기 위해서 라푼젤의 긴 머리카락을 사용했다.

10 마녀가 말한 것과는 달리 바깥세상이 아름다웠기 때문에 그녀의 눈을 믿을 수 없었다는 이야기이다.

11 사건은 어젯밤 Bakersville 중학교에서 발생하였다.

12 교장 선생님이 달려와 발견한 것은 Jocelyn과 유리창이 깨진 진열장이었다.

13 교장 선생님은 Shirley를 범죄 현장으로 데리고 갔다.

14 그는 Bakersville 중학교의 교장 선생님이다.

15 금메달이 있던 자리에 시 한 편이 놓여 있었다는 의미이다.

창의사고력 서술형 문제   p.104

|모범답안|

01 (A) take care of

 (B) his mother doesn't like dogs

 (C) her family loves dogs

02 who my favorite actor was / when he was born / if Tom Cruz was married

01 오늘 나는 내 개, Pony를 걱정했었다. 내가 이번 주말에 할머니를 방문해야 하기 때문에 나는 내 개를 돌보아 줄 수 있는 누군가를 찾아야 했다. 먼저 나는 Tony에게 내 개를 돌보아 줄 수 있는지 물어보았다. 불행히도, 그는 나를 도울 수 없었다. 왜냐하면 그의 엄마는 개를 싫어하기 때문이다. 나는 무엇을 해야 할지 몰랐다. 그 때, Tony가 수민을 추천해 주었다. 왜냐하면 그녀의 가족이 개를 매우 좋아하기 때문이었다. 나는 수민에게 전화를 했고 그녀에게 도움을 청했다. 그녀는 이번 주말 동안에 나를 도와줄 수 있다고 말했다. 나는 매우 기분이 좋았고 정말로 그녀에게 고마웠다.

단원별 모의고사   p.105~108

01 ②

02 (1) win the first place   (2) at the moment

 (3) rush over   (4) running across   (5) bring, back

03 ①

04 (1) A thief stole the gold medal yesterday.

 (2) Can you help me blow up these balloons?

 (3) Will you send me some pictures of our talent show?

05 ②, ④

06 He was looking for his baseball glove.

07 Spot took it.   08 (C) → (A) → (B) → (D)

09 ⑤   10 ③

11 (A) his smartphone   (B) the house

 (C) a sandwich   (D) the refrigerator

12 ③   13 ③   14 ④

15 Can you tell me where he is?

16 something important   17 ②   18 ③

19 ②

20 She saw someone running away from the case.

21 He went home a little before nine.

22 "Did you hear the window break?"   23 ⑤

01 다른 사람으로부터 무언가를 훔치는 사람을 일컫는 말은 thief(도둑)이다.

02 bring back: ~을 돌려주다, at the moment: 그때, rush over: 달려가다, 달려오다, run across: ~을 가로질러 뛰다, win first place: 일등을 하다

03 문장에 공통으로 들어갈 말은 flash이며 '섬광, 번쩍임' 또는 동사로 '번쩍이다, 빛나다'를 의미한다.

04 steal: 훔치다, blow up: ~을 불다, talent show: 장기 자랑

05 (A)는 추측을 나타내는 표현으로 ②, ④번과 바꾸어 표현할 수 있다.

06 Brain은 그의 야구 글러브를 찾고 있었다.

07 Spot이 Brian의 야구 글러브를 가져갔다.

08 (C) 도움 요청 → (A) 수락 및 질문 → (B) 대답 → (D) 추측 표현

09 ⑤번의 A는 도움을 요청하고 있으므로 이에 대한 대답이 이어져야 한다.

10 (A)는 동사 lost, (B)는 '문자를 보냈다'라는 과거동사 texted, (C)는 긍정문에서 '어딘가에'를 뜻하는 somewhere가 적절하다.

11 Brian은 그가 그의 스마트폰을 찾을 수 없어 혼란스러웠다. 그는 엄마에게 이것을 찾는 것을 도와주실 것을 요청하였다. Brain은 스마트폰이 집안에 있을 것이라고 확신하였다, 왜냐하면 그는 몇 분 전에 친구에게 문자 메시지를 보냈기 때문이다. 그는 부엌에서 샌드위치를 만들고 있었다. 그래서 그의 엄마는 부엌을 다시 한 번 확인했다. 마침내 그의 엄마는 이것을 냉장고 안에서 찾아내셨다.

12 Do you know how far the school is from here?라고 쓰는 것이 적절하다.

13 의문사가 없는 의문문은 if나 whether를 이용하여 간접의문문을

14 when she has to move out이라고 쓰는 것이 적절하다.

15 tell의 직접목적어로 '의문사+주어+동사' 어순의 간접의문문을 써서 문장을 완성할 수 있다.

16 -thing으로 끝나는 부정대명사는 형용사의 수식을 뒤에서 받는다.

17 두 문장 모두 시간과 관련된 것이므로 when이 적절하다. ⓐ에는 간접의문문을 이끄는 when이, ⓑ에는 시간의 부사절을 이끄는 when이 쓰인다.

18 범인이 누구인지 모르는 상황에서 학교에 있었던 학생들을 인터뷰하는 것으로 보아 ③번이 가장 적절하다.

19 (A)의 쓰임은 to부정사의 부사적 용법 중 목적에 해당한다. ① 명사적 용법 중 목적어 ② 부사적 용법 중 목적 ③ 진주어 ④ 형용사적 용법 ⑤ 명사적 용법 중 주어

20 번개가 쳤을 때 Jocelyn은 누군가가 진열장에서 달아나는 것을 보았다.

21 Harry는 아홉시 조금 전에 집으로 갔다.

22 창문이 깨지는 것이므로 지각동사 hear의 목적격보어로 완료를 나타내는 broken이 아니라 break가 적절하다.

23 장기 자랑 대회에서 누가 1등을 했는지는 위 글을 읽고 알 수 없다.

Frindle

교과서
Reading

확인문제   p.112

1 T   2 T

확인문제   p.113

1 T   2 T   3 F   4 T   5 F

교과서 확인학습 A   p.114~115

01 was excited about, was worried about
02 was famous for
03 should have a good dictionary, can look up
04 the meanings, means
05 entire town, agreed, its meaning
06 satisfied, did I agree, himself
07 On, decided   08 took out, From
09 asked, to use   10 During
11 held up, extra, to borrow   12 pleased
13 but, already has   14 found, funny, to use
15 In, became, cool word
16 said to, getting out of hand, to stop saying
17 stop it, as   18 no choice
19 took out, asked, to sign, date
20 I'll give, to you, is over   21 hates
22 began, with   23 punish, for using
24 things worse
25 to use, more and more   26 spread to nearby
27 Shortly after, wrote, on, knew about it
28 covered, found out about
29 By the time, graduated from, used
30 flew by, received   31 Inside it, found
32 signature from   33 yellow note . It said

1 Nick Allen was excited about starting fifth grade, but he was worried about one thing—Mrs. Granger's English class.

2 Mrs. Granger was famous for her difficult vocabulary lessons.

3 In the first class, Mrs. Granger said, "Everyone should have a good dictionary. You can look up the meanings of new words in it."

4 "Mrs. Granger? Who decides the meanings of words? I mean, who decided that 'dog' means an animal that barks?" Nick asked.

5 "You did, Nick. You, me, and the entire town and country. We all agreed. That gives the word its meaning."

6 Nick wasn't satisfied. "When did I agree?" he said to himself.

7 On the way home, he decided to test Mrs. Granger's idea.

8 He took out a pen and said, "From today, this is a *frindle*."

9 The next day, he asked five friends to use the word *frindle*.

10 During class, Nick said, "Mrs. Granger, I forgot my *frindle* today."

11 His friend, John, held up a pen and said, "I have an extra *frindle*. Do you want to borrow my *frindle*?"

12 Mrs. Granger was not pleased.

13 She said, "Your new word is cute, but it already has a perfectly good name — a pen."

14 Nick's classmates found this funny and began to use the word more and more.

15 In just three days, it became the cool word at school.

16 Mrs. Granger said to Nick after class, "This is getting out of hand. Can you tell your friends to stop saying *frindle*?"

17 "I'm sorry, but I can't stop it. It started as my word, but now it's the students' word."

18 "Very well. Then I have no choice."

19 Mrs. Granger took out an envelope and asked Nick to sign and date the back.

20 She said, "I'll give this letter to you when all this is over."

21 Nick thought, "She really hates me."

22 Next week, Mrs. Granger began a war with *frindle*.

23 She said that she would punish any student for using it.

24 But this only made things worse.

25 The students wanted to use the word more and more.

26 *Frindle* quickly spread to nearby middle and high schools.

27 Shortly after, a local newspaper reporter wrote an article on the situation and everyone in town knew about it.

28 A month later, a national television station covered the news and everyone found out about *frindle*.

29 By the time Nick graduated from elementary school, most students in the country used the word.

30 Time flew by and Nick turned 21. One day, he received a package.

31 Inside it, he found a pen, an envelope and a dictionary.

32 The envelope had his signature from fifth grade.

33 The dictionary had a yellow note. It said, "Check page 541."

01 agree

02 (1) bark   (2) signature   (3) envelope   (4) package

03 (1) I was excited about the school trip to Jejudo.
   (2) I felt relaxed after the math test was over.

04 (1) David was so tired that he couldn't meet us last night.
   (2) They are so tall that they can touch the ceiling.

05 (1) I want you to eat vegetables.
   (2) The doctor advised my father to exercise regularly.

06 (1) to do   (2) to borrow   (3) interesting

07 He was excited about starting fifth grade.

08 She wanted her students to have a good dictionary.

09 Students can look up the meanings of new words in it.

10 *frindle*   11 He created a new word, *frindle*.

12 Mrs. Granger was Nick's English teacher.

13 친구들이 *frindle*을 말하는 것

14 (D)–(A)–(C)–(B)

15 She asked him to sign and date the back of the envelope.

01 주어진 단어는 반의어 관계를 나타낸다. agree: 동의하다, disagree: 반대하다

04 'so ~ that 주어 can't 동사원형'은 'too ~ to V'와 같으며 '너무 ~해서 …할 수 없는'이라는 의미로 쓰인다. '~ enough to V'은 'so ~ that 주어 can 동사원형'으로 풀어쓸 수 있고 '…하기에 충분히 ~한'이라는 의미이다.

05 want와 advise는 목적격보어로 to부정사를 취하는 동사이다.

06 (1), (2) encourage와 want는 to부정사를 목적격보어로 취하는 동사이다. (3) find는 5형식 동사이며 상황은 흥미를 유발하는 주체이므로 interesting이라고 쓰는 것이 옳다.

07 Nick은 5학년이 시작되는 것이 신났다고 하였다.

08 선생님께서는 학생들이 좋은 사전을 갖기를 원하셨다.

09 Granger 선생님에 따르면, 학생들은 새로운 단어의 뜻을 사전에서 찾을 수 있다.

10 Nick이 지어낸 *frindle*이라는 단어를 의미한다.

11 선생님의 생각을 시험하기로 결심한 Nick은 새로운 단어인 *frindle*을 만들었다.

12 Nick의 영어 선생님은 Mrs. Granger였다.

13 친구들이 *frindle*을 말하는 것을 멈춰달라고 말하는 선생님의 요청에 그렇게 할 수 없다고 답하고 있다.

14 (D) 선생님께서 *frindle*과의 전쟁을 시작 → (A) 그 단어를 사용하는 학생을 벌 줄 것이라 말함 → (C) 이것은 상황을 더 악화시킴 → (B) 학생들은 그 단어를 점점 더 사용하고 싶어 함

15 선생님은 봉투를 하나 꺼내어 Nick에게 뒷면에 서명을 하고 날짜를 적게 했다.

단원별 예상문제

p.120~124

01 ②　　　　**02** (1) took out　(2) look up
(3) have no choice　(4) out of hand　(5) hold up
03 ①　　　　**04** ②　　　　**05** ③
06 (1) James spends more and more time playing the computer games.
　(2) My English teacher is famous for funny class.
07 ⑤　　　**08** ③　　　**09** ③　　　**10** ⑤
11 ②　　　**12** who gave you this letter　**13** ③
14 The teacher makes me nervous.
15 decided the meanings of words　　　**16** ③
17 She was famous for her difficult vocabulary lessons.　　　**18** ④
19 He was worried about Mrs. Granger's English class.
20 ④　　　　**21** [C]–[B]–[A]
22 펜을 *frindle*이라고 부르는 것　　　**23** ③
24 She was not pleased.　**25** ③　　**26** ④
27 ②　　　**28** ③　　　**29** ②
30 She will give it to Nick when all this is over.

31 She said that she would punish any student for using the word, *frindle*.
32 The students wanted to use the word more and more.　　　**33** ⑤
34 Most students in the country used the word, *frindle*.
35 He found a pen, an envelope, and a dictionary.
36 ⑤

01 '누군가가 법을 어기거나 무언가를 잘못했기 때문에 고통을 주다'는 punish(처벌하다)를 말한다.

02 take out: 꺼내다, get out of hand: 손을 쓸 수 없게 되다, hold up: 잡다, look up: (사전 등에서) ~을 찾다, have no choice: 선택의 여지가 없다

03 date: (동) 날짜를 적다, (명) 날짜

04 주어진 문장에서 cover는 '보도하다'를 의미하며 이와 같은 의미로 쓰인 것은 ②번이다. 나머지는 모두 '덮다, 가리다'를 뜻한다.

05 pleased: 기쁜

06 more and more: 점점 더

07 cause는 to부정사를 목적격보어로 취하는 동사이다. 따라서 to be more careful이라고 쓰는 것이 적절하다.

08 would like는 to부정사를 목적격보어로 취하는 동사이다. 따라서 '네가 나를 초대하면 좋겠다'고 하였으므로 would like you to invite me라고 쓰는 것이 적절하다.

09 'so ~ that 주어 can't 동사원형'은 'too ~ to 동사원형'과 같다.

10 make는 목적격보어로 동사원형을 취하는 사역동사이다.

11 의문사가 없는 의문문의 간접의문문은 의문사 대신 if나 whether를 사용하여 만들 수 있다.

12 의문사이자 주어 역할을 동시에 하는 의문대명사를 이용하여 간접의문문을 만들 수 있다.

13 let은 사역동사로 목적격보어를 동사원형을 취한다.

14 make는 5형식으로 쓰일 수 있다. 이때 목적어를 설명하는 목적격보어가 형용사임에 유의하자.

15 단어의 의미를 결정하는 것을 말한다.

16 온 마을과 나라가 동의한 것을 의미하므로 ③번이 가장 적절하다.

17 Mrs. Granger는 어려운 어휘 수업으로 유명했다.

18 누가 단어의 의미를 결정하는지 궁금해 한 것은 Nick이다.

19 Nick이 걱정한 것은 Mrs. Granger의 영어 수업이다.

20 ① agree ② difficult ③ new ⑤ famous의 반의어이며 ④는 entire와 같은 의미이다.

21 펜을 *frindle*이라고 부르기로 함 - [C] 친구들에게 단어 *frindle*을 사용해 달라고 부탁하고 수업시간에 *frindle*을 가져오지 않았다고 말함 - [B] 이에 친구가 *frindle*이라는 단어를 사용하며 빌리겠냐고 물어봄 - [A] 이 말을 들은 선생님은

pen이라는 좋은 이름이 있다고 말해줌.

22 Nick이 요청한 대로 펜을 *frindle*이라고 부르는 것을 의미한다.

23 a perfectly good name은 pen을 의미하며 나머지는 모두 *frindle*을 의미한다.

24 선생님은 새로운 단어에 대해 즐거워하지 않았다.

25 '빌리다'라는 의미의 borrow라고 쓰는 것이 적절하다. lend는 '빌려주다'라는 의미이다.

26 Nick의 교실에 반 친구들이 몇 명이나 있는지는 알 수 없다.

27 get out of hand는 '감당할 수 없게 되다'라는 의미이다. 따라서 '제지할 수 없게 되다'라는 의미의 ②번이 가장 적절하다.

28 stop은 동명사를 목적어로 취하는 동사로 '~하는 것을 멈추다'라는 의미로 사용해야 하므로 saying, (B) ask는 to부정사를 목적격보어로 취하는 동사, (C) want는 to부정사를 목적어로 취하는 동사이다.

29 Nick은 자신의 단어로 시작된 것이 이제는 그 학생들의 단어가 되었다고 하였다. 따라서 ②번이 글의 내용과 일치한다.

30 이 모든 것이 끝나면 선생님이 이 편지를 Nick에게 주실 것이라고 하였다.

31 선생님께서는 *frindle*이라는 단어를 사용하면 어떤 학생이든 벌을 줄 것이라고 말했다.

32 선생님이 *frindle*과의 전쟁을 시작하자 학생들은 그 단어를 더욱 더 사용하고 싶어 하였다.

33 *frindle*이라는 단어가 인기를 얻었을 때 Nick의 감정은 위 글을 읽고 알 수 없다.

34 Nick이 초등학교를 졸업할 때쯤에는 그 나라의 대부분의 학생들이 그 단어를 사용했다.

35 Nick이 소포 안에서 발견한 것은 펜 한 자루, 봉투 한 장, 그리고 사전 한 권이었다.

36 ⓐ는 '보도하다, 방송하다'라는 의미로 쓰였다. ①, ③ ~을 덮다 ② ~을 씌우다 ④ (책의) 표지 ⑤ 방송하다, 보도하다

교과서 파헤치기

Lesson 7

단어 TEST Step 1   p.02

01 작가	02 배낭	03 완벽한
04 관련성, 연관성	05 여행	06 상
07 차이점	08 섞다	09 믿다, 신뢰하다
10 모험	11 전통적인	12 설명하다
13 간단한, 단순한	14 우정	15 특히
16 ~와 달리	17 진실, 사실	18 거짓말하다
19 광고	20 가치가 있는	21 공상
22 신념, 생각	23 강력하게	24 들어 올리다
25 현명하게	26 식사	27 증명하다
28 나타내다, 표현하다		29 해결하다, 풀다
30 남색	31 추천하다	32 지루한
33 감동적인	34 의견	35 예를 들면
36 ~로 가득한	37 ~을 바탕으로	38 지금부터
39 기다려, 멈춰	40 선택하다	41 지금
42 ~을 확인하다	43 그만한 가치가 있는	

단어 TEST Step 2   p.03

01 trust	02 author	03 perfect
04 touching	05 express	06 boring
07 trip	08 navy	09 adventure
10 purple	11 novel	12 opinion
13 advertisement	14 pocket	15 simple
16 award	17 worth	18 especially
19 meal	20 friendship	21 strongly
22 lift	23 solve	24 prove
25 explain	26 traditional	27 difference
28 mix	29 fantasy	30 recommend
31 belief	32 unlike	33 wisely
34 truth	35 check out	36 look for
37 from now on	38 make a choice	
39 for example	40 full of	41 based on
42 right now	43 hold on	

단어 TEST Step 3   p.04

1 trust, 신뢰하다, 믿다   2 opinion, 의견   3 mix, 섞다

4 lift, 들어 올리다   5 truth, 진실, 사실   6 meal, 식사

---

7 express, 나타내다, 표현하다   8 lie, 거짓말하다

9 pocket, 주머니   10 recommend, 추천하다

11 advertisement, 광고   12 connection, 관련성

13 explain, 설명하다   14 prove, 증명하다

15 award, 상   16 desert, 사막

대화문 TEST Step 1   p.05~06

Listen & Speak 1-A

recommend a good movie / really liked / haven't seen, yet / number one, right now

Listen & Speak 1-B

help / looking for, backpack, recommend one / How about, the most popular color these days / My old backpack, different color / How about, navy, has side pockets, looks good, take

Listen & Speak 2-A

got, new smartphone / really happy with / What, like most about it / takes great pictures

Listen & Speak 2-B

How did, like, trip / happy with / Where, visit / visited / Where else did, go / wonderful place / Sounds like, perfect trip / walking up, was difficult / I'm sure, worth it

Real Life Talk – Step 1

can you recommend / Why don't, my favorite / What, like about / delicious, recommend / How, the prices / think, too / Sounds like, How, like the service / little slow / check it out / problem, Enjoy

Real Life Talk – Step 2

recommend a book for me / How about / What do you like / main character, special / Sounds, read

대화문 TEST Step 2   p.07~08

Listen & Speak 1-A

Brian: Can you recommend a good movie?

Emily: Try Star Wars. I really liked it.

Brian: Oh, I haven't seen it yet.

Emily: It's the number one movie right now.

Listen & Speak 1-B

W: May I help you?

B: Yes. I'm looking for a backpack. Can you recommend one?

W: How about this red one? Red is the most popular color these days.

B: My old backpack was red, so I want a different color.

W: How about this navy one? It has side pockets.

B: Oh, that looks good. I'll take it.

Listen & Speak 2-A

Sue: Tom, you got a new smartphone.

Tom: Yes, I did. I'm really happy with it.

Sue: What do you like most about it?

Tom: I love the camera. It takes great pictures.

Listen & Speak 2-B

Jack: Hi, Suji. How did you like your trip to Gyeongju?

Suji: I was very happy with it.

Jack: Where did you visit?

Suji: I visited Cheomseongdae. It was great.

Jack: Where else did you go?

Suji: Bulguksa. It was a wonderful place.

Jack: Sounds like the perfect trip.

Suji: Yeah, but walking up to Seokguram was difficult.

Jack: But I'm sure it was worth it.

Real Life Talk – Step 1

Brian: Mina, can you recommend a good pizza restaurant?

Mina: Why don't you try Antonio's? It's my favorite.

Brian: What do you like about it?

Mina: The food is delicious. I recommend the bulgogi pizza.

Brian: How are the prices?

Mina: I think the prices are good, too.

Brian: Sounds like a good restaurant. How do you like the service?

Mina: It's a little slow on the weekends.

Brian: Okay. I'll check it out. Thanks.

Mina: No problem. Enjoy your meal!

Real Life Talk – Step 2

Amy: Yujin, can you recommend a book for me?

Yujin: How about The Little Prince?

Amy: What do you like about the book?

Yujin: I like the main character. He is very special.

Amy: Sounds good. I'll read it.

본문 TEST Step 1   p.09~10

01 are, doing

02 watching, on, computer

03 How, it

04 Don't, so boring that

05 sorry to hear

06 mad, advertisement said

07 believe everything that, read

08 lied on, for, back

09 Hold, lie because, opinions

10 not following you

11 express, feelings like

12 that, not, facts, proven

13 For example, check, on

14 the connection with

15 Let, explain, favorite   16 It's, *Gump*

17 Let's, its advertisement, say

18 says, Awards including   19 uses facts unlike

20 Do, see, difference   21 exactly, says, ad

22 Aren't, both opinions

23 question, like, expressing opinions

24 ad, award, movie won   25 check, on, fact

26 From, on, trust, with

27 that simple, mix, with

28 have, make, choice, both

29 Got, watch, rest, with

30 no thanks, rest

본문 TEST Step 2   p.11~12

01 What are, doing

02 watching the movie, on

03 How, it

04 Don't, so boring that, to cry

05 sorry to hear that

06 mad, advertisement, it, The Most Exciting Movie

07 can't believe everything that you read

08 lied on, ask for my money back

09 Hold on, lie because, used opinions, facts

10 not following you

11 express people's feelings

12 that, true or not, can be proven

13 For example, check that on the map

14 the connection with

15 Let me explain   16 It's

17 Let's look for its advertisement

18 It says, including   19 uses facts unlike

20 the difference   21 exactly, says, says

22 Aren't, both opinions

23 words like, usually expressing opinions

24 award which the movie won

25 check that on the Internet

26 From now on, trust, with

27 that simple, mix facts with opinions

28 make a smart choice based on both

29 to watch the rest

30 no thanks, the rest of

1 Emma: Kyle, 뭐 하고 있니?

2 Kyle: Emma. 나는 컴퓨터로 영화 "Y-Men 7"을 보고 있어.

3 Emma: 어때?

4 Kyle: 묻지 마. 너무 지루해서 울고 싶어.

5 Emma: 유감이야.

6 Klye: 난 정말 화가 나. 영화 광고에는 이것이 "올해의 가장 흥미진진한 영화"라고 쓰여 있었어.

7 Emma: 음, 넌 네가 읽는 것을 모두 믿을 수는 없어.

8 Kyle: 그들은 광고에 거짓말을 한 거야. 돈을 환불해 달라고 해야겠어.

9 Emma: 기다려, Kyle! 그들은 사실이 아닌 의견을 사용했기 때문에 꼭 거짓말을 한 것은 아니야.

10 Kyle: 뭐라고? 네 말을 이해하지 못하겠어.

11 Emma: 의견은 "사막은 아름다워."와 같이 사람들의 감정을 표현하는 것이야.

12 그것이 사실인지 아닌지 말할 수는 없어. 하지만 사실은 증명할 수 있어.

13 예를 들면, "아타카마 사막은 칠레에 있다."는 사실이야. 넌 그것을 지도에서 확인할 수 있어.

14 Kyle: 알겠어…. 하지만 그게 영화와 무슨 관련이 있니?

15 Emma: 설명해 줄게. 네가 가장 좋아하는 영화가 뭐니?

16 Kyle: "Forest Gump"야.

17 Emma: 좋아. 그 영화의 광고를 찾아보자. 뭐라고 쓰여 있니?

18 Kyle: "Best Picture를 포함하여 아카데미 6개 부문 수상작"이라고 쓰여 있어.

19 Emma: 알겠니? "Y-Men 7" 광고와는 달리 사실을 사용하고 있어.

20 차이를 알겠니?

21 Kyle: 잘 모르겠어. "Y-Men 7" 광고는 "Most Exciting Movie"라고 쓰여 있고 "Forest Gump" 광고는 "Best Picture"라고 쓰여 있잖아.

22 둘 다 의견 아니니?

23 Emma: 좋은 질문이야, Kyle. 사람들이 'best'나 'most'와 같은 말을 사용할 때, 그들은 대개 의견을 표현하는 거야.

24 하지만 "Forest Gump" 광고에서 "Best Picture"는 영화가 받은 상이야.

25 우리는 인터넷에서 그것을 확인할 수 있어. 그건 사실이야.

26 Kyle: 아하! 지금부터 사실로 이루어진 광고만 믿겠어.

27 Emma: 그렇게 간단하지는 않아. 대부분의 광고는 사실과 의견이 섞여 있어

28 그러니 그 둘을 바탕으로 현명한 선택을 해야 해.

29 Kyle: 알겠어! Emma, "Y-Men 7"의 남은 부분을 나와 함께 볼래?

30 Emma: 고맙지만 사양할게. 영화의 남은 부분 잘 봐!

1 Emma: What are you doing, Kyle?

2 Kyle: Oh, Emma. I'm watching the movie, *Y-Men 7* on my computer.

3 Emma: How is it?

4 Kyle: Don't ask. It's so boring that I want to cry.

5 Emma: I'm sorry to hear that.

6 Kyle: I'm so mad. The movie advertisement said it was "The Most Exciting Movie of the Year."

7 Emma: Well, you can't believe everything that you read.

8 Kyle: They lied on the advertisement. I'm going to ask for my money back.

9 Emma: Hold on, Kyle! They didn't really lie because they used opinions, not facts.

10 Kyle: Huh? I'm not following you.

11 Emma: Opinions express people's feelings like, "The desert is beautiful."

12 You can't say that it's true or not. But, facts can be proven.

13 For example, "The Atacama Desert is in Chile," is a fact. You can check that on the map.

14 Kyle: Okay…. But what's the connection with movies?

15 Emma: Let me explain. What's your favorite movie?

16 Kyle: It's *Forrest Gump*.

17 Emma: Okay. Let's look for its advertisement. What does it say?

18 Kyle: It says, "Winner of 6 Academy Awards including Best Picture."

19 Emma: See? It uses facts unlike the *Y-Men 7* advertisement.

20 Do you see the difference?

21 Kyle: Not exactly. The *Y-Men 7* ad says "Most Exciting Movie" and the *Forrest Gump* ad says "Best Picture."

22 Aren't they both opinions?

23 Emma: That's a great question, Kyle. When people use words like "best" or "most," they are usually expressing opinions.

24 But in the *Forrest Gump* ad, "Best Picture" is the award which the movie won.

25 We can check that on the Internet. That's a fact.

26 Kyle: Aha! From now on I'm only going to trust ads with facts.

27 Emma: It's not that simple. Most ads mix facts with opinions.

28 So you have to make a smart choice based on both of them.

29 Kyle: Got it! Emma, do you want to watch the rest of *Y-Men 7* with me?

30 Emma: Thanks, but no thanks. Enjoy the rest of the movie!

구석구석지문 TEST Step 1 p.19

Listen and Speak 2 - C

1. How do you like
2. not happy with
3. not
4. too heavy

Think and Write

1. fantasy novel
2. was written by
3. the main character
4. magic school, adventures
5. especially like, friendship
6. so interesting that, put, down
7. strongly recommend

Project

1. folk village
2. is located in
3. Korean traditional houses
4. can watch
5. a fun place
6. traditional houses
7. will be exciting

구석구석지문 TEST Step 2 p.20

Listen and Speak 2 - C

1. A: How do you like your bicycle?
2. B: I'm not happy with it.
3. A: Why not?
4. B: It's too heavy.

Think and Write

1. *Harry Potter* is a fantasy novel .
2. It was written by J. K. Rowling.
3. *Harry Potter* is the main character of the book.
4. When Harry goes to magic school , his adventures begin.
5. I especially like the friendship of Harry and his friends.
6. The book was so interesting that I couldn't put it down .

7. I strongly recommend it to everyone.

Project

1. Korean folk village
2. Facts: It is located in Yongin.
3. There are Korean traditional houses.
4. Visitors can watch nongak and jultagi.
5. Opinions: It's a fun place in Yongin.
6. Korean traditional houses are beautiful.
7. Nongak and jultagi will be exciting.

9 mop, 대걸레로 닦다　10 rush, (급히) 행동하다
11 talent, 재능　12 clue, 단서, 실마리
13 bronze, 청동　14 detective, 탐정　15 steal, 훔치다
16 lightning, 번개

단어 TEST Step 1　　p.21

01 공포	02 게시하다, 공고하다	
03 깨진, 부서진	04 목마른	05 청동
06 깃털	07 (급히) 움직이다, 서두르다	
08 섬광, 번쩍임	09 시	10 이상한
11 천둥	12 단서, 실마리	
13 걱정하는, 두려워하는		14 냉장고
15 문자 메시지를 보내다; 문자		16 손자국
17 ~ 안에	18 보물	19 범죄
20 위험한	21 훔치다	
22 낯선 사람, 모르는 사람		23 탐정
24 궁금해 하다	25 호의, 친절, 부탁	26 전화를 걸다, 부르다
27 갑자기	28 발자국	29 도둑
30 번개	31 나르다, 옮기다	32 대걸레로 닦다
33 교장	34 재능	35 ~을 돌보다
36 몇몇의, 조금의	37 지금, 곧, 당장	38 일등을 하다
39 더 이상 ~ 않다	40 집에 가는(오는) 길에	
41 달려가다	42 곤경에 빠지다	43 그 순간에, 그때에

단어 TEST Step 2　　p.22

01 footprint	02 silver	03 bronze
04 lightning	05 stranger	06 carry
07 refrigerator	08 dangerous	09 suddenly
10 wonder	11 feather	12 broken
13 talent	14 crime	15 rush
16 poem	17 flash	18 clue
19 thief	20 lose	21 handprint
22 principal	23 favor	24 thirsty
25 horror	26 steal	27 strange
28 detective	29 inside	30 water
31 mop	32 treasure	33 post
34 thunder	35 a few	36 on the way home
37 not ~ anymore		38 right now
39 take care of	40 at the moment	
41 bring ~ back	42 get into trouble	
43 rush over		

단어 TEST Step 3　　p.23

1 anyway, 어쨌든　2 footprint, 발자국　3 horror, 공포
4 principal, 교장　5 crime, 범죄　6 thief, 도둑
7 else, 또 다른　8 flash, 섬광, 번쩍임

대화문 TEST Step 1　　p.24~25

Listen and Speak 1-A

ask, favor / Sure / wash the dishes / problem

Listen and Speak 1-B

do me, favor / take care of, going to visit / I'm sorry but I can't / what shoud I do / Why dont you, loves / call, right now

Listen and Speak 1-C

do me a favor / help me mop / problem, Sorry, can't

Listen and Speak 2-A

baseball glove / under the table / not, anymore / guess, took / he is

Listen and Speak 2-B

have passed. at th end of, wonderful year, a few, be in the same class, stranger, each other

Listen and Speak 2-C

what I'm doing / I guess, playing / wrong, Guess / guess, working on / right

Real Life Talk - Step 1

can't find, Can you help me / Are you sure, inside / texted, a few minutes / Where were, at the time / was making / somewhere / already checked / let's check it again, it is, refrigerator / greastest / welcome

Real Life Talk - Step 2

help me find / did, see, last / On / guess, took, see its footprints

대화문 TEST Step 2　　p.26~27

Listen and Speak 1-A

Emily: Jinsu, can I ask you a favor?

Jinsu: Sure. What is it?

Emily: Can you help me wash the dishes?

Jinsu: No problem.

Listen and Speak 1-B

Narae: Tony, can you do me a favor?

Tony: Sure. What is it, Narae?

Narae: Can you take care of my dog this weekend?
　　　My family is going to visit my grandmother in Busan.

Tony: Oh, I'm sorry but I can't. My mom doesn't like dogs.

Narae: Oh, what should I do?

Tony: Why don't you ask Sumin? Her family loves dogs.

Narae: Okay. I'll call her right now.

Listen and Speak 1-C

A: Can you do me a favor?

B: Sure. What is it?

A: Can you help me mop the floor?

B: No problem. / Sorry, I can't.

Listen and Speak 2-A

Brian: Did you see my baseball glove?

Jane: Yes, I saw it under the table.

Brian: Really? It's not there anymore.

Jane: Then I guess Spot took it.

Brian: Oh, there he is. You bad dog, Spot!

Listen and Speak 2-B

G: Good morning, classmates! Nine months have passed so fast, and we are almost at the end of this school year. We all had a wonderful year. I guess only a few of us will be in the same class next year. Don't be a stranger. Say hello when we see each other, okay? Thank you.

Listen and Speak 2-C

A: Guess what I'm doing.

B: I guess you're playing the piano.

A: You're wrong. Guess again.

B: I guess you're working on the computer.

A: That's right.

Real Life Talk - Step 1

Brian: Mom, I can't find my smartphone. Can you help me find it?

Mom: Are you sure you lost it inside the house?

Brian: Yes. I just texted my friend a few minutes ago.

Mom: Where were you at the time?

Brian: In the kitchen. I was making a sandwich.

Mom: Then I guess you left it somewhere in the kitchen.

Brian: I already checked the kitchen, Mom.

Mom: Well, let's check it again. Oh, here it is. Inside the refrigerator.

Brian: Thanks, Mom. You are the greatest!

Mom: You're welcome, honey.

Real Life Talk - Step 2

A: Can you help me find my baseball glove?

B: Okay. Where did you see it last?

A: On the bench.

B: I guess a dog took your baseball glove. I can see its footprints on the bench.

01 ran across, wet   02 need, help

03 eighth grade student

04 best detective, whole

05 something wrong   06 has stolen, for

07 took, to, scene

08 case with, broken

09 bronze, still there

10 missing, poem, its place   11 Where did, go

12 low, catch, too

13 when this happened

14 after, rounds, rushed over

15 wonder who else was

16 practicing for, call them

17 ninth grade, curly

18 thirsty, completely, thunder, away

19 see, thief's face

20 only, thief's back, short

21 eighth grade, with long

22 aloud, flash, like, scared

23 hear, break   24 too loud, going, win

25 seventh, short blonde

26 wrong, moves, little, outside

27 anything strange

28 How could, loud

29 on, way home

30 heard, singing, badly, anyone

31 need, anymore, turned to

32 bring, back, into, trouble

01 ran across, wet

02 need your help

03 an eighth grade student

04 the best detective, whole

05 something wrong, asked

06 has stolen, for, talent show

07 took, to, scene

08 was a case, broken

09 bronze, were still there

10 missing, a poem, its place   11 Where did, go

12 high and low, too slow

13 when this happened

14 after, making my rounds, rushed over, like

15 who else was here

16 practicing for, call them

17 ninth grade, with short curly

18 practicing, become thirsty, stepped outside, to get, It, completely, Suddenly, thunder, broke, Lightning followed, a second, two, saw, running away

19 thief's face

20 only saw, back, short

21 eighth grade, with long black

22 reading, aloud, went outside, next to, flash, like a horror movie, scared, ran straight

23 hear, break   24 too loud, was going to win

25 seventh, short blonde

26 wrong, moves, a little before, take, outside, until

27 hear anything strange

28 How could   29 on the way home

30 heard someone singing

31 need to hear anymore, turned to

32 bring the medal back, get into, trouble

1 Reese 교장은 젖은 운동장을 달려왔다.

2 "Shirley! Shirley! 네 도움이 필요하구나!"

3 Shirley는 Bakersville 중학교의 8학년 학생이었다.

4 그녀는 또한 그 마을 최고의 탐정이었다.

5 "무슨 일이 있나요?" Shirley가 물었다.

6 "누군가 장기 자랑 대회 금메달을 훔쳐갔어!"

7 Reese 교장은 Shirley를 범죄 현장으로 데려갔다.

8 유리창이 깨진 진열장이 있었다.

9 은메달과 동메달은 그곳에 그대로 있었다.

10 하지만 금메달은 사라졌다. 그 자리에는 시가 있었다.

11 내일은 장기 자랑 대회. 금메달은 어디로 갔을까?

12 구석구석 찾아라. 당신은 나를 잡을 수 없어. 당신은 너무 느려.

13 Shirley는 "언제 이 사건이 일어났는지 말씀해 주시겠어요?"라고 물었다.

14 "어젯밤 9시가 조금 넘은 후에. 내가 순찰을 돌고 있었을 때 비명 소리가 들렸어. 나는 달려가서 Jocelyn과 이 상태 인 진열장을 발견했지."

15 "어젯밤에 또 다른 누가 여기 있었는지 궁금해요."

16 "Sylvia와 Harry가 있었어. 그 두 사람 또한 장기 자랑을 위해 연습 중이었어. 내가 그들을 내 사무실로 부르마."

17 Jocelyn은 빨간색 짧은 곱슬머리를 가진 9학년 학생이었다.

18 "저는 제 노래를 연습하고 있었는데 목이 말랐어요. 저는 물을 가지러 교실 밖으로 나갔어요. 완전히 어두웠어요 갑자기, 커다란 천둥소리가 났어요. 저는 도둑이 그 순간에 유리창을 깼다고 생각해요. 번개가 바로 뒤따랐고 1~2초 정도 밝아졌어요. 그때 저는 누군가가 진열장에서 도망치는 걸 봤어요."

19 "도둑의 얼굴을 봤나요?"

20 "아니요, 도둑의 뒷모습만 봤어요. 하지만 그 도둑은 짧은 머리였어요."

21 다음은 8학년 학생인 Sylvia였다. 그녀는 긴 검은색 머리에 키가 컸다.

22 그녀는 말했다. "저는 교실에서 큰 소리로 제 시를 낭송하고 있었어요. 비명 소리를 듣고 밖으로 나갔어요. 진열장 옆에 한 소녀가 있었어요. 번개의 번쩍임과 어우러져 그것은 공포 영화 같았어요. 저는 겁이 나서 곧장 집으로 달려갔어요." "

23 "창이 깨지는 소리를 들었나요?"

24 "아니요, 천둥소리가 너무 컸어요. 음, 제가 그런 게 아니에요. 저는 어쨌든 1등을 할 거였으니까요."

25 7학년인 Harry는 짧은 금발을 가지고 있었다.

26 그는 말했다. "이봐요, 사람을 잘못 짚었어요. 저는 제 춤 동작을 연습하고 있었어요. 저는 9시 조금 전에 집에 갔어요. 저는 그때까지 교실 밖으로 한 발자국도 나가지 않았어요."

27 "이상한 소리라도 들었나요?"

28 "제가 어떻게 듣겠어요? 제 음악 소리가 정말 컸어요."

29 "집에 가는 길에 누군가를 보았나요?"

30 "아니요, 누군가가 노래를 정말 끔찍하게 부르는 소리는 들었지만 누구도 보진 못했어요."

31 Shirley는 "더 이상 들을 필요는 없겠네요."라고 말했다. 그리고 나서 그녀는 도둑을 향했다.

32 "정말 곤경에 빠지기 전에 금메달을 돌려주는 게 어때요?"

1 Mr. Reese, the principal, ran across the wet playground.

2 "Shirley! Shirley! I need your help!"

3 Shirley was an eighth grade student at Bakersville Middle School.

4 She was also the best detective in the whole town.

5 "Is there something wrong?" asked Shirley.

6 "Someone has stolen the gold medal for the talent show!"

7 Mr. Reese took Shirley to the scene of the crime.

8 There was a case with a broken window.

9 The silver and bronze medals were still there.

10 But the gold medal was missing. There was a poem in its place.

11 Tomorrow is the talent show. Where did the gold medal go?

12 Look high and low. You can't catch me. You're too slow.

13 Shirley asked, "Could you tell me when this happened?"

14 "A little after nine last night. I was making my rounds when I heard a scream. I rushed over and found Jocelyn and the case like this."

15 "I wonder who else was here last night."

16 "Sylvia and Harry. They were also practicing for the talent show. I'll call them to my office."

17 Jocelyn was a ninth grade student with short curly red hair.

18 "I was practicing my song and I became thirsty. I stepped outside the classroom to get some water. It was completely dark. Suddenly, there was a loud sound of thunder. I think the thief broke the window at that moment. Lightning followed right after and it became bright for a second or two. Then I saw someone running away from the case."

19 "Did you see the thief's face?"

20 "No, I only saw the thief's back. But the thief had short hair."

21 Next was an eighth grade student, Sylvia. She was tall with long black hair.

22 She said, "I was reading my poem aloud in the classroom. I heard a scream and went outside. There was a girl next to the case. With the flash from the lightning, it was like a horror movie. I got scared so I ran straight home."

23 "Did you hear the window break?"

24 "No, the thunder was too loud. Well, I didn't do it. I was going to win first place anyway."

25 Harry, a seventh grader, had short blonde hair.

26 He said, "Hey, you got the wrong guy. I was practicing my dance moves. I went home a little before nine. I didn't take one step outside the classroom until then."

27 "Did you hear anything strange?"

28 "How could I? My music was really loud."

29 "Did you see anyone on the way home?"

30 "No, I heard someone singing really badly, but I didn't see anyone."

31 Shirley said, "I don't need to hear anymore." Then she turned to the thief.

32 "Why don't you bring the medal back before you get into some real trouble?"

Project

1. treasure hunters
2. have hidden, something delicious
3. where, follow the steps
4. look for, near, under
5. pick up, walk to the back
6. third locker from the left
7. is locked, to open, yourself

Think and Write

1. put her in
2. grew up, long hair
3. to climb up
4. world outside
5. heard Rapunzel singing beautifully
6. Come down
7. who is telling the truth, was confused
8. made up, cut, came down
9. faced, for the first time, What a beautiful world

Check Up

1. you, me a favor
2. Sure
3. help me blow up
4. problem

Project

1. To the treasure hunters,
2. Hello. We have hidden our treasure in the classroom. It is something delicious.
3. Do you want to know where it is? Then follow the steps.
4. First, look for a plant near the window. Look under the plant. You'll find a key.
5. Second, pick up the key and walk to the back of the classroom. You'll see the lockers.
6. The treasure is in the third locker from the left.
7. It is locked, so use the key to open it. Got it? Help yourself.

Think and Write

1. When Rapunzel was a baby, a witch put her in a tall tower.
2. Rapunzel grew up in the tower. She had long hair .
3. The witch used it to climb up the tower.
4. The witch always said, "The world outside is very dangerous."

5. One day, a prince heard Rapunzel singing beautifully.

6. He said, "Come down. The world outside is wonderful."

7. Rapunzel said, "I don't know who is telling the truth." Rapunzel was confused.

8. Finally, she made up her mind. She cut her hair and came down from the tower.

9. When she faced the world for the first time, she couldn't believe her eyes. " What a beautiful world !"

Check Up

1. A: Can you do me a favor?
2. B: Sure. What is it?
3. A: Can you help me blow up these balloons?
4. B: No problem.

Lesson S

단어 TEST Step 1   p.40

01 (개가) 짖다	02 퍼지다, 확산되다	03 소포
04 보도하다, 덮다	05 날짜를 적다; 날짜	06 동의하다
07 서명	08 빌리다	09 멋진
10 의미	11 전체의, 온	12 완벽하게
13 봉투	14 상황	15 졸업하다
16 처벌하다, 벌주다	17 안에, 내부에	18 지역의, 지방의
19 의미하다	20 받다	21 기사
22 재미있는	23 학년	24 급우, 반 친구
25 인근의, 가까이의	26 기자	27 여분의, 추가의
28 결정하다	29 기쁜, 기뻐하는	30 신이 난
31 만족하는	32 어휘	33 전쟁
34 사전	35 선택의 여지가 없다, 대안이 없다	
36 ~이 끝나다	37 그때까지, ~할 때까지	
38 ~을 꺼내다	39 쥐다, 잡다	40 ~에 대해 걱정하다
41 집으로 가는 길에	42 ~로 유명하다	43 ~에 신이 나다

단어 TEST Step 2   p.41

01 bark	02 mean	03 envelope
04 borrow	05 signature	06 grade
07 receive	08 cool	09 date
10 pleased	11 meaning	12 punish
13 article	14 extra	15 satisfied
16 excited	17 funny	18 situation
19 spread	20 graduate	21 package
22 inside	23 local	24 decide
25 perfectly	26 reporter	27 dictionary
28 cover	29 nearby	30 quickly
31 entire	32 vocabulary	33 war
34 agree	35 more and more	
36 be famous for	37 have no choice	
38 hold up	39 look up	40 out of hand
41 by the time	42 on the way home	
43 be worried about		

단어 TEST Step 3   p.42

1 graduate, 졸업하다   2 envelope, 봉투
3 agree, 동의하다   4 entire, 전체의   5 meaning, 의미
6 vocabulary, 어휘   7 extra, 여분의
8 article, (신문의) 기사   9 classmate, 급우

10 package, 소포　11 reporter, 기자

12 signature, 서명　13 borrow, 빌리다

14 situation, 상황　15 punish, 처벌하다

16 dictionary, 사전

01 excited, fifth grade, worried

02 famous for, difficult, lessons

03 class, dictionary, up, meanings

04 meanings, decided, means, barks

05 entire, agreed, its meaning

06 satisfied, agree, himself

07 On, decided , test　　08 took out, From

09 asked, use, word　　10 During class, forgot

11 held up, extra, borrow　　12 not pleased

13 but, already, perfectly

14 found, funny, use, more

15 In, became, cool word

16 getting, hand, stop saying

17 stop, as, word　　18 have no choice

19 took out, sign, date　　20 give, when, over

21 thought, hates　　22 Next, began, with

23 punish, for using　　24 only, things worse

25 to use, more　　26 spread to nearby

27 Shortly after, wrote, knew

28 later, covered, found out

29 By, graduated from, used

30 flew by, one, received

31 Inside, found, envelope

32 signature from, grade　　33 note, said, Check

01 was excited about, fifth grade, was worried about

02 was famous for, vocabulary lessons

03 should have a good dictionary, can look up, meaning, new words

04 the meanings, means, barks

05 entire town, agreed, its meaning

06 satisfied, did I agree, said to himself

07 On, decided　　08 took out, From

09 asked, to use　　10 During class, forgot

11 held up, extra, to borrow　12 was not pleased

13 but, already has, perfectly

14 found, funny, to use, more and more

15 In, became, cool word

16 said to, after class, getting out of hand, to stop saying

17 stop it, as, students' word　18 no choice

19 took out, asked, to sign, date

20 I'll give, to you, is over　　21 thought, hates

22 began, with　　23 punish, for using

24 made things worse

25 to use, more and more　　26 spread to nearby

27 Shortly after, wrote, on, knew about it

28 A month later, covered, found out about

29 By the time, graduated from, most students, used

30 flew by,One day, received

31 Inside it, found, envelope, dictionary

32 signature from fifth grade　33 yellow note, It said

1 Nick Allen은 5학년이 시작되는 것이 신났지만, 한 가지가 걱정되었다. 그것은 Granger 선생님의 영어 수업이었다.

2 Granger 선생님은 어려운 어휘 수업으로 유명했다.

3 첫 번째 시간에 Granger 선생님은 말했다. "모두 좋은 사전을 가지고 있어야 해요. 여러분은 사전에서 새 단어의 뜻을 찾을 수 있어요."

4 "Granger 선생님? 단어의 뜻은 누가 정하나요? 그러니까, '개'는 짖는 동물을 뜻한다고 누가 정했나요?" Nick이 물었다.

5 "네가 그랬지, Nick. 너와 나, 그리고 온 마을과 나라가 말이야. 우리 모두가 동의했단다. 그게 그 단어에게 의미를 부여하는 거야."

6 Nick은 마음에 들지 않았다. "내가 언제 동의했지?" 그는 혼잣말을 했다.

7 집에 가는 길에 Nick은 Granger 선생님의 생각을 시험하기로 결심했다.

8 그는 펜을 하나 꺼내서 말했다. "오늘부터 이것은 'frindle' 이야."

9 그 다음날 Nick은 다섯 명의 친구들에게 단어 'frindle'을 사용해 달라고 부탁했다.

10 수업 중에 Nick이 말했다. "Granger 선생님, 오늘 'frindle' 을 빠뜨리고 왔어요."

11 Nick의 친구인 John이 펜을 하나 들고서는 말했다. "나한테 여분의 'frindle'이 있어. 내 ' frindle'을 빌리 고 싶니?"

12 Granger 선생님은 즐거워하지 않았다.

13 선생님이 말했다. "너희들의 새 단어는 귀엽지만, 그건 이미 'pen'이라는 완벽하게 좋은 이름이 있단다."

14 Nick의 학급 친구들은 이것을 재미있어 했고 더욱 더 그 단어를 사용하기 시작했다.

15 단지 3일 만에 학교에서 그것은 멋진 단어가 되었다.

16 Granger 선생님은 수업 후에 Nick에게 말했다. "점점 손을 쓸 수 없게 되어 가는구나. 네 친구들에게 'frindle'을 말하는 것을 멈춰달라고 말해 줄래?"

17 죄송하지만, 멈추게 할 수가 없어요. 그건 제 단어로 시작됐지만, 이제 그건 학생들의 단어예요."

18 "좋아. 그러면 선택의 여지가 없구나."

19 Granger 선생님은 봉투를 하나 꺼내더니 Nick에게 뒷면에 서명을 하고 날짜를 적게 했다.

20 선생님은 말했다. "이 모든 것이 끝나면 내가 이 편지를 너에게 줄게."

21 Nick은 생각했다. "선생님은 내가 정말 싫은가봐."

22 다음 주에 Granger 선생님은 'frindle'과의 전쟁을 시작했다.

23 선생님은 그 단어를 사용한다면 어떤 학생이든 벌을 줄 것이라고 말했다.

24 하지만 이것은 상황을 더 나쁘게 만들 뿐이었다.

25 학생들은 그 단어를 더욱 더 사용하고 싶어했다.

26 'frindle'은 근처의 중학교와 고등학교로 빠르게 퍼져 나갔다.

27 곧 지역 신문 기자가 그 상황에 관한 기사를 썼고, 마을의 모든 사람들이 그것에 관해 알게 되었다.

28 한 달 후에 한 전국 텔레비전 방송사에 서 그 소식을 다루었고, 모든 사람들이 'frindle'에 관해 알게 되었다.

29 Nick이 초등학교를 졸업할 때쯤에는 이 나라의 대부분의 학생들이 그 단어를 사용했다.

30 시간은 흘러 Nick은 21살이 되었다. 어느 날 Nick은 소포를 하나 받았다.

31 소포 안에는 펜 한 자루, 봉투 한 장, 그리고 사전 한 권이 있었다.

32 봉투에는 5학년 때의 그의 서명이 있었다.

33 사전에는 노란색 쪽지가 있었다. "541쪽을 확인해 봐."라고 적혀 있었다.

본문 TEST Step 4~Step 5   p.49~52

1 Nick Allen was excited about starting fifth grade, but he was worried about one thing—Mrs. Granger's English class.

2 Mrs. Granger was famous for her difficult vocabulary lessons.

3 In the first class, Mrs. Granger said, "Everyone should have a good dictionary. You can look up the meanings of new words in it."

4 "Mrs. Granger? Who decides the meanings of words? I mean, who decided that 'dog' means an animal that barks?" Nick asked.

5 "You did, Nick. You, me, and the entire town and country. We all agreed. That gives the word its meaning."

6 Nick wasn't satisfied. "When did I agree?" he said to himself.

7 On the way home, he decided to test Mrs. Granger's idea.

8 He took out a pen and said, "From today, this is a *frindle*."

9 The next day, he asked five friends to use the word *frindle*.

10 During class, Nick said, "Mrs. Granger, I forgot my *frindle* today."

11 His friend, John, held up a pen and said, "I have an extra *frindle*. Do you want to borrow my *frindle*?"

12 Mrs. Granger was not pleased.

13 She said, "Your new word is cute, but it already has a perfectly good name — a pen."

14 Nick's classmates found this funny and began to use the word more and more.

15 In just three days, it became the cool word at school.

16 Mrs. Granger said to Nick after class, "This is getting out of hand. Can you tell your friends to stop saying *frindle*?"

17 "I'm sorry, but I can't stop it. It started as my word, but now it's the students' word."

18 "Very well. Then I have no choice."

19 Mrs. Granger took out an envelope and asked Nick to sign and date the back.

20 She said, "I'll give this letter to you when all this is over."

21 Nick thought, "She really hates me."

22 Next week, Mrs. Granger began a war with *frindle*.

23 She said that she would punish any student for using it.

24 But this only made things worse.

25 The students wanted to use the word more and more.

26 *Frindle* quickly spread to nearby middle and high schools.

27 Shortly after, a local newspaper reporter wrote an article on the situation and everyone in town knew about it.

28 A month later, a national television station covered the news and everyone found out about *frindle*.

29 By the time Nick graduated from elementary school, most students in the country used the word.

30 Time flew by and Nick turned 21. One day, he

received a package.

31 Inside it, he found a pen, an envelope and a dictionary.

32 The envelope had his signature from fifth grade.

33 The dictionary had a yellow note. It said, "Check page 541."

MEMO

적중100

영어 기출 문제집

정답 및 해설

동아 | 이병민